MW00637416

Prelude to Waterloo:
Quatre Bras

Prelude to Waterloo: Quatre Bras

The French Perspective

Andrew W. Field

Pen & Sword
MILITARY

To Mandy, my saviour

First published in Great Britain in 2014 by
PEN & SWORD MILITARY
An imprint of
Pen & Sword Books Ltd
47 Church Street
Barnsley
South Yorkshire
S70 2AS

Copyright © Andrew W. Field, 2014

ISBN 978-1-78346-384-8

Typeset by Concept, Huddersfield, West Yorkshire, HD4 5JL.
Printed and bound in Malta by Gutenberg Press Ltd.

Pen & Sword Books Ltd incorporates the imprints of Pen & Sword Archaeology, Atlas, Aviation, Battleground, Discovery, Family History, History, Maritime, Military, Naval, Politics, Railways, Select, Social History, Transport, True Crime, and Claymore Press, Frontline Books, Leo Cooper, Praetorian Press, Remember When, Seaforth Publishing and Wharncliffe.

For a complete list of Pen & Sword titles please contact
PEN & SWORD BOOKS LIMITED
47 Church Street, Barnsley, South Yorkshire, S70 2AS, England
E-mail: enquiries@pen-and-sword.co.uk
Website: www.pen-and-sword.co.uk

Contents

List of Illustrations

List of Plates

Introduction

The idea for this book came from my membership of the Napoleonic Wars Forum (www.napoleonicwarsforum.com). A review of Mike Robinson's *The Battle of Quatre Bras 1815* was posted that sparked a discussion on the merits of the book. I had been on a battlefield tour of Quatre Bras and Waterloo with a group that included Mike a couple of years previously and had subsequently bought and enjoyed reading his account of the battle. As my own particular interest is the French perspective on the 1815 campaign I was rather disappointed that he had generally ignored this angle and restricted himself to an otherwise detailed and fascinating account from the British and allied perspective, but one that gave so little information on their opponents. To be fair he acknowledged this shortfall in the introduction of his book, writing:

> Despite my best efforts, little of value could be found in French sources ... I chose therefore, to concentrate on events seen from the allied side of the hill, using French accounts to corroborate where necessary. It is for this reason that there is no examination of the inactivity of the French on the morning of 16 June, no analysis of the peregrinations of General d'Erlon and no space devoted to the increasingly desperate flow of orders from Imperial Headquarters to Marshal Ney.

Given that it would be natural for British readers to be most interested in the British perspective, I was therefore pleasantly surprised, and a little reassured, to see that the comments on the forum reflected my own. Reviews of his book on other websites criticised him for failing to include any detail on the French forces, personalities, tactics or strategy and this convinced me that there was a growing demand for a more objective view of history, and particularly accounts that draw on the experience and perspectives of all protagonists. This interest often evolves into a broader study of the campaign and, in the case of 1815, beyond an apparently insatiable appetite for books on Waterloo, has also manifested itself in a demand for further detail on all aspects of the campaign including the battles of Ligny and Quatre Bras, both of which were to have a critical role in determining the way the campaign was to climax at Waterloo. Indeed, for a full understanding of Waterloo, a study of the whole of the short campaign is vital.

For some inexplicable reason, French officers and soldiers were nowhere near as prolific in writing about their experiences in either volume or detail as their British and allied counterparts, and because of this it is true to say that there are few detailed and atmospheric first-hand accounts of the fighting at Quatre Bras. In fact, many French officers and soldiers, who wrote at length on their experiences at Waterloo, allocate only a few lines to Quatre Bras, and given how cataclysmic Waterloo was in their experience, it is perhaps unsurprising that Quatre Bras was completely overshadowed by it. Consequently, there is no scope to deal with that battle in the same way that I was able to do in *Waterloo: The French Perspective*, for which I was able to draw on a reasonably-sized pool of French eyewitness accounts. Quatre Bras was a much smaller affair and, due to what was perceived as prevarication and lack of resolve in the higher levels of command, the battle was viewed with frustration by those French soldiers who fought there. In fact, as we shall see, the action at Quatre Bras did deliver some significant strategic success for the French, but for the soldiers who fought there it felt like a defeat, and the strategic success it brought fell well short of Napoleon's somewhat over-inflated hopes. The failings of that day were considered by many French historians to be a major contributing factor to the disastrous defeat at Waterloo.

We must accept then, that there is substantially less eyewitness detail of the fighting from the French side than the allied, and this will give us far less clarity on some of the tactical aspects of the battle. The ebb and flow of the fighting of a major battle, enhanced by the exciting yet terrifying accounts by those who were there, will always be of interest to students and enthusiasts of military history. Yet there is always significance to a battle beyond the intensity of the fighting and the direct outcome of the combat. What's more, it is inevitable that most interest tends to centre on the largest and most decisive battles, as it was these that almost inevitably had the greatest impact on the history of nations, both winners and losers. Consequently, the smaller battles and engagements that shaped subsequent events, but appear somewhat less significant, are often overlooked or neglected. And yet it is often these smaller battles that are important in understanding how or why the larger-scale engagements turned out the way they did. Thus Aspern-Essling and Znaim in 1809, and Smolensk in 1812, are overshadowed by Wagram and Borodino. This is particularly true for the campaign of 1815; the battles of Ligny and Quatre Bras, and the manoeuvring prior to and after these battles, had a significant effect on the outcome of Waterloo.

However, if Waterloo is studied in isolation it is quite possible to believe that Napoleon had a more than even chance of success; he appeared to hold the initiative as the attacker, he had a small but appreciable advantage in numbers, and an apparently more homogeneous and better-motivated army. But this most famous battle, fascinating as it is in itself, was shaped and arguably decided by the manoeuvrings, mistakes and outcomes of the previous three days, to the point where a full and comprehensive understanding of these three days brings the student of the campaign to the conclusion that Napoleon was almost inevitably going to lose at Waterloo. Whilst this is rather simplistic and established with the benefit of hindsight, it is hard not to argue that the sequence of actions and events suggests there was a certain inevitability about the outcome, even if it was not obvious at the time.

From the French perspective, the historical significance of the battle of Quatre Bras is out of all proportion to the relatively small numbers of troops involved and the little historical coverage it has attracted. Its progress and result had huge implications for the passage of events up to Waterloo, the result of that battle and therefore, by definition, the campaign itself.

The disaster of Waterloo two days later has understandably overshadowed this little-understood battle and contributed to the lack of detailed accounts by French participants. But more significantly, accounts and narratives by British and Dutch-Belgian historians concentrate on the *minutiae* of the fighting and give little or no consideration to Napoleon's overall strategy and the mistakes made by the emperor and Marshal Ney. Frankly, the battle was there for the French to lose rather than to win, and this situation was also largely due to the mistakes made by Wellington, whose legions of admirers find this difficult to acknowledge.

The main significance of Quatre Bras for the French is not the detail or even the result of the fighting, but the decisions and actions of Marshal Ney, who commanded the left wing of the French army during this critical period of the campaign. An examination of the unfolding events, their timings, Ney's decisions and Napoleon's orders and expectations are actually the key to understanding why the campaign was a crushing defeat for the French. The difficulty we face is in examining the evidence objectively, and not allowing ourselves to be swayed in our judgements by the huge benefit of hindsight or the apparently persuasive arguments of earlier critics.

In his own analysis of the campaign the famous Prussian strategist and military philosopher, Clausewitz, cautions against constantly asking 'what if', but demands that the decisions made by the various commanders on the ground must be judged on their merits, with particular attention paid to what they had been ordered to do, what they actually knew and what the situation really was when those orders were received.

The truth is, therefore, that plenty has been written in French about Quatre Bras, but relatively little of it covers the detail of the fighting at that battle. Instead the material is concerned with events from the crossing of the border into Belgium on 15 June, to the day after the battles of Quatre Bras and Ligny, which led to the debacle at Waterloo. There is no criticism of the energy, courage, determination or morale of the French soldiers and junior commanders. It is generally felt that a concentrated, devoted and veteran

French army, led by one of history's greatest military leaders, fighting against dispersed, somewhat surprised protagonists, leading less homogeneous yet superior forces, should have triumphed, and much thought and ink have been expended in analysing why they did not. The general conclusion is that the fault lies at the feet of the emperor and his senior commanders, and most analysis of the French performance concentrates on the mistakes that were made and the culpability of those who made them. This is the true French perspective of Quatre Bras and the days either side of it, and it is this that we must study if we are to fully understand that perspective.

Napoleon, of course, did not accept any blame for the failure nor heap any on his troops. As we have already discussed, he was convinced that the failure lay in the chain of command below him. In his memoirs he wrote:

> Never has the French soldier shown more courage, good will, and enthusiasm. He was full of the consciousness of his superiority over all the soldiers of Europe. His confidence in me was complete, and had perhaps grown greater; but he was touchy with his other chiefs and mistrustful of them ... The character of several generals had been softened by the events of 1814. They had lost something of that dash, that resolution and that self-confidence which had won so much glory for them and had contributed so much to the success of former campaigns.[1]

Such is the division of opinion that Napoleon generated amongst French historians that they fall clearly into two camps; those who believed Napoleon was a charismatic and popular leader and always showed him in a favourable light, and those who felt he was a power-crazed megalomaniac and missed no opportunity to show him in a poor light. French histories therefore need to be read with this in mind, and one analysis was often penned specifically to counter the views and criticism of another.

The situation is not helped by the fact that few of the key commanders on the French side left detailed accounts of their own actions or the campaign as a whole, and most of the accounts and correspondence that do exist were generated in response to the criticisms of others. This is true of Napoleon himself who, in exile on the island of St Helena, dictated his own account of the campaign, which heaped much of the blame for his defeat on his two lieutenants, marshals Ney and Grouchy.

Other than his official report on Waterloo that was published in the *Moniteur* in Paris on 21 June, Napoleon dictated two accounts of the 1815 campaign. The first was *La Campagne de 1815, ou rélation des operations militaires qui ont eu lieu en France et en Belgique, pendant les Cents Jours, écrite à Ste Hélène, par géneral Gourgaud.* This was published in English in 1818 and although the title credited it to General Gourgaud, it is universally accepted as being Napoleon's own account. It immediately drew a barrage of criticism from Marshal Grouchy in particular, but also Marshal Ney's son, the Duke of

Elchingen. Both men immediately set about producing their own accounts to justify their own, or their father's, actions.

Napoleon dictated *Mémoires pour servir à l'histoire de France en 1815* to General Bertrand in exile on St Helena and it was published in 1820. This account was essentially a justification of his own performance, heavily, and in places clumsily, clouded by all the advantages of hindsight, and was again used to deflect much of the blame for the failure of the campaign onto his two key lieutenants. Admirers of Napoleon did not hesitate to base much of their analysis of the campaign on these memoirs, without choosing to compare them with other accounts, and they have essentially taken Napoleon's words as the unchallengeable truth. The emperor's detractors, meanwhile, were predictably quick to criticise, but in the words of the American historian John Codford Ropes, whose thorough, objective and critical analysis of the entire campaign is a 'must' for any serious student of 1815, few memoirs have been subjected to 'more harsh and unjust criticism'. In fact, these memoirs should not be written off because of some fanciful claims, as running through them is an incisive and compelling argument to support his central thesis that demands further study rather than peremptory dismissal. Before we explore Napoleon's approach to recalling events, it must be remembered that his memoirs were written in exile and from memory; he had no records or references, nor other perspectives of the campaign. Some understanding of this is necessary for an objective study of the detail in these memoirs.

Ropes's *The Campaign of Waterloo* was published in 1892. It is one of the later analyses of the 1815 campaign and thus was able to consult all the contemporary evidence, some of which was not available to those who had written before. He could thus objectively (given that he was an American) analyse all the information that was available and identify where previous critics had missed key facts or evidence. He was then well placed to consider the honesty and manner in which Napoleon wrote his memoirs. He has this interesting view:

> Our purpose at present is to call attention to a peculiarity of Napoleon's which may serve to explain the existence in his memoirs of very definite statements which are apparently very wide of the truth. This peculiarity is, that while his orders to his lieutenants were often very general in their character, – pointing out clearly enough, it is true, the thing to be aimed at, or the danger to be feared, – but leaving entirely to the officer the course to be adopted if the emergency was to arise, – yet these orders never seemed to have been retained in Napoleon's memory in the shape in which they were given, but what he did recall about them was his expectation that, on receiving his order, his lieutenant would act in such or such a manner. This expectation, that such or such action would be taken by his lieutenant on receiving such or such an order, was all that

was left in his mind; and, when he came to write his narrative, he would often (at any rate) state that he had given definite instructions to such or such an effect, when all he had really done was to give a general order, from the giving of which he expected such or such a course of action to be taken by his subordinate.[2]

Ropes goes on to give some examples of this, stressing that whilst Napoleon no doubt forgot the exact detail of the order, he clearly recalled its substance and what he expected the recipient to do. Ropes concludes by saying that this 'is certainly to be distinguished from deliberate misrepresentation'. As my own narrative progresses, it is left to the reader to decide the extent to which Napoleon failed to make it clear in his orders what he expected of his subordinates.

Interestingly, Clausewitz, in his own critical analysis of the campaign, draws heavily on Napoleon's memoirs. However, this is not because he accepts that what Napoleon says happened is entirely accurate, but because they clearly reveal the inner workings of Napoleon's mind and allow him to bring the critical events of the campaign into sharper focus, perhaps in much the same way as Ropes interprets them above.

As Ney was executed by the reinstalled Louis XVIII just months after Waterloo he could not answer the emperor's criticism nor give his own account of the campaign. It fell to his son to take up the torch on his behalf and try to justify his father's performance and counter the accusations that appeared in Napoleon's memoirs and the accounts of the campaign that drew upon them. The value of his intervention comes in the correspondence that he had with his father's own lieutenants and which he subsequently published in *Documents inédits sur la Campagne de 1815*, giving us information and insight from those officers that might otherwise not have been available to us. Included in this publication was an account of the whole campaign written by Colonel Heymès, Ney's *Premier* (i.e. senior) ADC, who wrote it to protect his former commander's reputation in light of Napoleon's criticism.

Although Marshal Grouchy spent many years trying to clear his own name, his earliest accounts were written in exile in the United States. Having only his own personal correspondence to base his defence on, it is widely proven that some of his claims and recollections contain errors which undermine key aspects of his argument. When writing in your own defence, whether you are Napoleon or one of his lieutenants, it is unlikely that your own account is not somewhat heavily biased in your own favour!

Marshal Soult, the army's chief of staff, is not entirely free of blame for some of the shortcomings of the French performance, and although he was probably best placed to write a full and clear account of the campaign from the French perspective, he did not do so. He had had only a basic education and he never found writing easy; although he started his memoirs, he struggled to progress and he gave up before he reached 1815. His contributions to the many years of argument and debate that followed the catastrophe were restricted by his return to favour with the monarchy and he was careful not to jeopardise his position with a detailed account of his participation in the campaign. Consequently, he made little contribution to the debate and we have little more than his various orders and correspondence that remain in the archives to help us.

Whilst I am confident that the following account of the battle is the most detailed available from the French perspective, I cannot compete with the number of eyewitness accounts given in Mike Robinson's book by allied participants. However, for French historians, the real controversy that surrounds Quatre Bras relates more to the circumstances that surround it than to the detail or outcome of the fighting. Examining the causes of the failure and its implications is not only good history but, for British audiences at least, will also give a whole new perspective on the battle and explain its true importance when considering the campaign as a whole.

I have therefore deliberately avoided too much detail on the allied perspective, as this is comprehensively covered by Mike Robinson and it seems pointless to repeat it all. However, there are places where my own interpretation differs from Mike's; I do not wish to be drawn in to a lengthy discussion and readers can make up their own minds. Needless to say, there are also many volumes available on the armies of the opposing forces and I refer the reader to the bibliography if they want more information on this aspect of the campaign. I have tried to restrict myself to using sources and information that are not commonly available for this popular campaign and to give a new perspective on some familiar events. I earnestly hope that there is something new for all readers, irrespective of their own level of knowledge.

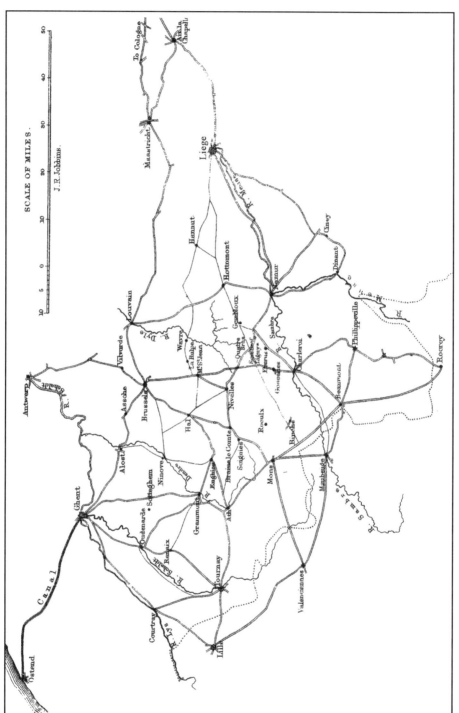

SCALE OF MILES.

J. R. Jobbins.

Map 1. The Whole Theatre.

Chapter 1

Setting the Scene

After his stunningly successful return from exile that found him back in the Tuileries in March 1815, Napoleon faced a monumental challenge in retaining power. The Congress of Vienna that had met the previous year to shape the new, post-Napoleonic Europe was still in session and the French emperor's overtures for peace were quickly and disdainfully rejected. By the Treaty of Chaumont, each of the allies pledged to put an army of 150,000 men into the field until he was driven from power. By June 1815 well over 600,000 men were approaching the borders of France, with more following or being mobilised. Napoleon, despite his herculean efforts, could muster fewer than half that number in the front line. To get the better of such overwhelming forces would require almost a miracle; Napoleon set about trying to create one.

Napoleon's Plans
Given the very real internal and external threats that he faced, Napoleon felt he had little option but to take the initiative and attack his enemies before they could concentrate all their forces against him. What's more, his forté was certainly the offensive; his military genius was based on audacious and daring enterprises. The only two armies that were fully mobilised and concentrated were the Anglo-Netherlands army of Wellington and Blücher's Prussians. The former had a strength of about 100,000 men and the latter around 130,000, to oppose to his own 120,000. What's more, the British lines of communication ran towards Ostend, Antwerp and the sea, whilst those of the Prussians ran towards Liège, Maastricht and Prussia; in opposite directions to each other. Through Gourgaud's account of the campaign, Napoleon expressed his plan thus:

> The Prussian army, having intimation of the enemy's intentions eight or ten hours before the English, would accordingly be first concentrated. Hopes were even entertained of attacking the Prussians before their four corps were united, or of obliging them to fall back in the direction of Liège and the Rhine, which was the line of their operations; and by thus separating them from the English, to create an opportunity for new operations.
>
> In these calculations, the characters of the enemy's commanders were much to be considered. The hussar habits of Marshal Blücher, his

activity and decided character, formed a strong contrast to the cautious disposition, the deliberate and methodical manner of the Duke of Wellington. Thus it was easy to foresee, that the Prussian army would be first concentrated, and also that it would evince decision and promptitude in hastening to the aid of its ally. If Blücher had had only two battalions ready to act, he would have employed them in support of the English army; but there was reason to believe, that Wellington, unless his whole army was prepared for action, would not attack the French to assist Blücher. All these considerations rendered it desirable, that the attack should be commenced against the Prussian army; it necessarily followed, that it would be first concentrated, which was in reality the fact.[1]

Napoleon's aim was undoubtedly to destroy each of these armies in succession, force them away from each other along their lines of communication and then to occupy Brussels. He hoped that such a blow would dissolve the coalition and might even bring peace; after all, the emperor of Austria was his father-in-law and the interest of distant Russia was largely theoretical. To concentrate such an army, he could only cover the rest of his frontiers with very weak detachments, albeit with the grand title of 'army'. These bodies, too feeble to resist a determined enemy, were designed to impose upon and delay them, buying him time to achieve his key victories in Belgium.

General Carl von Clausewitz, the famous military historian and strategist, in his analysis of the campaign, summed up Napoleon's situation:

> The fundamental concept that Bonaparte adopted for the campaign was to burst forth with an attack on the Allied armies in Belgium and on the Meuse, because they were the first ones present and thus the first ones capable of being brought to battle; because they were the closest and thus the first ones that could be reached; and because they were commanded by the most enterprising leaders and therefore the ones to be feared most. He therefore assembled a disproportionate part of his army against them … There was certainly nothing better for him to do: This was indeed the only way – given his extremely difficult and precarious situation – for him to attain a more solid position. Only by splendid victories over Blücher and Wellington, the two generals in whom the Allied sovereigns placed their greatest confidence, and by the total destruction of their armies, could he strike a blow that would cause admiration in France, dismay amongst the Allies, and astonishment in Europe. Only then could he hope to gain time and increase his power by a few more steps, thus becoming more of a match for his opponents. If he failed to gain this victory, or if it did not deter the Allies from immediately invading France, then it would be impossible for him to save himself from a second downfall.[2]

There is no doubt that if Napoleon had been successful in destroying these two armies, the morale of the allies would have been seriously affected. After their defeat, Napoleon could have turned with part of his army against the next developing threat with a huge moral advantage. It could certainly be argued that the determination of the allies would have been shaken to the point where they were prepared to make an accommodation with France, but at worst it would still buy the emperor considerable time; the time he needed to secure his position. And it is certainly true to say that a great victory would have galvanised the majority of France behind him.

A brilliant victory over the two armies in the Netherlands was therefore Napoleon's most urgent requirement. To achieve this he needed to destroy them individually, so they could not unite and defeat him using their superior numbers. His strategy therefore had to be to advance in such a way that firstly ensured that an encounter was certain, and secondly ensured that he did not force, or encourage, them to unite. Thus, his march into the Kingdom of the Netherlands was not aimed primarily at capturing Brussels, as many allied leaders and commanders thought, but to engineer a confrontation with Wellington or Blücher in such a way as to give him the greatest chance of destroying their armies one after the other. The capture of Brussels was almost irrelevant if the allied armies remained intact. His march on the capital of the Netherlands, therefore, was almost the bait that he used to force the allies into battle.

Napoleon had four lines of operation from which to choose. He could concentrate at Valenciennes and advance on Brussels via Mons, destroying Wellington before the Prussians could move to his support. He could concentrate at Maubeuge and move on Brussels through Charleroi, striking at the junction between the two allies and defeating them separately. On the right he could descend the Meuse towards Namur and fall on the Prussians, cutting their lines of communication; or he could sweep even further east, again threatening their lines of communication. Wellington clearly feared the first of these options, but Napoleon felt that such a move would merely push the British commander into the arms of the Prussians and he would risk having to fight them concentrated. Napoleon chose to fall on the central point, conveniently marked by the main Charleroi to Brussels *chaussée* (main road), hoping to destroy Blücher before Wellington could come to his support.

The Swiss strategist Antoine Henri Jomini, who wrote a political and military history of the campaign that was first published in 1839, wrote:

> Napoleon's taking the field, and his first plan, may be regarded as among the most remarkable operations of his life: nine corps of infantry or cavalry cantoned from Lille to Metz, were, by marches skilfully concealed, to concentrate in front of Charleroi, at the same moment with the

guard's arrival there from Paris. These movements were combined with so much precision, that 120,000 men were assembled on the Sambre, as by enchantment, on the 14th June.[3]

Whilst the concentration was not as faultless as Jomini implies, it was still a remarkable achievement; whilst the allies knew that the French army was assembling in the north, its strike did come as something of a surprise and Wellington in particular, unsure whether the advance on Charleroi was a deception, refused to nominate his own concentration point until he was certain, thus prompting Wellington's comment on the 15th that Napoleon had stolen a march on him. Although Blücher was able to concentrate more quickly than Wellington, even he was unable to ensure his whole army was concentrated for the first battle.

If Napoleon did not know the exact composition and location of his enemy's corps, he knew that in general terms the Prussians were cantoned from Charleroi to Liège, and that the Anglo-Netherlands army was distributed between Ath and Brussels, with advance guards towards Mons and Tournay. Napoleon believed that it would take Wellington two days to concentrate his army and Blücher probably more than twenty-four hours. The point of junction of these two armies was on the main road leading from Charleroi to Brussels, and it was here that he planned to strike, hoping to be able to profit from their dispersal and defeat them sequentially. In order to achieve this, success absolutely depended on audacity and celerity.

Allied plans

On 3 May, Wellington and Blücher met at Thirlemont to discuss their strategy to defeat Napoleon. At this time they were both building up their forces with a view to an offensive into France in concert with the other allied armies, probably in July. However, given that this process was still far from complete, and complicated by the mutiny of the Saxon forces that were under Prussian command, their first thoughts were on how to counter a French offensive launched to try and catch them unprepared.

Wellington was certainly a great commander, but he was very much a politicised and politically astute general. He therefore saw his priorities as the need to protect the capital of the Kingdom of the Netherlands, Brussels, and to protect the exiled French king, Louis XVIII, who was in Ghent. His conviction was that the French would attack via Mons, and this was based on the premise that Napoleon's priority was the capture of Brussels.

As Napoleon had three distinct options for advancing on Brussels through the Anglo-Dutch deployment area, Wellington would be unable to cover all of them in sufficient strength. His plan therefore saw his army concentrating well back from the frontier so that he could then deploy it to the threatened route, allowing the French to advance virtually unopposed until this was complete, and giving the Prussians time to march to his assistance. Wellington was therefore trading space, giving up Netherlands territory, for the time required to concentrate his army and receive support.

In contrast, Blücher needed to protect his communications with Prussia. One of the main roads along which he did this was known as the Roman Road that ran comparatively close to the frontier between modern-day Belgium and France. As he also wanted to manoeuvre in coordination with Wellington, his plan was to concentrate forward, around Fleurus and Sombreffe, and to fight a battle there, in order to protect this important route, or to march west and support Wellington along the main road from Namur towards Nivelles that passed through Sombreffe.

By the time of Thirlemont, therefore, both commanders already had their own plans in place, although they were diametrically opposed: Wellington concentrating in depth and Blücher forward. But the priority now was to agree a plan that saw them coordinating their efforts with a view to concentrating an overwhelming force against Napoleon. The intelligence they had available at that time hinted that any French offensive would be focussed on western Belgium rather than the Meuse valley, suggesting that Wellington's forces would be engaged first. Thus, although at their meeting at Thirlemont the principle of mutual support was agreed, their expectation was that Napoleon would advance against Wellington. If this had happened, the Prussians could be trusted to move to Wellington's assistance and the issue of their forward concentration became irrelevant. However, if Napoleon was to attack the Prussians first, or at the junction of the two armies, the fact that Wellington would firstly need to be convinced that any French attack in this area was not a feint, and then need to concentrate his army and march to support the Prussians, suggested that the Prussians were almost inevitably going to be left somewhat in the lurch.

By the end of May, both allied armies were complete and ready to start the campaign. As no threat had developed, when Blücher made an official visit to the Netherlands between 28 and 30 May, all the talk was of an allied offensive into France; all thoughts of coordinating defensive arrangements had been forgotten and the dichotomy between forward and rearward concentrations was no longer an issue. Just a few days before Napoleon launched his offensive, Blücher had written to his wife, 'We shall soon enter France. We might remain here another year, for Bonaparte will never attack us.'[4]

The *Armée du Nord*
In my previous book, *Waterloo: The French Perspective*, I avoided a unit-by-unit breakdown of the *Armée du Nord* as this is already available in no end of other excellent books. Instead I attempted to give a comprehensive account of the motivations and morale of the army, as this was to have a great impact on its performance in victory and defeat. This moral component, and its subtle

but significant differences within the command structure, is fundamental in understanding the French perspective of this fascinating campaign.

I do not wish to repeat the whole of my previous work and so I refer readers to that book for a full understanding. However, for those that have not read it I would like to recap the key points that it raises.

After Napoleon's abdication in 1814, the army quickly became disillusioned by the return of the monarchy, which reduced its size, failed to recognise its considerable achievements and replaced experienced, capable officers with those whose loyalty was to the king. A large number of officers were placed on half pay and many of those who were suspected of being too Bonapartist were harassed and kept under observation. It soon became clear to Napoleon that, if he were to make a return to France, he would have the support of the army, but if such a return was to be successful he also needed the support of a fair proportion of the population. Luckily for him, Louis and his court appeared to have learnt nothing during their exile. Instead of embracing the new France that the revolution and imperial rule had brought, they were determined to bring back the old ways, reinstating many institutions of the *ancien régime* and placing émigrés in key positions of power. In a short time the new king managed to alienate a large proportion of the population. Napoleon's return in March 1815 was quick and bloodless, thanks mainly to the support of the army that unhesitatingly rushed to his banner. A lieutenant sums up the reaction of the army to Napoleon's return:

> We heard as we were on the march that Napoleon had disembarked in Provence with a small band of men from the island of Elba, and that he was marching directly on Paris ... and that we also marched on Paris ... '*Vive l'empereur!*' At this moment, there was joy, delirium throughout the regiment, everyone cried with pleasure. In a moment the silver *fleurs de lys*, distributed by M. Le duc d'Angoulême, were broken and strewn on the ground.[5]

Facing the overwhelming numbers of the allied forces, whose governments refused to acknowledge Napoleon's right to rule, the emperor immediately set to work reconstituting the army in its old image.

The vast majority of the soldiers had an unconditional love for Napoleon. Lacking education or responsibility to anyone other than themselves, and with a sense of duty that was exclusively to him, it was an uncomplicated decision to cast off the *fleur de lys* and transfer their loyalty to the emperor without any soul-searching or feelings of guilt or betrayal. This was particularly true for the older soldiers, who still remembered the days of victory before the humiliation of defeat, many of whom had personal grievances with the enemies of France.

The younger soldiers, of which there were many, had experienced only fleeting moments of glory and the final humiliation of invasion. They had vengeance in their hearts and, having spent many hours listening to the stories of veterans, and with the passion of youth, they too wanted their share of sacrifice and glory.

The junior officers, those at the company level, were mostly younger and more impressionable and, like the younger soldiers, they wanted the glory and promotion that came with campaigning. For them, there was little attraction in peacetime soldiering, particularly amongst a veteran army. Here there was also a need to prove themselves, and as their loyalty and responsibility was to their soldiers, with whom they spent much of their time, they too were likely to transfer their loyalty without too much hesitation. Thus for them, the aura and draw of the emperor was as strong as it was amongst the soldiers.

More senior regimental officers, and the more junior general officers, felt themselves in a much more sensitive position. Many, despite their love for the emperor, felt that their sense of honour demanded that, as they had sworn loyalty to the king, they had no option but to serve him until he gave up the throne. Colonel Combe wrote, 'The return of the emperor in 1815 placed us in a cruel alternative between our feelings for him and our duty to our new sovereign.'[6] The dilemma they faced is well described in many other memoirs. Colonel Nöel tells us:

> The inhabitants of Dauphiné and the army supported the emperor; but for me, I deplored this event [his return] with all sensible men. I foresaw, and this was not difficult, all the ills that he would attract on France, and the first would be civil war.
>
> I realised exactly what the situation was. My duty was to remain at my post, my self-interest to go to the emperor. I had made my oath to the Monarchy; whilst this government remained the lawful government, I would serve it.[7]

As the army flocked to Napoleon, Louis fled to Belgium. Many officers now saw this act as releasing them from their oath of loyalty to him, and felt that they were now free to serve Napoleon with a clear conscience. But not only were the middle-ranking officers concerned by their oaths of allegiance, many could also see the possible consequences of Napoleon's return and the impossibility of emerging victorious against the military might of almost the whole of the rest of Europe.

For the marshals and more senior generals, the decision to join Napoleon or stay loyal to the king was an even more difficult one. Initially, the king had showered those marshals and generals who swore allegiance to him with awards and titles, whilst those who were not prepared to transfer their loyalty so easily went into retirement. Once many of the old émigrés had returned, however, the 'new' imperial aristocracy that had been created by Napoleon, including the marshals and generals, quickly found themselves snubbed and insulted. Some of these senior officers stayed loyal to the king and went into exile with him, many retired and refused to serve, whilst others only reluctantly felt they should fight to protect France. It seems comparatively few – those with the most intimate connections with Napoleon – enthusiastically attached themselves to his cause. The implications of these divided loyalties will be examined later.

The soldiers of 1815 were not exclusively the young conscripts with which Napoleon had been forced to fight the campaigns of 1813 and 1814; they were now older, had endured much hardship and were accustomed to war. In the short period of peace after his abdication many tens of thousands of prisoners of war had been released from Britain, Prussia, Austria and Russia, and the beleaguered garrisons throughout the German states that had been denied to him in 1814 had also returned. Some of these men were no longer fit to serve, but many others had returned keen to avenge the privations and humiliations they had suffered.

Captain Chapuis commanded a company in the 85th Line:

This regiment only had two battalions, totalling a little more than 900 men; but what you are not aware of is that these men, commanded by the brave Colonel Masson, came from the 3rd Regiment of Tirailleurs of the Guard a few days before our entry into campaign, were proven and resolute soldiers prepared to fight to the finish. At the peace in 1814, most had come from the English pontoons, in which a long and terrible torture had been their fate; they looked forward to the moment when they could come face to face with their torturers.[8]

The regimental commander of the 22nd Line seemed content with what he saw.

Our regiments are fine and animated by the best spirit; the emperor leads us; we hoped that we would take our revenge with dignity.[9]

But in the accounts of others we can see just a hint that the spirit of the soldiers went beyond an enthusiasm that was normal in well-motivated troops. General Foy commanded a division in the 2nd Corps and observed, 'The troops show no patriotism or enthusiasm, but a true rage for the emperor and against his enemies. None of them doubt the triumph of France.'[10]

The confidence of the troops in the emperor was absolute, as *chef d'escadron* Lemonnier-Delafosse explains.

Napoleon was at their head. The influence that he had on the spirit and courage of the soldiers was truly incomprehensible: a single word, a gesture, sufficed for their enthusiasm and to confront the most terrible dangers with a blind joy. If he ordered a movement at the wrong time that struck the soldiers as reckless or rash, they said he knew what he was doing, and they dashed forward to their deaths to the cry of '*Vive l'empereur!*'[11]

We are beginning to see that the army had a much higher number of veterans than had been the case for many years, it had strong morale, absolute faith in the emperor and, despite the short time Napoleon had had to pull it together, it was well constituted: particularly strong in the quality and quantity of its cavalry and artillery. But we are also beginning to sense that there was something extraordinary, something not quite right, about the psyche, or the spirit, of the army.

Certainly, given the negligence it had suffered under Louis, and the little time Napoleon had had to reorganise and motivate it, there were bound to be some significant issues with the army's cohesion and level of training. Regiments had received large numbers of recalled soldiers and volunteers, and officers returning from retirement on half pay. An anonymous general who fought at Waterloo wrote:

> The soldiers, arriving from all directions, knew nothing; they hardly knew their officers and were not known by them. They had much individual élan, but little communal: also the cavalry, which above all was in need of this élan, was itself very good; whilst the infantry, composed of similar elements, and having as much individual bravery, had need of several months of these manoeuvres and of that brotherhood which binds together one type of soldier with another and makes the strength of this arm. Time was lacking to give them this moral advantage which had been present in the highest degree in the troops of the camps of Boulogne, in the campaigns of Austerlitz and Jena, and which already left something to be desired in the campaign of Wagram! Several generals and officers of the headquarters, arrived at the opening of the campaign, were hardly mounted, and they had no knowledge of their troops when they marched on the enemy.[12]

The lack of cohesion and training that this implies is certainly important, but given the enthusiasm and motivation of the army, this in itself is not sufficient to have made it the fragile instrument that was to fall apart so disastrously at Waterloo. The most significant issue is made very clear in virtually all the writings of more junior officers after the disaster. Captain de Brack of the Imperial Guard Lancers summed up the feeling of the army:

> The French army of the Hundred Days was not of the pure imperial sort. Already the few months of peace and the Restoration had changed it; the passive obedience, silent, respectful, confident, had been impaired. Its march, on campaign, was no longer cheerful firmness, heedless of ill, enthusiastic, the first cause of our success. Selfishness and treason circulated in its veins, and it had the feeling of their vile fever.[13]

This suggests that behind the thin veneer of confidence and homogeneity, there were some far more fundamental problems that were gnawing like a cancer at the heart of the army. Once again, the writings after the battle were quick to identify its cause; Lemonnier-Delafosse again:

> Although the entire army was superb and full of enthusiasm, it was necessary to inject new blood into its leadership; but the emperor ... made the mistake of putting it back under its old leaders.
>
> Most, despite their speeches to the king, had not ceased to speak in support of the imperial cause; but nevertheless they did not appear disposed to serve with the enthusiasm and devotion that the circumstances demanded. These were no longer the men who, full of youth and ambition, were generous with their lives to gain promotion and fame; they were men tired of war, and, having achieved the highest positions, enriched by the spoils of war or the generosity of Napoleon, had no other desire than to enjoy their fortune peacefully in the shadow of their laurels.[14]

The prevarication and clash of loyalties felt by the officers was not understood by the simplistic approach and attitudes of the soldiers. They remembered the treason of some senior officers before the fall of Paris, the way some of the marshals had forced Napoleon's abdication and, more recently, the failure of many marshals and senior officers to immediately rally to the emperor, to whom they owed their wealth and rank. Furthermore, the hesitation of many middle-ranking officers to lead their soldiers over to Napoleon on his return was simply not understood. All of this resulted in an increasing distrust of the officers by the rank and file, even before the campaign opened, and festered as the war began and imaginary slights, incompetence and real betrayal became evident. Sergeant Mauduit summed up the feelings of the soldiers, '... a great fault had been committed, in employing certain commanders, for whom the words 'glory' and *'patrie'* no longer had the same significance as for their subordinates'.[15] Later, he goes on to say:

> The subaltern officers and soldiers alone, with very rare exceptions, had conserved the sacred instinct for war, the thirst for combat!
>
> Too many of our generals were no longer worthy of commanding such troops; some of them traitors on the inside, spoke against the triumph of our arms; others, incapable, indecisive and lacking spirit, went into battle half-heartedly.[16]

The result is a clear difference in motivation and spirit between the soldiers and many senior officers. The soldiers were confident and ready to die for Napoleon; yet many of their officers were split in their loyalties between the king and the emperor, wanted peace, foresaw the terrible consequences of fighting virtually the whole of Europe, and yet felt compelled, in spite of all this, to defend their country against foreign invasion. Soldiers did not maintain the same feelings of duty, obligation and honour as their officers and were therefore much quicker in declaring for Napoleon. It was no doubt this that sowed the seeds of suspicion between many officers and the soldiers, who doubted the devotion and loyalty of their superiors. However, it must be taken into account that much of this analysis is based on the testimony of those who wrote on the campaign after their defeat, when many were looking for scapegoats and excuses. There is plenty of evidence to support their claims, but the extent to which this feeling permeated the whole of the army must remain a matter of conjecture.

What is clear from contemporary evidence is that distrust in their officers and perhaps the extraordinary circumstances in which they found themselves, manifested itself in a lack of discipline among the rank and file, of which there are many examples. The distrust turned to growing anger and suspicion as the campaign progressed and the consequences of bad luck, treason and incompetence appeared, to the soldiers at least, to realise their gloomiest predictions. The fact that many of these were the frictions of war that are omnipresent in all conflict were conveniently ignored by the soldiers to justify, in retrospect, their worst excesses and fragile morale.

Colonel Gordon was one of a number of prominent officers who deserted during the first days of the campaign and whose actions served to justify the suspicion of the soldiers. He was the chief-of-staff to General Durutte, commander of the 4th Division in d'Erlon's 1st Corps. Immediately after his desertion he wrote:

> The spirit of the soldiers is terrible, they are maniacs, and I am sure that the first consequence of their rout will be horrible indiscipline and a thousand excesses. Even in France they had started pillaging and speaking loudly of burning property if the army was obliged to retreat. This army is lost ...[17]

But how the army saw itself is illustrated by this piece, written by Lieutenant Martin of the 45th Line:

> Never had the army set off on its march with more certainty of victory. Of what importance to us was the number of our enemies? We counted in our ranks soldiers grown old in victory, who had spent some years as prisoners which had made them even more formidable. A thousand humiliations added anger to their natural valour. Their faces, burnt by the sun of Spain or the ice of Russia, lit up with the prospect of battle. They surely wanted peace, but they wanted a glorious peace, having re-established the Rhine as the border of France.[18]

But perhaps the most objective view of the *Armée du nord* is given by Houssaye when he writes:

> Such was the army of 1815 – impressionable, critical, without discipline, and without confidence in its leaders, haunted by the dread of treason, and on that account perhaps, liable to sudden fits of panic; it was never-theless, instinct with warlike aspirations and loving war for its own sake, fired with a thirst for vengeance; it was capable of heroic efforts and furious impulses; it was more impetuous, more excited, more eager for the fray than any other Republican or Imperial Army after or before it. Napoleon had never before handled an instrument of war, which was at once so formidable, and yet so fragile.[19]

Chapter 2

Napoleon, Ney and Soult

Before we examine the battle of Quatre Bras and the operations that led up to it, it is important that we examine the motivations, capabilities and mindset of the two principal actors, Napoleon and Marshal Ney, as they play a large part in our understanding of why things turned out the way they did. Just as the various manoeuvres, skirmishes and deployments prior to a battle determine its shape, so these traits shape the way these key commanders made their decisions and acted. Given the criticism that Napoleon heaped on some of his lieutenants after the campaign, principally Ney and Grouchy, we need to try and empathise with the central characters in order to judge whether such criticism is justified.

From humble origins Ney had enjoyed a meteoric rise through the ranks of the French army. Joining the 4th Hussars in 1790 aged twenty-one, he was a sergeant major just two years later and commissioned the same year. As a cavalry commander he quickly established himself as a leader of dash and courage. The future Marshal Bernadotte commented, 'Ney will go far if he doesn't kill himself first.' He fought under Moreau in these early stages and was no admirer of the young Bonaparte as the future emperor first started to establish his reputation. Ney was made *général de brigade* at twenty-six, after only five years in the army, and *général de division* in 1799. By this time he had shown himself to be a leader of guile, in his capture of Wurzburg and Mannheim, and a determined and effective commander of an advance- or rear-guard. He had already been wounded a number of times.

His achievements soon came to the notice of Napoleon and, although his allegiance to Moreau, who some saw as Napoleon's rival for power, could have caused lasting damage to his career, the future emperor realised that this was a man he needed. In 1802 Ney's growing reputation was enhanced by his invasion of Switzerland and from then on he took a leading role in most of Napoleon's campaigns, fighting against Austria in 1805, Prussia in 1806 and Russia in 1807. Throughout these campaigns he showed himself to be a brave and aggressive commander, but there were also occasions, most notably at Jena and during the winter of 1807, when he could be rash and prepared to ignore orders, even from the emperor himself. Sent to Spain in 1808, he performed well when under Napoleon's direct command, but once the emperor had returned to France, Ney became an unruly subordinate to both Soult and Massena. Happiest in action, he quickly gained a reputation as thoroughly insubordinate, quarrelsome and uncooperative. Eventually relieved of his command in 1811 by an exasperated Massena, he was recalled to France to face the wrath of Napoleon.

As frustrated as Napoleon must have been by Ney's behaviour in Spain, the emperor was soon to have need of him. Once again under the supervision of Napoleon, Ney led a corps into Russia in 1812 and took a leading role at both Smolensk and at Borodino. Perhaps his crowning achievement was his command of the army's rear-guard during the retreat. Cut off from the main body and presumed lost, he led it back to the army to the astonishment and approbation of all. His reputation amongst the rank and file was unrivalled except by Napoleon himself.

Ney's command of the rear-guard in Russia had shown that he was at his best with his back to the wall, fighting almost as an equal amongst his men with outstanding courage and resolve. But as the war continued into Germany, his suitability for the highest levels of command came under scrutiny. Whilst the surprise of his corps at Lutzen could hardly be blamed solely on him, he did not appear to fully comprehend his crucial role at Bautzen as the commander of the left wing and was humiliated as an independent army commander at Dennewitz. At the latter battle, he was accused of 'acting like a lieutenant in a general's cloak', showing no understanding of the wider strategic implications of the situation whilst becoming fixated by the lower-level tactical direction of the battle. He could not resist getting drawn into the fighting and this was a charge he faced many times in his career, perhaps confirming his unsuitability as an independent, high-level commander. After his defeat he was severely criticised by Napoleon and it is evident that this was deeply felt. These shortcomings were to be evident in 1815.

After his failure at Dennewitz, Ney was drawn back under Napoleon's direct control and was present at the climactic battle of 1813 at Leipzig, where he commanded the northern sector of the battlefield. Another example of poor judgement resulted in him being overwhelmed by superior numbers and, in desperate fighting, he was shot in the shoulder and eventually evacuated from the battlefield.

It was January 1814 before Ney was fit to rejoin the army. Threatened by invasion, Napoleon welcomed him back and gave him command of two divisions of the Young Guard. Although he fought with his usual bravery operating directly under Napoleon's eye, at the battle of Craonne Ney once again showed his predilection for committing his troops too early in a rash attack and they paid a terrible price. The French historian Robert Margerit wrote of Ney in 1814 that 'he re-entered France sick of fighting, sick of Napoleon, sick of a regime that was incompatible with peace.'[1] As the allied armies bore down on Paris, Ney took a leading part in forcing Napoleon to abdicate. It was also he who delivered the abdication to Czar Alexander.

Ney was quick to be courted by the returning Louis XVIII and enjoyed the opportunity to relax with his family and bask in the glory of his military reputation and the honours he had earned (*Duc d'Elchingen* and *Prince de la Moskowa*). However, he quickly became disillusioned by the policies and behaviour of the *émigrés* who ignored his advice and treated him, and particularly his wife, with contempt in court. When Napoleon's escape from Elba was announced he found himself in a difficult position; apparently snubbed by the new regime, yet horrified by the potential implications of Napoleon's return, he seemed to foresee the catastrophe that awaited France. Bound by his oath of loyalty he was one of the first of Napoleon's former marshals to offer his sword to the king, famously promising to bring Napoleon back to Paris in an iron cage. However, as he travelled south he reflected on the slights he had suffered under the Bourbons, the glory and rewards heaped upon him by Napoleon and saw for himself how the whole army and even much of the population rejoiced in Napoleon's return. He increasingly began to question his own loyalties and when he was finally approached by Napoleon's emissaries, he quickly transferred his allegiance back to the emperor he had been instrumental in deposing.

Although apparently embraced by Napoleon, the emperor, after an initial warm welcome (perhaps more to feed the enthusiasm of the assembled soldiers than as a true display of reconciliation), then appeared to keep Ney at arm's length. Napoleon had clearly not forgiven the marshal for his leading role in the revolt of the marshals and his abdication of the previous year, and his apparent rehabilitation was nothing more to Napoleon than a popular move that would help to re-establish his rule. On his return to Paris, Ney found the emperor 'too busy' to see him and he was sent off around the north of France and the Swiss frontier rallying support. On his return he was given a frosty reception by Napoleon and he must have realised that he had still to earn the emperor's forgiveness. In the following weeks Ney was almost ostracised from the centre of events and we can only begin to imagine what was going through his mind; whilst perhaps he was clear on the reason, he must have agonised over what would be the outcome of it all. He had seriously compromised himself with the Bourbons and should Napoleon fall the consequences to himself could be fatal, and yet he seemed to have gained nothing from throwing in his lot with the emperor.

Ney fulfilled only a bit-part during the pomp and ceremony of the awarding of the regimental eagles on the *Champ de Mai* and he returned home convinced that he did not feature in the emperor's plans. He no doubt realised that the emperor's loyalty and trust in him was badly, if not irrevocably, shaken. On 4 June he left Paris for his country estate of Coudreaux. But just as he had resigned himself to the fact that he would take no part in the upcoming campaign, on 11 June Ney received a letter from Marshal Davout, the minister for war. It included a note from Napoleon which said, 'Send for

Marshal Ney and tell him that if he wishes to be present for the first battles, he ought to be at Avesnes on the fourteenth.'

Ney must have been stunned to receive such a summons. Perhaps unsurprisingly, he was horribly ill-prepared to go on campaign and was still unsure about how he would be employed. He had only a single *aide*, Colonel Heymès, and few horses. Heymès takes up the story:

At 9am on the morning of the 12th, after having sent off his horses and war carriages, the marshal entered his carriage with Colonel Heymès, his senior *aide de camp*. He left by post ...

The marshal arrived at Laon at 10pm; the emperor was asleep and he did not see him.

On the 13th, the marshal spent the night at Avesnes; he arrived there in the morning, immediately joined the emperor and dined with him.

On the 14th, all the post horses were reserved for the emperor's service and the marshal was unable to obtain any. It was only at 10am that he finally found some local horses and was able to leave Avesnes; but the road was so bad, so full of troops and his horses pulled him so slowly that he did not reach Beaumont until 10pm. The emperor was sleeping and he could not see him. There were no lodgings for him so M. D'Aure, the army *intendant général* offered him a room where he spent the night.

On the 15th, the troops set off on their march and the emperor left Beaumont at 2am. The marshal did not immediately follow him, having to wait until he acquired some horses.

However, having learnt, about 10am, that Marshal Mortier had remained sick in this town, Ney went to see him and bought two horses from him. Colonel Heymès arranged things so they could start off, followed by a domestic, the carriages remaining in Beaumont.

The marshal, moving along the marching column, was acclaimed in the most flattering way by the old soldiers who rejoiced in having the '*rougeot*' amongst them, who had so often led them to victory.

At 7pm, the marshal rejoined the emperor beyond Charleroi, at the junction of the roads to Brussels and Fleurus.

'Hello Ney,' this Prince said to him, 'I am pleased to see you: you are to take command of the 1st and 2nd Infantry Corps ...'

The wishes of the marshal had been answered; he had a command, but he forgot that there is nothing worse for a general than to take command of an army the day before a battle. He left the emperor and an hour later he was at the head of the II Corps ...[2]

Napoleon's late decision to employ Ney suggests a number of possibilities, and had a number of implications, which should not be ignored. It is intriguing to reflect on whether these also went through Marshal Ney's mind.

Firstly, Napoleon found himself short of employable and trustworthy marshals. Some had refused to serve him, some had remained loyal to the king and went into exile with him, some were prepared to serve, but could not be trusted, and others were getting too old to campaign. Only Grouchy was deemed worthy of immediate promotion; d'Erlon, Vandamme, Gérard, and probably others, aspired to being awarded the baton, but no doubt Napoleon wanted that ambition to motivate them on the coming campaign. Davout, although probably the most effective fighting marshal, was appointed as minister of war; Soult, a proven, effective army commander, was employed as the army chief-of-staff and Suchet, one of the few marshals whose reputation was actually enhanced in Spain, was charged with facing down the Austrians as commander of the Army of the Alps. This left only the tough-fighting Mortier and the newly-promoted Grouchy available for field commands in the *Armée du Nord* (as the main army had been named).

It is quite possible that when he recalled Ney, Napoleon had still not decided how, or perhaps even if, he was going to employ him. After all, despite his warm welcome on the 13th at Avesnes, Napoleon had not offered Ney a command less than thirty-six hours before the army crossed the border into Belgium. Was it possible that Napoleon only relented after he was informed that Mortier's illness prevented him from campaigning, and thus that the emperor was forced to appoint Ney against his better judgement? Whilst we may never know, perhaps this thought also occurred to Ney.

Throughout his campaigns Napoleon had been given many examples of Ney's shortcomings as a commander; indeed, in 1808 he had likened the marshal's understanding of Napoleonic strategy to that of 'the most recently joined drummer boy'.[3]

However, Napoleon well knew and valued Ney's personal courage and example. Well directed and supervised, there were few better men to person- ally lead a decisive attack, and, possibly for this reason alone, Napoleon felt that Ney was of real value on the battlefield. If Mortier had been fit, Ney might well have been employed as one of Napoleon's ADCs, who had tradi- tionally been used to lead desperate attacks that were designed to swing the battle in Napoleon's favour. Of Waterloo, Napoleon wrote in his memoirs:

> Marshal Ney received the honour of commanding the big attack in the centre. It could not have been entrusted to a braver man, nor to one more accustomed to this kind of thing.[4]

In his epic book, *The Campaigns of Napoleon*, David Chandler suggests another, perhaps more subtle reason for rehabilitating Ney.

> Nevertheless, Napoleon's decision to appoint Ney to high command in 1815 was an act of considerable cunning. Not only was Ney the hero of the French army, he was also a figure of propaganda for use against the

Bourbon cause. On the one hand it was a calculated blow against King Louis XVIII's prestige to re-employ the former Bourbon commander in chief; on the other, Ney's preferment might serve to persuade other servants of the Bourbons that their acts of desertion in 1814 could be overlooked in return for new tokens of devoted service to Napoleon's cause. Thus on political grounds there was quite a lot to recommend Ney's appointment in 1815 ...[5]

Finally, Napoleon was well aware of Ney's popularity throughout the army and since the retreat from Moscow his bravery had been a legend in the army; Colonel Heymès has already told us of the reception the marshal received as he passed the marching troops. On 13 March, Ney had his whole command, some 6,000 men, parade just outside Lons-le-Saulnier, where they had marched to confront Napoleon. Here, in one large square, Ney announced that the Bourbon cause had been lost forever and that he was going to march them to join the emperor. Whilst some officers chose to leave, the vast majority were ecstatic and the marshal's popularity was manifest. Sergeant Major Sylvain Larreguy de Civrieux of the 93rd Line Regiment was only nineteen years old and witnessed the expression of this affection: 'The ranks instantly broke up, the cavalry abandoned their horses, and we surrounded the Prince of the *Moskowa* to embrace him, shake his hand, touch his uniform, his sword ...'[6]

But one more important factor must also be taken into account: whatever Ney's failings as a senior commander, and whatever his enthusiasm and psychological readiness for war, he was certainly ill-prepared to take up such a position. He took command of his wing on the afternoon of 15 June, just as the lead elements were moving into contact, a day after the army had crossed the frontier and the day before a major action. He had only one ADC, with another on the way to join him, and no headquarters or staff officers. Colonel Heymès was therefore required to act as chief of a non-existent staff and Ney had to use officers of the various cavalry regiments to transmit his orders. He did not know who his subordinate commanders were, let alone the composition of their formations. This was hardly adequate preparation for such a significant command.

So what was Napoleon getting when he chose to re-employ Marshal Ney, and what frame of mind was the marshal in going into the campaign? Napoleon well knew the true worth and failings of probably the most popular and charismatic of his subordinates. By nature he was an inspirational leader, popular with his troops, energetic and aggressive. As a battlefield commander he was fearless (as his nickname of the 'bravest of the brave' suggests), but often rash and impulsive. As a subordinate he could be sullen, insubordinate and uncooperative. His record suggests that he was ill-fitted for independent command; often failing to see the bigger picture and rarely prepared to stand back and make calm, rational decisions, especially in a crisis. In 1815 he was thrust, unprepared and at short notice, into the midst of operations with no headquarters or staff officers. He was certainly distracted and possibly pre-occupied with what his fate would be, totally bound up as he was with the outcome of the campaign and Napoleon's own fate. It will be interesting to see how these traits became manifest in this, his last campaign.

There is no need to examine Napoleon's career in a book with such a narrow focus and it is probably fair to say that both admirers and even detractors would agree that whatever his other faults he stands as one of history's greatest military leaders. But 1815 was some years after he reached the pinnacle of his military accomplishments, which are generally agreed to be between 1805 and 1807, and it is the extent to which his strategic genius and his physical and psychological health declined from that period which often most occupies the minds of historians of the 1815 campaign. In 1809 Austria had given a far better account of herself than in previous campaigns and Napoleon's invasion of Russia in 1812 had been a disaster which destroyed his veteran army. But his genius still burned brightly; against all the odds he rebuilt a huge army in 1813 and was only beaten by overwhelming allied numbers and the relative incompetence of his lieutenants. With France invaded the following year, Napoleon, with a small, rather polyglot army, performed magnificently, and although finally overwhelmed and forced to abdicate, is credited with fighting one of his finest campaigns.

At his first abdication in 1814 therefore, Napoleon had been campaigning almost non-stop for over two years with all the physical and mental stresses and strains that this would have imposed upon him, and it should be remembered that each of the three campaigns he had fought in had ended in defeat. It is impossible for us to fully understand the impact this had on him and perhaps we should forgive him if, exiled to the small island of Elba, he took the opportunity to relax. However, on arrival in his new kingdom, he immediately set himself to work improving the rundown economy, infra-structure and quality of life of the island. This energy dwindled only when he understood that he would not be joined by his wife and son, and his activity reduced with his disappointment and depression.

However, his mood lifted again as he learnt of the situation in France and began to believe that a return was viable. Certainly, when he did return, the speed with which he marched on Paris and the energy and decisiveness with which he put the country onto a war footing after the neglect of the Bourbons was reminiscent of him at his peak. As we shall see, the detail of his planning for the upcoming campaign did not suggest that his intellect had in any way been impaired, and although he was accused of a lack of decisiveness at critical points in the four days of operations leading up to Waterloo, we must wait to examine the evidence before we decide if these charges are appropriate.

However, there is no doubt that Napoleon's sojourn on Elba altered his physical condition; many of his closest followers noticed the changes on his return. Colonel Crabbé, who later served on Ney's staff, wrote on 15 June, 'The emperor appears tired to me. He is very fat, seems out of breath and sometimes struggles to mount his horse.'[7] Adjutant commandant Petiet, who served in imperial headquarters, leaves us this description:

> During his sojourn on Elba, Napoleon's stoutness had increased considerably. His head had acquired a great volume, it was sunken into his shoulders and he was fatter than normal for a man of forty five. Also, it was noticeable that during this campaign he did not remain mounted as long as on previous ones. When he dismounted, either to examine his maps, or to send or receive information, his staff made available a small table of light wood and a rough seat of the same sort on which he sat and remained there for long periods.[8]

Whilst some described his stoutness and unhealthy appearance, a number of different maladies have also been attributed to Napoleon, including haemorrhoids and dysuria (a urinary disease), whilst David Chandler, a much-respected Napoleonic historian, believes, from his symptoms, that he was suffering from acromegaly (a disease of the pituitary gland, among the symptoms of which are fits of lassitude and spasms of over-optimism), although there appears to be no corroborating evidence for this. Although he did seem to be suffering physically from one or more ailments, he displayed great energy at times during this short campaign.

However, whilst there is some evidence of physical resilience, and Napoleon's intellect seemed as sharp as ever, there remain concerns over his judgement and decisiveness. Perhaps his state of mind is a better indication of his performance during the 100 days than his health? Whilst we have seen how Napoleon criticised his lieutenants for their lack of enthusiasm and energy, the emperor appears to be guilty of bouts of apathy. He later wrote, 'I sensed that Fortune was abandoning me. I no longer had in me the feeling of ultimate success, and if one is not prepared to take risks when the time is ripe, one ends up doing nothing – and, of course, one should never take a risk without being sure that one will be lucky.' Once again, the reader will need to decide whether, on the evidence presented, the Napoleon of 1815 was the same as the Napoleon of 1805.

In his final campaign, it is claimed that one of Napoleon's biggest handicaps was the absence of his very experienced and trusted chief-of-staff, Marshal Berthier. Indeed, Berthier had served as the emperor's chief-of-staff, or the *major-général* as his post was properly called, for eighteen years, and had long proven to be the perfect foil for the emperor's genius. He had the ability to translate Napoleon's schemes and verbal briefings into lucid, understandable and comprehensive orders and had organised a system to ensure that those orders got to the right destinations in a timely manner. His decision not to join Napoleon on his return has been widely, but never convincingly, debated. Berthier himself did not get the opportunity to enlighten us as he died in mysterious circumstances in Bamberg on 19 May, before the campaign opened. His controversial replacement was to be Marshal Jean de Dieu Soult, *Duc de Dalmatie*.

Soult had proven to be an extremely capable independent army commander and was clearly very ambitious. He was one of the last marshals to pledge allegiance to Louis after Napoleon's first abdication and was initially judged as untrustworthy by the royalists. However, his reputation for hard work and organisational skills eventually saw him appointed Minister for War. Soult found himself in an impossible position; although admired by the king he was seen by Bonapartist officers as a traitor, and many royalists believed this too. His failed attempts to counter Napoleon's march on Paris further entrenched the opinions of both parties and Soult was forced to resign.

Content to retire to his estates, Soult rejected Napoleon's initial approaches. But he was too good a soldier for the emperor to ignore, and Napoleon also probably saw him as a political prize. But Soult's ambition and reluctance to stand back as immense events were happening around him forced him to rethink and he finally accepted the emperor's invitation. His appointment as *major-général* has been widely criticised; it was certainly true that he had proved himself a more able field commander than Ney or Grouchy, and also that he had the most experience in fighting against the British, but it was not true that he had no experience as a staff officer. He had spent ten months as *major-général* to King Joseph in Spain between 1809 and 1810 (including the coordinating role that led to the battle of Ocaña, probably the greatest French victory in the Peninsula, and the invasion of Andalusia) and for a few months in 1813 he had worked for the old master, Berthier himself. Soult also had proven administrative skills, evident both in Spain and as minister of war to Louis, so although there may have been better candidates, the appointment was not as inexplicable as many have maintained. Napoleon, who as we have heard was very critical of the performance of most of his key subordinates after Waterloo, actually praised Soult as his *major-général*. Even the French historian Thiers, a fierce supporter of the emperor in his criticisms against his lieutenants after the end of the campaign, wrote that Soult, 'possessed most of the qualities of a chief-of-staff, less the "clarity of spirit" and experience of this position, but did not, like Berthier, double or triple the despatch of orders in order to be sure of their safe delivery.'[9] The implications of this latter failing were quick to manifest themselves as the campaign opened. General Guyot, commander of the Heavy Cavalry division of the Imperial Guard, put it like this, 'If the enthusiasm [of the army] was clear, its organisation lacked efficiency. Marshal Soult, who had replaced Marshal Berthier as *major-général*, did not have the same precision, nor the same speed in writing out

Napoleon's orders; his messengers – their horses in particular – were of mediocre quality.'[10]

Colonel Crabbé, who started work in the headquarters before being allocated to Ney as an ADC, wrote:

> 12 June. I am presented to Marshal Soult who is at St Quentin. The atmosphere in General Headquarters is not that which reigned there when Prince Berthier was found at its head. There was, it seemed, less strictness, less calm and efficiency. There were also less qualified officers.[11]

As the army chief-of-staff, Soult was responsible for writing and distribution of the orders and direction given for the army by Napoleon. As such, we must also examine the clarity and precision of Soult's work if we are to judge Napoleon's performance during this short campaign, for it is vital that we are clear on whose fault it was if there were any omissions or mistakes in the orders and direction given to Marshal Ney and the other senior commanders of the left wing.

Chapter 3

Initial Moves – 13 and 14 June

Having positioned most of his army along the northern frontier of France, Napoleon left Paris early in the morning of 12 June. Travelling via Laon, he stopped at Avesnes on the 13th, where he met his senior commanders and issued the following movement order, which aimed to concentrate the army for its strike into the Kingdom of the Netherlands.

ORDER OF THE DAY
Avesnes, 13 June 1815.
Position of the Army on the 14th.

The Imperial Headquarters will be at Beaumont. The infantry of the Imperial Guard is to be bivouacked a quarter of a league in front of Beaumont, and to form three lines; the Young Guard, then the Chasseurs, and then the Grenadiers. The Duke of Treviso [Mortier] will reconnoitre the site of this camp: he will ensure that everything is in its place; artillery, trains, baggage, etc.

The First Regiment of Foot Grenadiers is to proceed to Beaumont.

The cavalry of the Imperial Guard will be posted in the rear of Beaumont; but the furthest corps must be within a league of that city.

The Second Corps will take position at Leers, that is to say, as near as possible to the frontier without crossing it. The four divisions of this army corps will assemble and bivouac on two or four lines; the headquarters in the centre; the cavalry in advance, guarding all the approaches, also without passing the frontier, but ensuring it is respected by the enemy's partisans, who might seem inclined to cross it.

The bivouacs are to be so placed that their fires may not be seen by the enemy: generals must prevent troops straying from the camp; and must ensure that each man is provided with fifty cartridges, four days allowance of bread, and half a pound of rice; that the artillery and trains are in good condition; and they must place them in order of battle. Thus the Second Corps will be in readiness at three in the morning of the 15th, to march on Charleroi, should it receive orders to that effect, and it may arrive there before nine o'clock.

The First Corps will take position at Solre-sur-Sambre and bivouac in several lines in a similar way to the Second Corps and take care that its bivouac fires are concealed from the enemy and that no one is allowed to

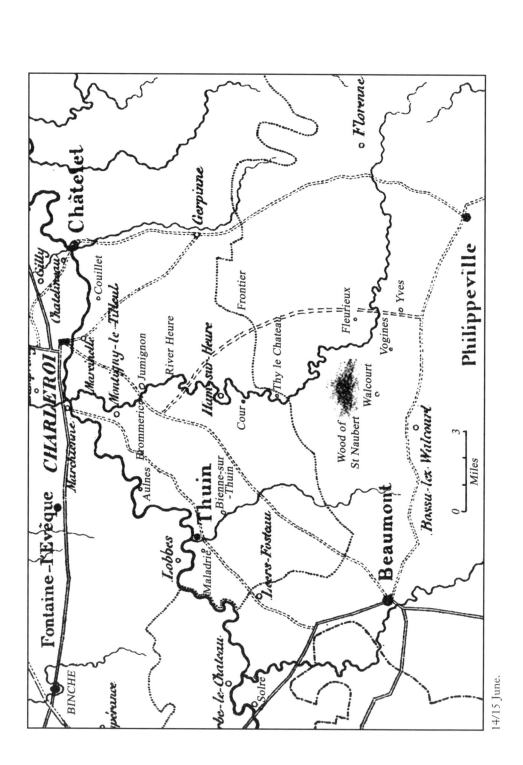

Fontaine-l'Évêque · CHARLEROI · Châtelet

BINCHE

Gilly (Chatelineau)

Couillet

Marchienne

Marcinelle

Montigny-le-Tilleul

Jumignon

Brommeric

Aulnes

Lobbes

Maladrie

Thuin

Bienne-sur-Thuin

Leers-Fostau

River Heure

Ham-sur-Heure

Cour

Cerpinne

Gerpinne

Frontier

Thy le Château

Fleurieux

Vogines

Yves

Wood of St Naubert

Walcourt

Bassu-lex-Walcourt

Beaumont

·be-le-Château

Solre

Philippeville

F. Florenne

0   3
Miles

14/15 June.

wander from the camp; its generals will satisfy themselves about the condition and supply of the ammunition and food carried by the troops, and that the artillery and ambulances are placed in their order of battle. The First Corps must likewise hold itself in readiness to follow the movement of the Second Corps at three o'clock on the morning of the 15th; thus, on the day after tomorrow, these two corps may manoeuvre in the same direction and cooperate with each other.

Tomorrow the Third Corps will take a position a league in advance of Beaumont, as near as possible to the frontier, without, however, crossing it, or allowing it to be violated by any party of the enemy. General Vandamme will keep everyone at his post, and will give orders for concealing the fires, so that the enemy may not observe them. His corps must also conform with the regulations prescribed to the Second Corps with respect to the ammunition, provisions, artillery, and trains, and must hold itself in readiness to march at three o'clock on the morning of the 15th.

The Sixth Corps will proceed in advance of Beaumont, and bivouac on two lines, at the distance of a quarter of a league from the Third Corps. Count de Lobau is to choose the ground, observing the general arrangements prescribed by the present order.

Marshal Grouchy will move the First, Second, Third and Fourth Corps of cavalry beyond Beaumont, and establish them in bivouac between that town and Walcourt, causing the frontier to be respected, prohibiting anyone from crossing it, or suffering themselves to be seen, and taking measures to prevent the fires from being observed by the enemy; he will hold himself in readiness to march on Charleroi, at three o'clock in the morning of the 15th, in case he should receive orders to do so, and to form the advance guard of the army.

He must direct the generals to ensure that all the cavalry troops have been provided with cartridges, that their arms are in good condition, and that they have each four days allowance of bread and half a pound of rice as has been ordered.

The bridge equipages are to be bivouacked behind the Sixth Corps, and in front of the infantry of the Imperial Guard.

The central park of artillery will halt in the rear of Beaumont.

The Army of the Moselle [Gérard's IV Corps] will take position tomorrow in front of Philippeville. Count Gérard will arrange it so that it may be in readiness to march the day after tomorrow, the 15th, at three in the morning, to join the Third Corps, and support its movement on Charleroi, according to the new order which will be given to him. But General Gérard must carefully guard his right flank and the head of his advance along all the roads from Charleroi and Namur. If the Army of the Moselle has any pontoons in its train, General Gérard must keep them as far in advance as possible so that they can be employed if the need arises.

The sappers and the means of transport that the Generals have collected will march at the head of the columns.

The sappers of the Imperial Guard, the Marine Artificers and the reserve sappers are to march after the Sixth Corps and at the head of the Guard.

All the corps must march in close order. In the movement on Charleroi, advantage must be made of all the routes, to overwhelm any enemy forces that may be inclined to attack the army or manoeuvre against it.

Only the Grand Headquarters will be at Beaumont. No other must be established there and the town must be free from all obstructions. The old regulations respecting the headquarters and equipages, the order of march and the policing of carriages and baggage, the laundresses and suttling women, must be enforced. A general order will be issued to that effect; but in the meanwhile, the generals commanding the army corps must make the necessary arrangements, and the Provost-Marshal must ensure that these regulations are executed.

The Emperor commands that all the arrangements contained in the present order shall be kept secret by the generals.

By order of the Emperor,
The Marshal of the Empire,
Major-Général, Duc de Dalmatie

Napoleon then travelled on to Beaumont, where he arrived during the afternoon of the 14th. No doubt disappointingly for him, he appears to have been met by indifference from the population. The cries of '*Vive l'empereur!*' from his escort as his carriage travelled through the streets of the small town were not taken up by the local townspeople. He immediately called for, and interrogated, the postmistress on the communications in the area and any news that had come from the Netherlands.

The concentration of the *Armée du Nord* on the 14th was undoubtedly an outstanding logistical operation, apart from the serious and unpardonable failure of imperial headquarters to send orders to Marshal Grouchy for the cavalry reserve. It was otherwise extremely well planned and as smoothly executed as could be expected of any complex military concentration; by the evening of the 14th, virtually all the formations of the army were in their allocated concentration areas apart from some of Gérard's divisions that had the furthest to march. The majority of the army was able to open the campaign 'well rested and well nourished.'[1] But it was not the same for Grouchy's cavalry; he wrote in his memoirs:

The result of their [the movement orders] non-transmission, or at least their non-arrival, was that several cavalry regiments had to march up to fifteen and twenty leagues a day to reach the frontier in time. Thus, on the 15th and 16th June, on the entry on campaign, men and horses were very tired.[2]

The Allies on 14 June

Although the French concentration was generally efficiently executed and Napolcon had gone to great efforts to carry it out in secrecy, the emperor and nearly all French writers have exaggerated the extent to which this concentration surprised Wellington and Blücher. Both commanders had very effective intelligence networks and were well aware the French were concentrating.

These networks had reported the intensive build-up of troops to the front of the Prussian outposts, and however hard the French tried to camouflage their presence, the Prussians received a steady trickle of information on their arrival. From the 12th, the forward formations were clear that a French offensive was imminent and this information was passed back up the chain of command. On the 13th Blücher ordered the North German Federal Corps to close towards his army, although there was no intention for it to reinforce it. Eventually, Steinmetz, one of Zieten's brigade commanders, was so convinced that the offensive was going to be launched on the 14th that the previous night he ordered his units to concentrate. By the 14th all the intelligence suggested that an attack was imminent and that night Blücher sent out orders to the II, III and IV Corps to concentrate at Onoz and Mazy, Namur and Hannut respectively, under cover of the I Corps. This would allow him to concentrate the whole of his army quite well forward around Fleurus in a relatively short time after receiving news of the outbreak of hostilities.

Still convinced that the move of the French army to their new concentration areas was a feint, Wellington took no such precautions and awaited fresh intelligence to confirm that Napoleon was not going to launch his offensive on Mons before he committed himself. His various corps, spread across a much larger area than the Prussians, would not only require more time to concentrate, but the Duke also sought unequivocal intelligence on which approach to Brussels Napoleon would use before he could decide where to do so. As the Prussian advance guards covered the route to Brussels from Charleroi, Wellington was more concerned about the approach from Mons, and this was where his main interest lay. This inevitable loss of time made it almost impossible to concentrate as far forward as the Prussians, making mutual support that much more difficult. If circumstances forced him to rush troops forward, there was considerable danger that they would be decisively engaged before they were fully concentrated. As we shall see, this was exactly what happened and Wellington was fortunate indeed to escape a mauling.

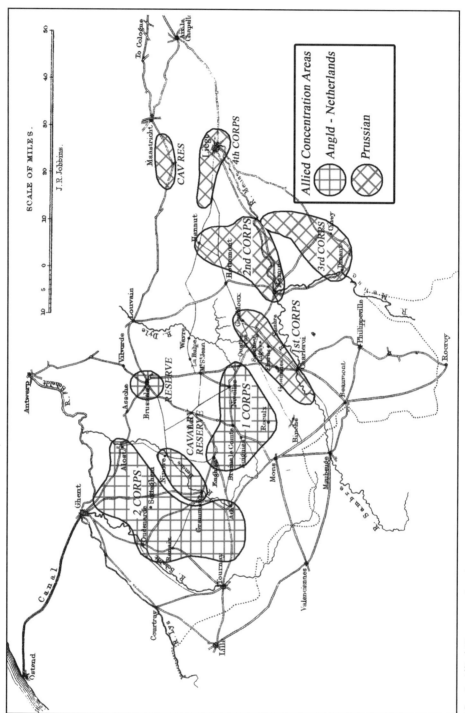

Map 3. Allied Concentration Areas.

Napoleon's Orders for the Offensive

That evening, Marshal Soult sent out the following detailed order which was to initiate hostilities:

ORDER OF MOVEMENT

Beaumont, 14 June 1815

Tomorrow, the 15th, at half past two in the morning, General Vandamme's division of light cavalry will mount their horses and advance along the Charleroi road: it will send out patrols in all directions to scour the country, and to capture the enemy's advanced posts; each patrol must consist of at least fifty men. Before the division moves, General Vandamme will see that it is provided with cartridges.

At the same hour, Lieutenant General Pajol must assemble the 1st Cavalry Corps and follow the movement of General Domon's division which will be under General Pajol's command. The divisions of the First Cavalry Corps are not to supply any detachments; they will be found by the Third Division. General Domon will leave his battery of artillery to march after the first battalion of the Third Corps of infantry. Lieutenant General Vandamme will give it the necessary orders.

Lieutenant General Vandamme will order the reveille to be beaten at half past two in the morning; at three he will march with his army corps in the direction of Charleroi. The whole of his baggage and followers must be posted in the rear, and must not commence their march until the Sixth Corps and the Imperial Guard shall have passed. They will be under command of the Commissary General, who will unite them to the baggage of the Sixth Corps and the Imperial Guard, and of the Grand Headquarters, and will give orders for their movement.

Each division of the Third Army Corps will have along with it its battery and trains: every other vehicle found in the ranks will be burnt.

Count Lobau will cause the reveille to be beaten at half past three o'clock, and he will order the Sixth Army Corps to march at four, to follow and support General Vandamme's movement. He will direct the troops, artillery, trains and baggage to observe the same order of march that is prescribed to the Third Corps.

The baggage of the Sixth Corps will be united with that of the Third Corps, under the orders of the Commissary General, as has been stated.

The Young Guard will beat the reveille at half past four, and will begin to march at five; it will follow the movement of the Sixth Corps on the Charleroi road.

The Foot Chasseurs of the Guard will beat the reveille at five o'clock and will begin to march at half past five, to follow the movement of the Young Guard.

The Foot Grenadiers of the Guard will beat the reveille at half past five, and will march at six, to follow the movement of the Foot Chasseurs. The order of march for the artillery, trains and baggage, prescribed for the Third Corps must be observed by the Imperial Guard.

The baggage of the Guard will be united to that of the Third and Sixth Army Corps, under the orders of the Commissary General, who will direct the movement of the whole.

At half past five in the morning, Marshal Grouchy will cause that corps of cavalry of the three which is nearest the road to mount and follow the movement on Charleroi. The two other corps will depart successively at the interval of one hour after each other; but Marshal Grouchy will be careful to make the cavalry march on the lateral roads, whilst the column of infantry will proceed along the principal road, to avoid confusion, and likewise that his cavalry maintain better order than it otherwise would. He will direct the whole of the baggage to remain behind, parked and collected, until the Commissary General shall give orders for its advance.

Count Reille will cause the reveille to be beaten at half past two in the morning, and order the Second Corps to march at three on the bridge at Marchienne-au-Pont, and will make arrangements for its reaching that place before nine in the morning. He must station guards on all the bridges over the Sambre, to prevent anyone from passing them. The posts will be relieved by the First Corps, but he must endeavour to anticipate the enemy on these bridges, to prevent their demolition, especially the bridge of Marchienne, to enable him to cross it, and which, should it be damaged, he must immediately have repaired.

At Thuin and Marchienne, as well as at all the villages on this road, Count Reille must interrogate the inhabitants respecting the positions and strength of the hostile armies. He must also take possession of, and examine the letters in the post offices and forward to the emperor such information as he obtains.

Count d'Erlon will put the First Corps in march at three in the morning, and will also direct it on Charleroi, following the movement of the Second Corps, the left of which it will gain as soon as possible to support it if necessary. He will keep a brigade of cavalry in the rear, to cover himself, and to maintain, by small detachments, his communication with Maubeuge. He will send patrols beyond that place, in the direction of Mons and Binche, as far as the frontier, to obtain information on the enemy, and to report anything they gain. These parties must be careful neither to compromise themselves, nor to cross the frontier.

Count d'Erlon will occupy Thuin, with a division; and should the bridge of that town be destroyed, he must immediately repair it. He must likewise plan and construct a bridgehead on the left bank. This division will also be responsible for the bridge at the Abbey at Aulne and Count d'Erlon must ensure a bridgehead is also constructed at this place.

The order of march prescribed to the Third Corps for the artillery, trains and baggage will be observed by the Second and First Corps, the baggage of which will be united, and will march on the left of the First Corps, under the orders of the most senior Commissary General.

The Fourth Corps (the army of the Moselle) has received orders to take position on this day in advance of Philippeville: if its movement is complete and the divisions that compose this army corps are concentrated, Lieutenant General Gérard will put them in march at three o'clock tomorrow morning, and direct them on Charleroi. He must be careful to maintain alignment with the Third Corps, with whom he will maintain communication, in order to arrive before Charleroi nearly at the same time; but General Gérard must clear his right, and will scour all the approaches leading to Namur. He will march in close order of battle, leaving at Philippeville all the baggage and followers so that his army corps will be better able to manoeuvre.

General Gérard will order the Fourteenth Division of cavalry, which will arrive today at Philippeville, to follow the movement of his army corps on Charleroi, where that division will join the Fourth Cavalry Corps.

Lieutenant Generals Reille, Vandamme and Gérard will communicate with each other using patrols and ensure they arrive before Charleroi at about the same time and concentrated. If possible, they will attach Flemish speaking officers to their advanced guards so that they may interrogate the local population and thus gain information; but these officers must be careful only to give out that they command patrols and do not mention the Grand Army in their rear.

Lieutenant Generals Reille, Vandamme and Gérard will direct all the sappers of their army corps (having along with them materials for repairing the bridges) to march after the first regiment of light infantry, and will direct the engineer officers to repair the bad routes, to open lateral communications, and to throw bridges over those streams which the infantry cannot conveniently ford.

The Marines and Sappers of the Guard and sappers of the reserve, will follow the lead regiment of the Third Corps: Lieutenant Generals Rogniat and Haxo will be at their head: they will take along with them only two or three carriages: the remainder of the park of engineers will march on the left of the Third Corps. If the enemy is encountered, these troops are not to be engaged, but generals Rogniat and Haxo will employ them in the works for crossing rivers, the construction of bridgeheads, repairing roads and openings etc.

The cavalry of the Guard will follow the movement on Charleroi, and set out at eight o'clock.

The Emperor will accompany the advanced guard on the Charleroi road. The Lieutenant Generals will be careful to send his Majesty frequent reports respecting their movements and the information they may obtain; they are aware that his Majesty's intention is to pass the Sambre before noon and to cross the army to the left bank of that river.

The bridge equipages will be divided into two sections; the first section will be divided into three parts, each consisting of five pontoons and five advanced guard boats to throw three bridges across the Sambre; to each of these subdivisions a company of *pontonniers* [bridging troops] will be attached; the first section will march in the train of the park of engineers after the Third Corps. The second section will remain with the reserve park of artillery, at the baggage column; it will have along with it the fourth company of *pontonniers*.

The Emperor's equipages and the baggage of Imperial Headquarters will be collected and put in march at ten o'clock. As soon as they shall be passed, the Commissary General will direct the equipage of the Imperial Guard and Third and Sixth Corps to depart: at the same time he will order the column of equipages of the reserve of the cavalry to march, and to follow the direction which the cavalry has taken. The trains of the army will follow the headquarters and march at the head of the baggage; but on no account should this baggage, the reserve parks of the artillery, or the second section of the bridge equipages advance within three leagues [about 8 miles] of the army, without an order from the *major général*, or pass the Sambre without orders to that effect.

The Commissary General will form divisions of this baggage and appoint officers to command them so that he may detach from them what may afterwards be required at headquarters or for the service of the officers.

The *Intendant General* will unite to this column of equipages the whole of the baggage and transports of the administration to which he will assign a place in the column. The carriages which may be delayed, will take the left and must not quit the rank in which they are placed except by order of the Quarter Master General.

The Emperor orders that all the equipage carriages which may be found in the columns of the infantry, cavalry or artillery shall be burnt, as well as the carriages of the equipage column which may quit their rank and disrupt their march without the express permission of the Quarter Master General.

For this purpose a detachment of fifty gendarmes shall be placed at the disposal of the Quarter Master General who, as well as the officers of the gendarmerie and the gendarmes, are responsible for the execution of these arrangements on which the success of the campaign may depend.

By order of the Emperor,
The Marshal of the Empire,
Major Général Duc de Dalmatie[3]

Essentially, Napoleon planned to advance in three columns; the left, consisting of Reille's 2nd Corps and d'Erlon's 1st Corps, would guard the army's left flank and cross the Sambre at Marchienne-au-Pont. The centre, consisting of most of Grouchy's cavalry, Vandamme's 3rd Corps, the Imperial Guard and Lobau's 6th Corps, would cross at Charleroi. The right column, consisting of Gérard's 4th Corps and a division of Grouchy's cavalry reserve would guard the right flank and also cross at Charleroi. Sensibly, the baggage would move under strict control to avoid it interfering with the combat formations.

Like the orders for the concentration of the army, these orders have been widely praised for their clarity and detail. Houssaye wrote:

> These orders are justly considered as perfect. Napoleon had never issued marching orders that were more carefully studied or better thought out, even in the happy days of Austerlitz and Friedland. Never had his genius been more brilliant, never had he exhibited to such perfection, his attention to detail, his broad grasp of the whole, his clearness and his mastery of the science of war.[4]

As we shall see, unfortunately for Napoleon, through a combination of treachery, accident and incompetence, they were not to be faithfully executed.

The Troops

For the troops, there was a mixture of excitement and apprehension; from the accounts we have, most appear to have been happy to be back on campaign.

> It was the first bivouac of the campaign. One could hardly sleep, but not because of the rain which stopped and started, but because everyone was discussing the operations of the next day. Each made the decisions of generals without understanding the big issues, and each bivouac found itself transformed into a council of war, which did not prevent these clever men from feeding the fires with wood and getting the marmites [cooking pots] boiling.[5]

It was not to be a particularly comfortable night; we have heard already that it rained, and as the soldiers did not have tents available, most were forced to lie in the open:

> This night, the soldier had the starry sky as the roof of his tent, for a mattress the grass on the edge of a wood, with leaves as his covers and the comforts of his pack to support his head![6]

Unlike their opposite numbers in Wellington's army, a very high proportion of the French soldiers were veterans of previous campaigns and knew how to make life in the bivouac and on the march more comfortable. Despite Napoleon's careful orders to ensure the troops started the campaign with some rations in their packs, the rice they had been issued was discarded to lighten the load they had to carry in the heat, and this was not all they threw away:

> On the 14th, the division continued its march, made a halt at Jeumont Heath and then moved on to Solre-sur-Sambre where it went into bivouac. There the soldiers of all the formations, knowing they were about to open the campaign, loosening the yoke of discipline, threw away their summer breeches and gaiters in order to lighten their pack as much as possible.[7]

Yet not everyone was able to rest; some men had to work. The 1st Cavalry Corps spent the night split between Boussu-sur-Heure and Walcourt, with the headquarters in the latter town. During the course of the evening a local man went to the headquarters to warn Pajol of the poor state of the roads along which they were due to advance the next day. The routes required repair before they could take artillery and in some places, even cavalry. The wood of Saint-Naubert had been blocked by trenches and *abattis* by the Prussians. Thanks to this information Pajol was able to send out parties of men to make the necessary repairs and this was accomplished before the advance started the next morning. Pajol was annoyed that the local *douaniers* (customs men), who had been allocated as guides, had failed to mention these obstacles.

Chapter 4

Morning, 15 June

After only a relatively short rest, given the hard marching of the day before, the soldiers were woken before daylight. Even for the men in the ranks who had experienced a wet, but warm bivouac, it seems that the rest was sufficient. 'The army was able to set off on their march after a rest of five hours; sufficient for the rank and file to recover from the fatigues of the previous day.'[1] Breakfast was normally taken during a break in the march if time allowed and therefore, once the *diane* had been beaten, it took little time for the troops to be ready to march:

> Getting to his feet at the first beat of a drum stick, the soldier returns to the front of his squad, where he quickly retakes his place at the arms stacks prepared before they were stood down; on the command he seizes his arms, the columns are formed and they are ready to set off. All this is an affair of a moment.[2]

When the troops had formed up, the emperor's proclamation to the army was read out.

> Soldiers! This is the anniversary of Marengo and of Friedland, which twice decided the fortunes of Europe. But then, as after Austerlitz, and as after Wagram, we were too generous; we believed the protestations and the oaths of the kings whom we had left on their thrones. Now, however, they have formed a League to overthrow the sacred rights of France. They have decided on the most unjust aggressions. Let us therefore march to meet them, for are not we and they still the same men?
>
> Soldiers! At Jena, the Prussians, so arrogant today, were three to one against you; at Montmirail you were one to six. As for the English, let those who have been their prisoners tell the tale of the miseries and tortures they suffered whilst cooped up on their prison hulks!
>
> Saxons, Belgians, Hanoverians, the forces of the Rhine Confederation, groan at being compelled to assist the cause of the kings who are enemies of justice and of the rights of the people. They know full well that this coalition will be insatiable. After having swallowed 12,000,000 Poles, 12,000,000 Italians, 1,000,000 Saxons, 6,000,000 Belgians, it will devour the second-tier States of Germany. Madmen! A moment of good fortune has made them blind. The oppression and humiliation of France are

beyond their powers, if they cross her frontiers it will be but to find their graves.

Soldiers! We shall be called upon to make forced marches, to fight battles, and to face dangers; but, with perseverance, victory will be ours; the rights, the honour, the happiness of our country will be regained.

For every Frenchman who has a heart, the time has come to conquer or to die![3]

However rousing the proclamation as we read it today, it is hard to be sure how carefully the tired soldiers listened in the damp, grey dawn, although at least one commanding officer assures us that it had the planned effect. 'I read the emperor's proclamation to my regiment . . . The words had the best effect; there was entire confidence in ultimate success that would force Europe to recognise our rights.'[4]

The Prussian Forces
The first forces the French would meet were those of the 1st and 2nd Brigades of General Zieten's 1st Prussian Corps (it should be remembered that in the Prussian army a brigade was the equivalent of a British or French division) and some of the Cavalry Reserve. Steinmetz's 1st Brigade was centred on Fontaine-l'Evêque, covering the crossings at Lobbes, Thuin and the abbey at Aulne. Pirch's 2nd Brigade, centred on Charleroi, covered the bridges at that place, Marchienne-au-Pont to the west and Châtelet to the east. Despite the efforts that the French troops had gone to in order to shield their bivouac fires from the Prussian outposts, the light was reflected off the low clouds and when the French crossed the frontier on the morning of the 15th, the Prussian outposts were formed up and under arms.

The Left Column
Reille's corps started off at the time prescribed by Napoleon's movement order (3am). For many units, the day started in similar fashion: '. . . first thing on the morning of the 15th, we had read to us a proclamation that the emperor addressed to his army before starting the campaign. After this lecture, which was our signal to march forwards, we headed for Thuin in Belgium.'[5]

There were four bridges to the front of 2nd Corps' front; those at Lobbes, Thuin, L'Abbaye d'Aulne and Marchienne-au-Pont. Of these, only the last was of real importance as the first three had poor access to major roads and the ground and routes were generally unsuitable for cavalry and particularly for artillery. The importance of the first three to the French was that if they were held they would protect the vulnerable left flank of the advancing army. The roads that the French were advancing over were poor; none were paved and they were muddy and rutted. Given that some had been blocked by the Prussians with various obstacles, the plan to move the sappers near the front of the advancing columns was a wise one and they were no doubt kept very busy.

Reille's advance was led by Bachelu's division supported by Piré's cavalry. These were followed by the division of Prince Jérôme and then Foy. Only half an hour after they set off, the advance guard, two battalions provided by the 2nd *légère*, was in contact with the Prussian outpost at the hamlet of Maladrie on the outskirts of Thuin, a small town built on the French (left bank) side of the Sambre that was occupied by the 3rd Battalion of the 2nd Regiment of Westphalian Landwehr. Only a small distance to the west was another bridge, near the village of Lobbes, that was also defended by a Prussian post. Lobbes was on the far (right) bank. This outpost and the village were manned by troops from the 2nd Battalion of the 1st Westphalian Landwehr Regiment commanded by Captain Gillhausen, supported by the 6th Uhlans. In the face of overwhelming numbers these troops could to do little but attempt to impose upon their attackers by making best use of natural defences and their superior knowledge of the ground. After the French started to develop their attack they had no choice but to retire; to stand and fight was to guarantee their destruction. Thuin occupied a particularly strong natural position, situated on a steep hill with old, but useful defences and narrow streets, and Major Monsterberg with his 3rd Battalion of the 2nd Westphalian Landwehr Regiment was able to put up a 'tenacious' resistance before being pushed back and practically destroyed; Monsterberg himself was captured. Lemonnier-Delafosse, General Foy's chief-of-staff, reported:

> ... however, these enemy forces did not stop our infantry, whose prompt and vigorous attack broke them and they ran from Thuin beyond the Rome Wood,[6] on the high ground above Marchienne-au-Pont.[7]

At about 7am, the Prussians attempted to fall back on Montigny where there were two squadrons of the 1st West Prussian Dragoons, who covered their retreat after this village was also taken by Bachelu's men. Unfortunately for the Landwehr battalion, the dragoons were overwhelmed by a sudden attack by Piré's troopers and the battalion was almost destroyed before it could reach Marchienne. Reille later wrote:

> At 3am on the 15th, it [the 2nd Corps] crossed the frontier and headed for Marchienne-au-Pont; the advance guard came into contact with a post of cavalry and infantry in front of Thuin with a Prussian battalion of about 800 men in the town itself. This battalion, pursued by cavalry, stopped for a time in the wood of Montigny-le-Tigneux, but having been pressed by the lead infantry, and the 200 cavalry it had with it being insufficient to support it properly, it was defeated with the loss of about 100 men killed or wounded and 200 prisoners.[8]

The remains of Captain Gillhausen's battalion made its way back to Fontaine l'Évêque where Steinmetz's 1st Brigade headquarters was located. The bridge at L'Abbaye d'Aulne fell to Reille's troops between 8 and 9 o'clock.

Once General Zieten was convinced that the whole of the French army was on the march he sent couriers to both Blücher and Wellington warning them of events and sent orders to his two forward brigades. The 1st (Steinmetz) was to retire via Courcelles to a position to the rear of Gosselies on the road to Brussels, and the 2nd was to protect the bridges at Marchienne, Charleroi and Châtelet to cover the flank of the 1st Brigade and hold up the French on the line of the Sambre. His 3rd and 4th Brigades were to move to Fleurus, close to the army's concentration point of Sombreffe.

Although marked by success, the taking of the bridges at Lobbes, Thuin and L'Abbaye d'Aulne, and the skirmishes with the Prussians along the river were a sideshow to the 2nd Corps' main advance on the vital crossing point at Marchienne. Whilst Bachelu busied himself with the pursuit of the Prussians along the river, Foy's division took up the lead towards the vital bridge at Marchienne. Reille had reached this bridge without too much delay, but now he failed to push home his advantage. The bridge was defended by the 2nd Battalion, the 6th Prussian Regiment, belonging to the 2nd Brigade. They had two guns in support and had barricaded the bridge but not destroyed it. Instead of attempting a *coup de main* against a well-organised but nervous defence, Reille waited until most of his forces had struggled along the poor roads to join him and his first two attempts on the bridge were repulsed. Napoleon's movement order had anticipated Reille arriving at Marchienne at 9am; at 8.30 Soult wrote to him.

Letter from Soult to Reille, bivouac of Jumignon,[9] 8.30am, 15 June.
M. le comte Reille, the emperor orders me to write that you should cross the Sambre if you do not have any enemy in front of you and to form in several lines, one or two leagues beyond in order to be across the main road to Brussels and to reconnoitre in strength towards Fleurus. M. Le comte d'Erlon will cross at Marchienne and form up in battle order on the Charleroi to Mons road, from where he will be able to support you if required.

If you are still at Marchienne when the present order reaches you, and that the move on Charleroi has not been possible, you are to operate via Marchienne, and to take up the position given above.

The emperor is moving beyond Charleroi. Immediately send a report to His Majesty of your operations and of what you are facing.
Le Maréchal d'empire, major général, Duc de Dalmatie[10]

The only new direction in this letter is the requirement for Reille to form up 'one or two leagues', that is 8 to 10 kilometres, up the Brussels road. This would take him to just beyond the town of Gosselies. It also informs him that the 1st Corps will cover his left flank and rear by facing and scouting towards Mons.

While Reille hesitated before Marchienne, d'Erlon's 1st Corps was slowly following him up. D'Erlon, who had been ordered to start his march at 3am, had not instructed reveille to be sounded until 4am.

> Solre-sur-Sambre, 14 June 'Evening'.
> The *diane* [reveille] is to be beaten at 4am precisely; the Order of the Day
> of the Army, dated the 14th, is to be read to the troops.
>   Signed d'Erlon

He could not, therefore, have started his march much before 4.30am, an hour and a half after he had been ordered. Although he gave no reason for this, the criticism he has received for this from some writers – Ropes is particularly damning – seems a little unfair. The 1st Corps had to wait until the whole of the 2nd Corps, which they were to follow, had moved off before they could start their march. As they both had the same start time and their bivouac areas were relatively close together, even if 1st Corps had been ready to move at 3am as ordered, it is unlikely that the whole of 2nd Corps would have set off. D'Erlon's troops had to wait for three infantry divisions, a cavalry division and all their artillery to start their march before they could follow. It is estimated that a corps covered 15 kilometres of road, that is, about a four-hour march from front to rear. In addition, the 2nd Corps were inevitably held up by the actions at Lobbes and Thuin and the poor road network did not allow the 1st Corps to take an alternative route.

It was a bleak start for some of 1st Corps's soldiers:

> On the 15th, before daybreak, we entered Belgium in gloomy, wet weather. The ground, soaked from the day before, sunk under our feet and tired out our infantry, for, when you advance to the attack, the roads are reserved for the artillery and cavalry, and the infantry has to march across the fields.[11]

As he advanced, d'Erlon relieved the 2nd Corps detachments that had continued to hold the various bridges along the Sambre after they had been captured, allowing those detachments to rejoin their parent formations. Captain Duthilt, ADC to General Bourgeois who commanded the 2nd Brigade of the 1st Division, tells us how part of the 1st Corps was thus deployed:

> On the 15th two divisions of the 1st Corps marched on Marchienne-au-Pont, the 1st Division remained as the rear-guard ... Our division slept at Thuin, a town where 7 to 800 Prussians had been beaten and put to rout by some of our companies of voltigeurs. Maréchal de Camp Gobrecht [commander of the 2nd Brigade of Piré's cavalry division] was left at

Solre-sur-Sambre and Bienne-sur-Thuin, the 3rd Lancers at the first of these posts, and the 4th Lancers at the second, to maintain communications with Maubeuge ... and also to watch out for any movement from the direction of Mons. This cavalry was to push patrols along the roads to Mons and Binche, and if it was forced to retire, either by the presence of the enemy or by an order of recall, it was to destroy the bridge at Solre and to move promptly to Thuin where the 1st Brigade of the 1st Division would wait for it.[12]

It was to be a dull day for d'Erlon's troops, but they were not to be completely sheltered from the horrors of war, as Lieutenant Martin explained.

Our corps was not engaged on this day; it followed that of Reille, who led the advance, and it was in their wake that I saw once more, for the first time for 18 months, the wounded and dead spread on the ground. This spectacle, which so vividly announced the upcoming return of such bloody scenes, made a big impression on me: my heart beat faster, it recalled it all. Why do I say this, since it did not prevent me from doing my duty?[13]

Sometime around 11am, d'Erlon received a similar letter to the one Soult had addressed to Reille at 8.30am.

Bivouac at Jumignon, 10am, 15 June.
M. le Comte, the emperor orders me to write that Comte Reille has received the order to cross the Sambre at Charleroi, and to form in several lines one or two leagues in front of this town across the main road to Brussels.
    The intention of his Majesty is that you should cross the Sambre at Marchienne, or at Ham [Ham was 6 kilometres from the river!], to move onto the main road from Charleroi to Mons, where you are to form up in several lines and to take position close to those of Comte Reille, maintaining your communications and sending patrols in all directions: Mons, Nivelle, etc. ...This movement should also be followed if Comte Reille is obliged to cross at Marchienne. Keep me informed of your operations and what you are facing; the emperor has passed Charleroi.[14]

Reille was not ready to attack Marchienne again until around midday. Under Foy's direction, 'the bridge was crossed by our skirmishers at the charge, supported by a deep column of infantry and the enemy started his retreat.'[15] However, most of the Prussian defenders had withdrawn in compliance with their orders and the small rear-guard defended the bridge without determination. By this time the central column had already seized the bridge at Charleroi over an hour before and Napoleon himself had crossed there. Although Reille could now start to get his corps across the river, this was to be a long and painful process. Not only was there a single, narrow bridge, approached by equally narrow streets, but he was still waiting for all his detachments covering the other captured crossings to be relieved by d'Erlon's men and to rejoin him.

The Centre Column

The morning did not get off to a very auspicious start for the centre column. Although Pajol's cavalry, who were to lead the advance, departed on time, the 3rd Corps, who were to follow them ahead of the Imperial Guard and 6th Corps, were not ready. The commander of this corps, General Vandamme, had taken lodgings in Beaumont on the 14th, but was told to leave and move closer to his corps on the arrival of imperial headquarters. He had left in a bad humour and moved to a country house that was difficult to find. Soult had sent only a single officer to Vandamme with the army's movement order and this officer searched in vain for Vandamme's headquarters, finally suffering a fall from his horse that broke his leg. With no one to pass the important message to, the morning found the 3rd Corps still quiet in their bivouacs.

General Rogniat, who had been ordered to join Vandamme's column, found this general ignorant of his orders. Expressing his astonishment at the inactivity, he informed Vandamme that he should immediately start his move on Charleroi. The abrasive Vandamme, indignant at Rogniat's tone, explained that he had received no orders from imperial headquarters. However, he immediately took the necessary steps to get his corps on the move, but it needed time to get 17,000 men up, concentrate them and get them moving. Despite his determination, this unfortunate incident put the 3rd Corps about three hours behind schedule and they did not set off on their march until about 6am, according to an officer of the 37th Line.[16] Not waiting for the 3rd Corps to get ready, the imperial guard started its march; the 6th Corps waited for Vandamme to get on his way before moving off themselves. To be fair to Vandamme, he marched his corps hard, despite the difficult country and poor roads, but a large proportion of the army suffered a long delay and this ensured that Napoleon's timetable was immediately undermined. The implications of only a single set of orders being sent to the 3rd Corps were to be significant.

The centre column was to be led by Grouchy's cavalry and, unlike those of the left and right, the centre had a number of parallel routes to choose from. Grouchy received specific instructions from the *major général*:

Beaumont, 15 June.
... Several routes lead to Charleroi from Beaumont; that of the right passes through Boussu, Fleurieux, Vogines and Yve, where it joins the main road from Philippeville to Charleroi. It is this route that you are to

take so as not to interfere with the other columns; but, before moving, ensure this route has been reconnoitred, and control your movement to conform with that of the left column, at the head of which General Pajol will be moving. I have warned General Gérard of the route you are to follow; his corps is formed up in front of Philippeville and will be moving on Charleroi from the same direction.

I must also inform you that a Prussian corps of 6,000 infantry is reported to be established at Jumignon. If this is true, the emperor wants this corps taken; manoeuvre accordingly ...

Le Maréchal d'empire, major général, Duc de Dalmatie

General Pajol had his corps mounted and ready to move at 2.30am. His mission was to clear the route for the central column. This followed, as far as Jumignon and Bommerée, the valley of the River Heure and the tracks on both sides of this valley. To achieve this he had the divisions of Soult (the marshal's younger brother) and Subervie from his own corps, as well as Domon's cavalry divison that was attached to him from Vandamme's corps. Less than two leagues from their bivouacs they encountered the Prussian outposts which were centred on Ham-sur-Heure. These outposts were not surprised; despite the precautions that Napoleon had prescribed a deserter, a drummer from the Imperial Guard no less, had presented himself to the outposts the previous night and warned them of the coming storm. This information had been sent back up the chain of command and had resulted in Marshal Blücher ordering the concentration of his army at Sombreffe. The desertion of General Bourmont in the early hours of the morning had confirmed this information.

Using subsidiary routes, each division advanced on a slightly different axis. Some of these were extremely difficult, but this avoided any mix-ups and confusion. Pajol himself marched at the head of Soult's division, where he was well placed to communicate with Vandamme to his right and the emperor to his left. The divisions on each flank were also ordered to maintain communications with the formations on their flanks. Warned of the Prussian post at Ham-sur-Heure, Pajol's deployment approached this position from left, right and centre, and in this way he hoped to capture it as he had been ordered by Marshal Soult's earlier message.

The first contact with Prussian sentries and weak patrols was made near Cour-sur-Heure; these withdrew quickly as Pajol advanced and it was at Ham-sur-Heure, where Pajol arrived towards 6am, that the first serious contact was made. Here the route was barricaded and defended by a Prussian battalion. A vigorous charge was sufficient to compel them to retreat, leaving a hundred prisoners in French hands.

Colonel Biot, one of Pajol's ADCs, had been attached to Subervie's division to lead its advance. Going ahead of the foremost troops into Thy-le

Chateau, Biot found Napoleon there with his escort conducting his own reconnaissance. The emperor, learning of Vandamme's late start, had taken the sappers and marines of the guard, as well as part of the Young Guard, and taken a lateral route to the left. Napoleon wanted to interrogate the *burg-mestre* (the mayor), and Biot was ordered to find him. However, he returned with a young man whom he had recognised earlier and spoken to, feeling he would have the information the emperor was interested in. Napoleon immediately recognised the man, who was called Duhaut, and said, 'Have you not served in the Gardes d'Honneur?'

'Yes, Sire.'

'And what do you do now?' replied the emperor.

'I am married, Sire.'

'Ah, Ah! You have done well; would you like to serve again?' The young man hesitated, but before he could properly answer, Napoleon pressed him and he was made a lieutenant in the cavalry. Biot, who recorded this story, comments, 'He was probably killed, for I did not hear of him again'![17]

An hour later, at 7am, Pajol approached Jumignon where soon after he met the emperor accompanied by the four Service Squadrons. No Prussians were found at this place and Soult continued his march towards Bommerée, where he met Domon's division. These two divisions continued their march side by side. It was at about this time that cannon fire was heard to the west; this was from Reille's engagements. Moving up onto some high ground, Pajol was able to watch this action, and while he was there he noticed some Prussians concentrating at the farm of La Tombe, near the village of Couillet to his east. Sending the 4th Chasseurs, commanded by Colonel Desmichels and supported by the 9th, to this place, the Prussian infantry took refuge in the buildings where the cavalry could not touch them. However, Colonel Biot, seeing the situation, sent over a howitzer, and, faced by this, the Prussian force, which turned out to be a company of the 28th Prussian Regiment, surrendered.[18]

Whilst this action held up Domon's men, Soult continued his advance as far as Marcinelle, on the southern outskirts of Charleroi. This village was connected to Charleroi by a dyke 300 paces in length, terminating at a bridge, the head of which was barricaded. Pajol wanted to take this post at a rush, but a strong force of Prussian skirmishers, hidden behind the hedges, the garden walls and in the houses, engaged the 1st Hussars that led the advance and a man was even killed and several wounded in Pajol's escort. Pajol had no option but to wait for some of Vandamme's infantry to come up, but he used the time to turn the Prussian position and to send General Amiel to try to find a ford where his cavalry could cross and continue the advance. Unfortunately, there was none. If Vandamme had started his march on time, Charleroi could have been in French hands at 7am. The full implications of his delay were now beginning to be felt.

Luckily, the sappers and marines of the imperial guard, led by Generals Haxo and Rogniat, arrived at Jumignon just as Napoleon learnt of Pajol's dilemma, and he sent them forward. Arriving with Pajol at 10.30am, he immediately ordered them to attack Marcinelle. Despite their relative numerical weakness, the élan of their attack was irresistible and the Prussians fell back into Charleroi and prepared to defend the barricade and palisade that blocked the bridge over the Sambre. However, the French quickly followed up their advantage and the sappers and marines stormed over the bridge, followed by Soult's cavalry with Pajol at its head. No attempt had been made by the Prussians to destroy the bridge and by 11.30am Charleroi and its precious bridge were in French hands.

Whilst Pajol's troopers and elements of the guard were pushing back the Prussian advance posts and seizing the bridge at Charleroi, Vandamme's troops were closing the gap between them. His lead elements approached the bridge at midday[19] and the whole corps took an hour to defile across the narrow bridge.

In contrast to the lukewarm reception even Napoleon himself had received at Beaumont, which was in France, there was a warmer welcome in Charleroi. Gourgaud noted that after crossing the border they were, 'received as friends'[20] and one of the staff officers in imperial headquarters reported:

> A great number of women in a crowd, moved in front of the troops, shouting, 'Long live the French, long live our compatriots! Give us the tricolour!' ... Having heard from the inhabitants of Charleroi that some Prussian officers who were garrisoned in the town had only managed to escape without having time to put on their breeches, I told the emperor this story which made him roar with laughter.[21]

The Right Column

Gérard's 4th Corps, three infantry divisions and a cavalry division, was furthest from Charleroi and not expected to be involved in any fighting that day. Gérard was to have concentrated forward of Philippeville and have set off at 3am, regulating his move with that of the 3rd Corps to his left and followed by Delort's 14th Cavalry Division. One of his main tasks was to protect the right flank of the advance, covering the approaches from Namur, around which it was known there was a corps of Prussians. The 4th Corps were to cross the Sambre at Charleroi.

However, not all Gérard's troops had reached Philippeville the day before and these required time to close up. Thus they were late forming up and did not gather on the heights of Florenne, their concentration point, until 7am. Gérard's movement orders did not leave his headquarters in Philippeville until 2am, only an hour before the troops were due to move out! Worse was to come. Gérard's 14th Division was commanded by General Bourmont, a noted royalist (he had once been imprisoned for being complicit in an attempt on Napoleon's life!), but one that had fought under Napoleon and had proven his combat ability the previous year in his successful defence of Nogent-sur-Seine, which had seen him promoted to *général de division*. Napoleon had only reluctantly agreed to give him a command after being urged to do so by Ney and Gérard, who had both sworn to answer for him. It was a decision all three of them were to regret.

Early in the morning of the 15th, before the corps was due to begin its advance, General Bourmont, accompanied by his chief-of-staff, Colonel Clouet, two of his staff officers and two ADCs, left his headquarters at Florenne and deserted to the Prussians. When Colonel Rumigny, who carried the movement orders for this division, arrived at that village, he was surrounded by soldiers shouting, 'We are betrayed, down with the traitors!'[22] This news had an almost catastrophic effect on the division as well as the corps, and it required passionate speeches by Gérard and General Hulot (the senior brigade commander who took over command of the division) to restore order. By this time there was no hope of the corps crossing the Sambre at 8am as Gérard's orders prescribed, and the best that could be hoped for was to march hard and try to make up as much time as possible.

Despite the impressive planning of Napoleon and his headquarters, and the detail laid down in their orders, a succession of problems had already disrupted their intended timetable; the result of accidents, incompetence and treachery. Many historians, mostly those who set out merely to criticise Napoleon, emphasise the incompetence, but those familiar with war will quickly realise that it was the inevitable 'friction' that comes with military operations. It is fair to conclude that a commander as familiar with the friction of war as Napoleon was probably satisfied with the morning's work.

Chapter 5

Afternoon, 15 June

The Left Column

Beyond Charleroi was a major road junction, with main roads leading towards Mons, Brussels and Namur. After its successful capture, Napoleon immediately sent Pajol's cavalry in pursuit of the retreating Prussians. Colonel Gourgaud, Napoleon's *premier officier d'ordonnance*, takes up the story:

> Hardly out of Charleroi, we saw an enemy column, infantry and cavalry, of twelve to fifteen hundred men, retiring in great disorder on the Brussels road. I pointed them out to Pajol who immediately sent the 1st Hussars after them, commanded by my friend General Clary [commander of the 1st Brigade of the 4th Division (Soult)]. I accompanied this regiment. The enemy infantry, to save themselves, dispersed into the large village of … [Gourgaud leaves this blank, but Prussian accounts name the village as Jumet]. We took a hundred prisoners and continued to pursue the cavalry [this was the 6th Uhlans] as far as Gosselies. There, some hidden Prussian infantry fired on us by platoon at fifteen paces. My frightened horse, swerving suddenly, fell with me into a ditch. I thought I would be captured, but the hussars did not abandon me; they stopped my horse and gave me the time to remount. The enemy infantry, after firing their volley and receiving ours, retired a little and I rejoined the 1st Hussars with my brave platoon. I discussed the situation with Clary; we deployed three squadrons in line on the plain with one remaining in column on the road. This move forced the enemy to reveal a large part of his force; we could distinguish eight to ten thousand men, infantry and cavalry.
>
> Being more than two leagues from Charleroi, and having a long village behind us, we began to skirmish, but as we started our withdrawal we lost a few hussars and an officer was killed. We captured three officers and ten lancers.
>
> The enemy followed us as far as the middle of the long village where we stopped. I left at the gallop to warn the emperor that it appeared as if the enemy held the route to Brussels in force.[1]

Zieten's troops were withdrawing east across the front of the French advance, leaving their southern flank vulnerable. Identifying that the main road to Brussels from Charleroi was a likely French axis, he had sent his 3rd

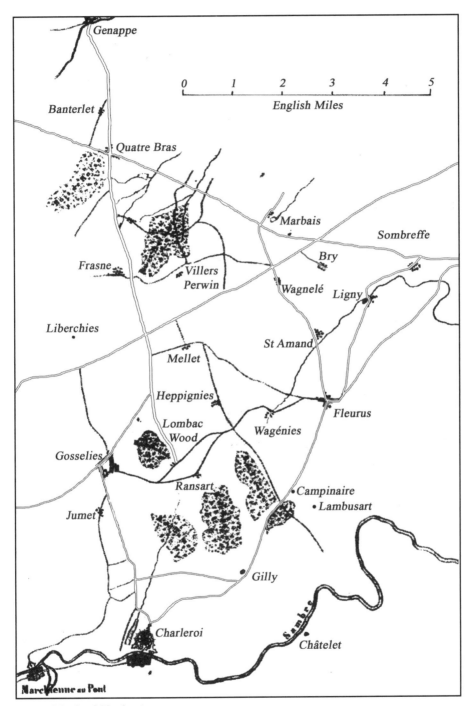

Map 4. North of Charleroi.

Brigade to occupy Gosselies, through which this road passed. The 6th Uhlans, commanded by Colonel Lützow, the former partisan leader, were also there, having been left by the Reserve Cavalry commander to maintain contact with Zieten's men. These were the troops encountered by Gourgaud and Clary.

Informed of this check by Colonel Gourgaud and concerned about the left flank of his own advance towards Fleurus, Napoleon sent Gourgaud to Reille to hurry his advance and vigorously attack the Prussian force occupying Gosselies. He then sent Lefebvre-Desnoëttes, with his two light cavalry regiments of the guard and two batteries, up this road to establish a block halfway between the two towns; he later reinforced them with a regiment of Duhesme's Young Guard. To ensure the left column was kept closed up and mutually supporting, Napoleon also had the following order sent to d'Erlon:

> Soult to d'Erlon, beyond Charleroi, 3pm, 15 June.
> M. *comte* d'Erlon, the emperor has ordered *comte* Reille to march on Gosselies, and to attack a body of the enemy that appears to have stopped there. The emperor's intention is that you are also to march on Gosselies to support *comte* Reille and to second his operations. However, you must continue to guard Marchienne, and you are to send a brigade onto the routes to Mons, ensuring it maintains its vigilance.[2]

When Reille finally came up on Gosselies, he deployed his artillery and opened fire. Pushing forward the 2nd *légère*, he took possession of the town. However, as soon as he pushed up the Brussels road he was strongly attacked and pushed back into the houses by Zieten's troops, which were being forced to bypass Gosselies to the north. Reille sent Piré's cavalry round the Moncaux wood to cut off the road to Brussels, but the Prussian troops had been able to continue their withdrawal towards Fleurus. Reille, having been joined by Marshal Ney, who had left his meeting with Napoleon at Charleroi with the cavalry of the guard, concentrated his corps around Gosselies.

The Centre Column
Having despatched the 1st Hussars towards Brussels, the remainder of Pajol's corps was directed along the main road towards Gilly and Sombreffe, towards which most of the Prussian defenders of Charleroi had retreated. Napoleon also sent forward the division of the Young Guard, less the regiment sent up the Brussels road, to support him. General Ameil, with the 5th Hussars, acted as the advance guard, but had not gone far when he came under fire from a Prussian rear-guard (General Pirch II's division) posted around Gilly. Grouchy went forward to reconnoitre the Prussian position. Hesitating because he thought the Prussians 20,000 strong, he was soon joined by Napoleon who, giving him the command of the right wing, declared it was only half that strength and ordered him to attack. Unfortunately, Napoleon

immediately left for Charleroi to hasten Vandamme's march, and it was not until he returned towards 6pm that the attack was launched.

Joining the troops as they prepared to launch their attack, Napoleon came across the 37th Line, one of whose officers reported:

> ... our divisions were massed on the plateau of Charleroi, where they waited for a time. Suddenly the emperor appeared on his horse in the middle of our columns. He addressed some words to the officer closest to him,
>
> 'What regiment?'
>
> 'Sire, the 37th'
>
> 'Ah! Gauthier's regiment? Your soldiers have poor greatcoats.'
>
> 'The Prussians have new ones.'
>
> 'They are there, go and take them!'[3]

Pirch had imposed on Grouchy and delayed his advance for several hours without firing a shot. However, as the French finally moved forward it soon became obvious that he was being outflanked and would be overwhelmed, so Zieten ordered him to withdraw. The French cavalry fell on the retreating infantry; one battalion was destroyed and another dispersed, but much of the Prussian force escaped, although their cavalry, trying to cover their with-drawal, was roughly handled by the overwhelming numbers of the French. Having gathered his division together, Pirch was again attacked and withdrew beyond Fleurus. In this attack, General Letort, now one of the emperor's ADCs, but long a commander of the Guard Dragoons, was killed leading the Service Squadrons, Napoleon's personal body guard, against the Prussian squares.

Grouchy was keen to capture Fleurus, which was only weakly defended, and then to drive on towards Sombreffe, but Vandamme, his troops exhausted after their forced marches and unaware that Grouchy had been given com-mand of the right wing, including his 3rd Corps, refused to carry out his orders and the opportunity was lost. The right wing bivouacked between Lambusart and Campinaire, 2 kilometres or so south of Fleurus.

The Right Column

With the delay imposed on the 4th Corps in getting the troops back into order and on the march, the poor state of the roads and the difficulties of passing such a high number of troops through the bottle neck of Charleroi, at 3.15pm orders were received to cross the Sambre at Châtelet, a small town about 5 kilometres to the east. This would considerably ease the congestion across the bridge at Charleroi and yet still give good egress to the routes heading towards Fleurus. A staff officer reported, 'Happily, no effort, no steps, had been made to destroy the bridge, which was not even defended.'[4] The small garrison had withdrawn when the Prussian rear-guard had made their stand at Gilly and so Gérard's troops were able to file across unhindered. If they had arrived earlier, they would have outflanked the Gilly position and may well have been able to cut the Prussians off. Although they had taken no active part in the offensive, by the end of the day they were just short of Fleurus, rejoining the main body of the right wing and well placed to take part in the operations planned for the 16th.

The Left Wing – Ney Takes Command

After leaving Grouchy to deal with the Prussian rear-guard at Gilly, Napoleon took up position at a key junction just to the north of Charleroi. Here he sat on a chair outside the Belle-Vue inn and watched the troops file past. Despite their cheers he soon fell fast asleep. He had decided to split his army into two wings and a reserve commanded by himself. The two wings, to be commanded by Ney (the left wing) and Grouchy (the right), would face Wellington and Blücher respectively and he would support one or the other with the reserve as the situation dictated. Each wing would be strong enough to hold its own against one of the allied armies, whilst the other wing, reinforced by the reserve, would defeat the other.

As he sat watching the troops march past he was finally joined by Marshal Ney. It was sometime around 4.30pm. It was certainly not 7pm as Colonel Heymès claims in his description of the meeting:

> At 7pm the marshal rejoined the emperor beyond Charleroi, at the junction of the roads to Brussels and Fleurus.
> 'Hello Ney', this prince said to him, 'I am pleased to see you; you are to take command of the 1st and 2nd Corps. General Reille is marching with three divisions on Gosselies. General d'Erlon is to sleep tonight at Marchienne-au-Pont. You will have with you Piré's light cavalry division. I also give you the two regiments of chasseurs and lancers of the Guard, but do not make use of them. Tomorrow you will be joined by the reserve heavy cavalry under the orders of General Kellerman. Go and push the enemy.'
> The wishes of the marshal had been answered; he had a corps. He forgot that there is nothing worse for a general than to take command of an army the day before a battle. He left the emperor and an hour later he was at the head of the 2nd Corps on the march; the skirmishers were in action, Gosselies had been passed.[5]

In his memoirs, Napoleon gives a rather different account of this meeting.

> Marshal Ney had just reached the battlefield. I immediately gave him the left composed of the 2nd and 1st Corps, of Lefebvre-Desnouëttes's cavalry division, and of General Kellerman's corps of heavy cavalry, comprising in all 47,800 men; and ordered him to charge like a bull at

anything he met on the Gosselies-Brussels road; to take up a position astride this road beyond Quatre Bras and to hold his position in the military sense, keeping strong advance guards on the Brussels, Namur and Nivelles roads.[6]

The difference between these accounts, in terms of how prescriptive Napoleon was to Ney in his direction on what to do with his command, is vital and will be discussed later. Most strategic analysts of the campaign give Napoleon's own account little credit; it smacks too much of hindsight and was written to strengthen the case against Ney. Despite the fact that the strategic importance of Quatre Bras (literally, 'four arms'; taking its name from the crossroads, forming four arms, leading to Namur, Charleroi, Brussels and Nivelles) was to become obvious, at this time Napoleon had too little information about the locations or intentions of either of his two protagonists to be so prescriptive in his instructions. This is thus likely to be a case of Napoleon pre-empting his later plan as he recalled the events in exile.

Leaving Napoleon, Ney immediately moved forward to join his command, meeting Reille as he was entering Gosselies. With this town in his hands, the road to Brussels was now open and four hours of daylight remained. He pushed forward Lefebvre-Desnouëttes's guard cavalry as an advance guard towards Frasnes and led Bachelu's and Piré's divisions forward to Mellet. Girard's division of the 2nd Corps was sent in pursuit of the Prussians that had been driven from Gosselies towards the east, whilst Foy and Prince Jérôme's divisions remained around Gosselies. A young officer in Foy's division wrote:

> After having crossed the Sambre at Marchienne-au-Pont, we took position in front of Gosselies to pass the night there. The day had been wet, the ground was soaked and the road was already ploughed up by the passage of our artillery and that of the enemy army that had retreated along it.[7]

Having had the whole of the 2nd Corps concentrated under his hand, Ney had now spread them out again, apparently cautious about advancing too much of his force ahead of the rest of the army and clearly forgetting or ignoring his instructions from Napoleon to push the enemy up the Brussels road. All he did was to order a reconnaissance to move towards Quatre Bras. Consequently, Lefebvre-Desnouëttes ordered General Colbert, commanding the Red Lancers, to send patrols forward towards Frasnes and as they moved forward they skirmished with some Prussian stragglers. However, when they reached the outskirts of Frasnes they found themselves under fire from some outposts manned by the 2nd Nassau-Usingen Regiment; the first contact the French had with Wellington's Anglo-Netherlands army.

From 1813 only the front rank of French cavalry lancer regiments were armed with lances; Napoleon felt that lances in the second rank could not be wielded effectively in close combat and so he had them armed with just carbines and sabres, allowing them to skirmish effectively. Faced by infantry in cover, the guard lancers dismounted some men and brought the Nassauers under skirmish fire. Under this fire from their front, and seeing that they were being outflanked by mounted squadrons to the west, the Nassauers withdrew towards their main body in the rear, covered by long-range artillery fire. The outflanking cavalry quickly closed with them and the Nassau regiment was forced to drive them off with volley fire. However, the lancers had succeeded in capturing some men and had even caused so many casualties amongst the horses of the artillery battery that the Dutch gunners struggled to get all their guns and caissons away (perhaps the French had deliberately aimed at the horses for this reason, rather than the more elusive gunners). The commander of the Guard Lancers, Lieutenant-General Count Édouard Colbert, pushed forward a reconnaissance as far as Quatre Bras itself, which he found apparently deserted, but lacking infantry and finding himself well forward of any support, he returned to Frasnes. Lefebvre-Desnouëttes later wrote a report to Ney on this action.

Frasnes, 9pm, 15 June.

Monsieur,

When we reached Frasnes, in accordance with your orders, we found it occupied by a regiment of Nassau infantry (some 1,500 men) and eight guns. As they observed that we were manoeuvring to turn them, they retired from the village where we had practically surrounded them with our squadrons. General Colbert even reached within musket shot of Quatre Bras on the high road, but as the ground was difficult, and the enemy fell back for support to the Bossu Wood and kept up a vigorous fire from their eight guns, it was impossible for us to carry it.

The troops which were found at Frasnes had not advanced this morning and were not engaged at Gosselies. They are under the orders of Lord Wellington, and appear to be retiring towards Nivelles. They set light to a beacon at Quatre Bras, and fired their guns a great deal. None of the [Prussian] troops who fought this morning at Gosselies have passed this way; they marched towards Fleurus.

The peasants can give no information about a large assembly of troops in this neighbourhood, only that there is a Park of Artillery at Tubize, composed of 100 ammunition wagons and twelve guns; they say that the Belgian army is in the neighbourhood of Mons, and that the headquarters of the Prince of Orange is at Braine-le-Comte. We took about 15 prisoners and we have suffered ten men killed or wounded.

Tomorrow at day break, if it is possible, I shall send a reconnaissance patrol to Quatre Bras so as to occupy that place, for I think that the Nassau troops have left it.

A battalion of infantry has just arrived [from Bachelu's division] and I have placed it in front of that village. My artillery has not joined me so I have sent orders for it to bivouac with Bachelu's division and rejoin me tomorrow morning.

I have not written to the emperor, as I have nothing more important to report to him than what I am telling your Excellency.

I have the honour, etc., L-D

I am sending you a non-commissioned officer to receive the orders of Your Excellency.

I have the honour to observe to your Excellency that the enemy has shown no cavalry in front of us and the artillery is 'light' [horse] artillery.

Whilst Lefebvre-Desnouëttes's cavalry pushed forward, Ney followed up and occupied Frasnes with Bachelu's division at about 9pm; a battalion of the 2nd *légère* was sent forward of the village to establish the outposts. The 2nd Corps had started their day sometime around 2am, had marched 40 kilometres and had a number of minor actions during the day; they were exhausted and had well deserved a rest. Heymès reported:

> ... the marshal occupied the village of Frasnes, situated on the main road to Brussels, a league from Quatre Bras, with Piré's light cavalry division and the infantry division commanded by General Bachelu. The two regiments of chasseurs and lancers of the Guard were in reserve behind this village. General Reille with two infantry divisions and their artillery remained at Gosselies where he passed the night. The divisions assured communications whilst awaiting the arrival of the 1st Corps which was to sleep at Marchienne-au-Pont.
>
> Night fell, the troops had been marching since 2am, information announced that ten battalions with artillery occupied Quatre Bras and that the English army manoeuvred to concentrate on this important point.[8]

The 1st Corps had marched all day but seen no action. Faced by the need to cover the left flank of the army by holding the crossings of the Sambre and patrolling down the roads towards Mons and supporting the 2nd Corps towards Gosselies, the divisions had inevitably become rather more spread out than the commander would have wished. In the evening, General d'Erlon wrote to Soult informing him of the locations of his divisions:

> Conforming with Your Excellency's order of 3pm, I moved on Gosselies. I found the 2nd Corps established there so placed my 4th division [Durutte] to the rear of this village and the 2nd [Donzelot] in front of Jumay [Jumet], a brigade of cavalry [Bruno's] in this place.
>
> The 3rd Division [Marcognet] has remained at Marchienne and the 1st [Quiot] at Thuin, my other brigade of cavalry [Gobrecht] is at Solre

and Bienne-sous-Thuin, so my troops are very spread out; I request Your Excellency to let me know if I can recall those that I have left in the rear ...[9]

Soult's response allowed d'Erlon to recall his most distant detachments and, whilst maintaining some patrols towards Mons, to concentrate the bulk of his corps across the Sambre.

> Soult to d'Erlon, Charleroi, 15 June.
>
> *M. le Comte*, the emperor's intention is that you concentrate your corps on the left bank of the Sambre and join the 2nd Corps at Gosselies, in line with the orders that you will be given on this subject by the Prince of the Moskowa.
>
> Also recall the troops that you have left at Thuin, Solre and that area. However, you are to always have numerous patrols on your left to cover the road to Mons.
>
> *Le maréchal d'empire, major général, Duc de Dalmatie*[10]

It is not known for sure what time this order reached d'Erlon, but he had now received unequivocal orders to 'join the 2nd Corps at Gosselies'. D'Erlon's troops were no doubt pleased with the opportunity to rest:

> The day drew to an end; we had been on our feet from 2am and had made a march of eight leagues without eating and made more tiresome by a suffocating heat. We bivouacked on the road to Brussels, a league in front of Charleroi.
>
> This night was better than the preceding one. It did not rain; the soldiers went to get wood and straw [Their foragers found 'several bottles of excellent old wine' in the cellar of a curate's house, 'that we drank to the health of the good priest'].[11]

*   *   *

With everything apparently now under control, and having been up since before 2am, Napoleon now took the opportunity to get some rest. His secretary wrote to Joseph, the emperor's brother, 'Monseigneur, it is 9pm. The emperor, who has been mounted since three o'clock this morning, has returned overwhelmed by fatigue. He has thrown himself onto his bed for a few hours rest. He is to rise again at midnight ...'

No doubt Soult was still working; receiving and preparing reports and orders. One of these was a situation report from Marshal Ney.

> Gosselies, 11pm, 15 June.
>
> Marshal,
>
> I have the honour to report to your Excellency that, in accordance with the orders of the emperor, I advanced with the cavalry of General Piré

and the infantry of General Bachelu to Gosselies this afternoon to dis-lodge the enemy from this point. The enemy made only slight resistance. After an exchange of 25 to 30 cannon shots, he retired through Heppignies to Fleurus. We have made 500 to 600 Prussian prisoners from the corps of General Zieten.

This is the situation of the troops:

- General Lefebvre-Desnoëttes, with the Lancers and Chasseurs of the Guard, at Frasnes.
- General Bachelu with the 5th Division at Mellet.
- General Foy with the 9th Division at Gosselies. [Prince Jérôme's division appears to have been forgotten, but is given by Gourgaud as being 'in the rear of the wood of Lambusart.']
- The light cavalry of General Piré at Heppignies.
- I do not know where General Reille is.
- General d'Erlon has sent to inform me that he is at Jumet with the greater part of his Army Corps. I have just sent him the instructions prescribed in your Excellency's letter of today's date. I annex to my letter a report received from General Lefebvre-Desnouëttes.

Accept Marshal, the assurances of my great regard, Ney.

Based on reports such as this, Soult produced a report summarising the operations of the day that would be sent back to Paris and published in the *Moniteur* on the 18th.[12]

On the 14th, the army was deployed as follows:

- Imperial Headquarters at Beaumont.
- The 1st Corps, commanded by General d'Erlon, was at Solre, on the Sambre.
- The 2nd Corps, commanded by General Reille, was at Ham-sur-Heure.
- The 3rd Corps, commanded by General Vandamme, was to the right of Beaumont.
- The 4th Corps, commanded by General Gérard, had arrived at Philippeville.

On the 15th, at 3am, General Reille attacked the enemy and moved on Marchienne-au-Pont. He had a number of engagements in which his cavalry charged a Prussian battalion and took 300 prisoners.

At 1am the emperor was at Jamioulx-sur-Heure.[13]

General Domon's light cavalry division cut up two Prussian battalions and took 400 prisoners.

General Pajol entered Charleroi at midday. The Sappers and Marines of the Guard were with the advance guard to repair the bridges; they were the first to enter the town. General Clary with the 1st Hussars moved towards Gosselies on the main road to Brussels, and General Pajol moved on Gilly, on the Namur road.

At 3pm, General Vandamme approached Gilly with his corps.

Marshal Grouchy arrived there with General Exelman's cavalry.

The enemy occupied a position to the left of Fleurus. At 5pm the emperor ordered the attack. The position was turned and taken. The four Service Squadrons of the Guard, commanded by General Letort, ADC to the emperor, broke three squares; the 26th, 27th and 28th Prussian Regiments were routed. Our squadrons sabred 4 or 500 men and took 1,500 prisoners.

During this time, General Reille crossed the Sambre at Marchienne-au-Pont and moved on Gosselies with the divisions of Prince Jérôme and General Bachelu. Attacking the enemy he made 250 prisoners and pursued them on the road to Brussels.

This day has cost the enemy five guns and 2,000 men, of which 1,000 are prisoners. Our loss is ten men killed and eighty wounded, most from the Service Squadrons who made the charges and three squadrons of the 20th Dragoons, who charged a square with the greatest determination. Our loss, whilst small in number, has been painful to the emperor for the serious wound to General Letort, his ADC, when charging at the head of the Service Squadrons. This officer is of the greatest distinction. He was struck by a ball in the stomach, and the surgeon fears that the wound will be mortal.

We have found several stores at Charleroi. The joy of the Belgians is difficult to describe. There are villages that have celebrated with dances in front of their liberators, and their happiness is heartfelt.

In the report of General Headquarters, the names of the most distinguished officers and soldiers will be included.

The emperor has given command of the Left Wing to the Prince *de la Moskowa*, whose headquarters this evening is at Quatre Bras on the road to Brussels.

The *Duc de Travise* [Mortier], whom the emperor had made commander of the Young Guard, has remained in Beaumont as he is sick with sciatica and is bedridden.

The 4th Corps commanded by General Gérard is arriving this evening at Châtelet. General Gérard has made known that Lieutenant General Bourmont, Colonel Clouet and chef d'escadron Villoutreys have deserted to the enemy. The *major génèral* has ordered that these deserters are to be immediately charged according to the law.

Nothing can describe the good spirit and enthusiasm of the army. It regards this desertion of a small number of traitors as a happy event which is out in the open.

As we shall see, Napoleon was generally satisfied with the day's achievements and thus the report is broadly accurate. On the night of the 15th Gourgaud gives the position of the French army as follows:

- Headquarters at Charleroi.
- The Left Wing of the army; headquarters at Gosselies.
- Vanguard at Frasnes.
- General Reille's corps stationed between Gosselies and Frasnes but with one division (Girard's) at Wagnies [Wangenies] in the direction of Fleurus.
- General d'Erlon's corps was between Marchiennes and Julmet [Jumet].
- The centre, consisting of Vandamme's corps and Grouchy's reserves of cavalry, lined the woods opposite Fleurus.
- General Gérard's corps, forming the Right Wing, had passed the Sambre and was in front of Châtelet.
- The Imperial Guard was echeloned between Fleurus and Charleroi. The Sixth Corps was in front of the latter town. Kellerman's corps of cuirassiers, with the great park of artillery, was on the left bank of the Sambre, behind Charleroi.[14]

The Allied Camp
Now that Napoleon's offensive was clearly coming through Charleroi, Blücher ordered his army's concentration around Sombreffe. He must have known that if he chose to give battle in the next twenty-four hours, the chances were that he would have to do so without the support of Wellington. It was clear that the Anglo-Netherlands army would not be able to concentrate and move its centre of gravity from the west to the east in time. Blücher was probably more concerned with ensuring his own IV Corps, that commanded by General Bülow, would join him the next day.

Wellington first received news of Napoleon's offensive from the Prince of Orange sometime around three o'clock in the afternoon, but the first formal report was received at about five. Although the report said that the attack was coming via Charleroi, Wellington continued to harbour the concern that this was merely a feint and that the real attack would come in the area of Mons. Consequently, at seven o'clock orders were prepared for the divisions to assemble and be ready to march as soon as the appropriate destination could be confirmed. The last of these orders were not despatched until 10pm and even at this time Wellington was unaware of the skirmish at Frasnes.

Luckily for Wellington, General Constant-Rebeque, the I Corps chief-of-staff, better informed of the situation by being much closer to the front, recommended the 2nd Netherlands Division, commanded by General Perponcher-Sedlnitzky, to concentrate at Quatre Bras. Shortly after this order was despatched, the movement orders arrived from Brussels directing that division to concentrate at Nivelles. Luckily for Wellington, the decision was taken to ignore these orders.

What Wellington did not realise is that through this hesitation and the withdrawal of Zieten's corps to the east, a 10-kilometre hole had opened up between his own left and the Prussian right; and the main Charleroi to Brussels road was virtually unprotected. It was only at ten o'clock, with Wellington at the famous Duchess of Richmond's ball, that he was finally convinced that the main French attack was coming from Charleroi and so gave orders for the army's concentration to be on Nivelles, with Brunswick and Nassau troops to march to Quatre Bras.

At this time Quatre Bras was occupied by just Colonel Prince Bernard of Saxe-Weimar's brigade of 4,700 men and two batteries (sixteen guns) of Perponcher's 2nd Netherlands Division. If the Prince of Orange and his staff had ensured the concentration of his forces in strict accordance with their orders, then on the evening of the 15th, and even during the morning of the 16th, Ney would have been able to occupy Quatre Bras completely unopposed.

Ney's Meeting with Napoleon

The key to Napoleon's next step was conveying his intent for the next day to his subordinates. The simplest way of doing this was to brief Ney and Grouchy face to face. Regrettably for our understanding of the campaign we cannot be sure that such a meeting actually took place.

Neither in his memoirs nor in Gourgaud's account of the campaign, which it is accepted that Napoleon dictated, does he mention a meeting. This is strange if he wished to confirm that Ney was clear on the need to seize the crossroads on the 15th or even the 16th. However, Marshal Ney's ADC and acting chief-of-staff, Colonel Heymès, should be a credible witness. He wrote that on the evening of the 15th:

> A position was taken up in front of Frasnes. After having given orders and recommending that everyone should stay alert, the Marshal returned alone to Charleroi where he finally arrived at midnight.
>
> The emperor returned there; Ney dined and conferred with him from midnight until 2am. The marshal was reprimanded for not having captured the position of Quatre Bras during the day ... He informed him of his plans and hopes for the day of the 16th, which was soon to begin ... All the officers of the Imperial Headquarters can attest to this.[15]

This statement seems unequivocal, especially from someone who wrote with the sole purpose of defending Ney against all the criticisms that were levelled against him; and yet many of Ney's supporters claim this meeting never took place. Colonel Charras, in his rather anti-Napoleon account of the campaign, accepts that Ney went to see Napoleon on the night of the 15th, 'to give an account of his operations and to ask the emperor for new instructions',[16] but gives no indication as to what he was told other than to claim that he could not have been given verbal orders to seize Quatre Bras, as he subsequently did not make efforts to do so until he received written orders the next day.

In his memoirs, Grouchy, who also takes a rather anti-Bonaparte stance in defending himself against the criticisms of the emperor, wrote:

> ... the Prince de la Moskowa had dined with Napoleon at Charleroi on the 15th, had conferred with him for part of the night of the 15th/16th and not rejoined his troops and headquarters at Gosselies until 2am on the morning of the 16th. The emperor hoped that Ney would seize Quatre Bras during the morning of the 16th, but he was clear that this position was not occupied by us when the marshal left him during the night.[17]

It is hard to believe that if these three individuals, who all had cause to deny such a meeting took place, admit that it did, then perhaps we should believe it. However, the big question is; what was discussed? Ropes, who is also convinced that the meeting did take place, finds it impossible to believe that Napoleon did not take the opportunity to order Ney to take Quatre Bras first thing in the morning. Napoleon still aspired to attack and destroy the Prussians first, and the operations of the day still suggested that the opportunity to do this might reveal itself on the 16th; there was evidence to believe that a substantial, but unknown Prussian force was gathering around Sombreffe, but there was insufficient information to suggest it was the whole army. If Napoleon hoped to advance against it in the morning, then for Ney to take and hold Quatre Bras, to prevent Wellington from intervening, was such an obvious requirement that it hardly needs debating whether or not it was discussed. But Ney's supporters are adamant that if Ney had been given the verbal order to do this, then a man of his character and reputation would have made the necessary arrangements immediately upon his return to his headquarters. This logic is hard to deny and yet this makes Ney's tardiness the next morning even more difficult to understand or explain.

Analysis
The Allies
Although Zieten's delaying action bought vital time for the concentration of both Wellington's and Blücher's armies, it cannot be considered entirely successful. As we shall see, neither of the two allied commanders was able to fully concentrate his troops before the first battles, yet considerable further delay could surely have been imposed on the French advance by destroying the bridges over the Sambre. The French found it surprising that none of these bridges had been destroyed and it seemed no preparations had been made to do so. Chesney wrote, 'No satisfactory explanation has ever been given of the

reasons of his [Zieten's] allowing the bridges, which were left on his flanks as he quitted Charleroi, to fall into the enemy's hands un-mined and without resistance.'[18] If the allies had wanted to buy time to cover their concentration, it would appear to have been a very wise precaution. The campaign in 1814 had been marked by the importance of seizing and holding bridges, or destroying them to cover a flank or to hold up the enemy. Wellington certainly needed time to concentrate his widely spread forces, but as this part of the frontier was covered by the Prussians it is quite possible that there was a lack of liaison. The Prussians, who had brought their corps closer together in the days prior to hostilities, did not require so much time and therefore may not have attached the same importance to it. However, bearing in mind that they planned on Wellington's support, this does seem to be a serious oversight.

It is possible that the bridges were not destroyed because the allies expected to use them for their own offensive into France, planned for July, but this is no reason not to prepare them for destruction in case of emergency. A Prussian report states that as the bridges were made of stone they could not be destroyed; this seems rather odd given the time they had to make the necessary arrangements. But not only had the bridges not been destroyed, what is even more surprising is that all three (Marchienne, Charleroi and Châtelet) seem to have fallen cheaply, with little attempt at a determined defence. A well-planned, well-prepared and resolute defence of such narrow defiles should have gone a long way to countering the considerable superiority in numbers that the French otherwise enjoyed. Thankfully for Napoleon, his plans to erect pontoon bridges were not required. Given the importance of speed for the emperor, if he had had to spend two or more hours erecting bridges before the main body of his army had been able to cross, on top of the time he actually lost, it would have had a significant impact on the following days.

Marshal Ney

We must not underestimate the difficulties faced by Marshal Ney in taking up his new command only once the campaign had already opened; perhaps the biggest of these was his lack of a proper staff. Initially at least, he lacked the means to gather information and to ensure his orders and instructions were written accurately and in detail, and then despatched to, and received promptly by, all the necessary formations under his command. This would have been a tall order for a divisional commander, let alone the commander of twelve divisions. Whilst he would have slowly gathered the necessary staff over the next few days, it would be no easy task to get the officers with the right experience and then quickly mould them into a headquarters that really understood what was required of it. He was lucky to have the division of guard cavalry close by, which was inevitably strongly officered, and from which he could draw messengers and order-carriers, but in no way did these constitute a staff and nor was he to have their use for long.

Immediately after taking command, the right thing for Ney to do was to get forward and start seeing the situation for himself, and this is what he did. Normally, whilst he was doing this, a commander would rely on his staff to stay behind and to coordinate movement, gather information and plan subsequent moves, but at this time Ney had only Colonel Heymès to attempt this, and he was an ADC, not a trained chief-of-staff. The chief-of-staff of any headquarters is a pivotal man for a senior commander; the executive officer who coordinates the activities of the whole force under his commander's orders. This key role required an appropriately trained and experienced officer. A wing commander such as Ney would normally have expected to have a lieutenant general to carry out these duties. There can be little doubt that Ney's failure to properly coordinate, hasten and execute the movements and concentration of his formations over these few days has its roots in this key shortfall.

We must now ask ourselves whether the almost universal condemnation of Ney for not occupying Quatre Bras on the 15th is fair, or whether this criticism comes wholly with the benefit of hindsight. There is no doubt that the crossroads was weakly held during the evening and that, with a little more determination, the single Netherlands brigade (of five battalions and a battery, about 4,700 men) could have been brushed aside. However, the evidence we have is very contradictory.

As Marshal Ney's defenders have all stated, he received no written orders to occupy the crossroads during the 15th. However, Napoleon claims that he gave Ney verbal orders to do so when the marshal was given command of the right wing when he arrived with the army at about 5pm.[19] But Colonel Heymès, who was present, claims that Napoleon only ordered Ney to 'push the enemy' and we have already cast doubt on Napoleon's account of this discussion. However, it will have been noted that in the Bulletin of the Army for the 15th, Ney's headquarters are put at Quatre Bras, which suggests this is where Soult, who is most likely to have composed this, believed Ney to be. The evidence therefore is not entirely conclusive, and it is quite possible that Ney, seeing the exhaustion of Reille's 2nd Corps, felt that asking them to march even further was too much. Although Bachelu's division was at Frasnes, the main body of the corps was around Gosselies, about 6 miles (about three hours' march to get the whole corps there) from Quatre Bras and we must not forget that Reille's corps had got up at 2.30am, started its march at 3am, and covered eight leagues during the day, fighting or skirmishing for a fair amount of the time.

Even if Napoleon did give Ney a clear verbal order to seize and occupy Quatre Bras when he arrived at about 5pm, we have also seen that the emperor did not appear to be too concerned that he did not; he doubtless felt that although the occupation had been delayed longer than he would have wished, there would still be time for Ney to accomplish this the following morning before sufficient allied troops could concentrate there to deny him. It appears, therefore, that Napoleon's discontent with Ney may well have been over the fact that he had not carried out his orders rather than the fact that it was strictly necessary for him to do so, and because Ney's hesitation seemed to indicate to the emperor a lack of that boldness and energy which he had always confidently expected from that marshal.

Many historians have also criticised Ney and d'Erlon for not ensuring that the 1st Corps was closed up on Gosselies as ordered by Soult. Unfortunately, the order is not timed so we cannot be absolutely sure when it was either despatched or received. In his account of the campaign, Pontécoulant, who was a junior officer in the imperial guard artillery and therefore could not have been an eyewitness to these events, claims it did not arrive before 10pm, suggesting that it was too late to be acted upon that day. During the evening of the 15th, d'Erlon had reported to Ney that his corps was concentrated around Jumet, just south of Gosselies. Ney, without a staff, had to trust the report from his subordinate and probably felt that this was acceptable, but the truth is that the divisions of the 1st Corps were far from concentrated, although during the night d'Erlon gave orders for his corps to move forward to Gosselies by 6am on the 16th.

Napoleon

Most of the writers that are critical of Napoleon condemn him for not ensuring that the strategically important posts of Quatre Bras and Sombreffe were in his hands by the end of the 15th. They maintain that holding these two points would have comprehensively cut the communications between Wellington and Blücher, as the road joining these points was the only really viable cross road between them, and that he would then have been free to destroy them individually. But this is to fundamentally misunderstand Napoleon's strategy; whilst the emperor might have wanted to take Quatre Bras to prevent Wellington from supporting his allies, if the French had also held Sombreffe Blücher would have realised that he could not support Wellington and in order to maintain communications and be able to achieve mutual support, both would have been forced to retire to the north, closer to Brussels, to re-establish them. Napoleon rightly predicted that Blücher would therefore fight his battle south of the Namur to Nivelles road in order to maintain his communications with Wellington, just as he wanted.

It appears then that Napoleon was quite content that Grouchy had not occupied Sombreffe, as the emperor had no intention of him doing so. On the right wing he was intently focussed on bringing the Prussians to battle and he wanted to do nothing that might induce them to withdraw because they felt they had lost their communications with Wellington. The emperor later wrote:

> The Emperor's intention was that his advance guard should occupy Fleurus, keeping his troops concealed behind the wood near this city; he took good care not to let his army be seen, *and, above all, not to occupy Sombreffe* [my emphasis]. This would of itself have caused the failure of all his manoeuvres; for then, Marshal Blücher would have been obliged to make Wavre the place for the concentration of his army, the battle of Ligny would not have taken place, and the Prussian army would not have been obliged to give battle [as it did] in its then not fully concentrated condition, and not supported by the English army.[20]

Napoleon clearly felt that he would be able to concentrate a sufficiently large force to confront the Prussians the next day if they wished to risk a battle, and believed that Wellington would be unable to join his ally because he would not be strong enough to push past Marshal Ney. Whilst he might well have expected Ney to have occupied Quatre Bras, the fact that he had not was not crucial, as Wellington was still not concentrated. However, it was necessary for Ney to occupy it early the next morning before allied reinforcements arrived.

In his orders for the 15th, Napoleon had specified that he wanted all his troops across the Sambre 'before noon'. This he had clearly failed to achieve; the division of heavy cavalry of the guard, half of Grouchy's cavalry reserve, an infantry division and cavalry brigade of the 1st Corps and half of Gérard's corps had not managed this. But whatever the criticisms of his detractors, that he was content with the achievements during the 15th is suggested by his memoirs, in which he wrote:

> All my manoeuvres had succeeded as I wished; I could now take the initiative of attacking the enemy armies, one by one. Their only chance of avoiding this misfortune, the worst of all, was to yield ground and rally on Brussels or beyond.[21]

Whatever the criticism of the armchair generals, Napoleon, who knew well that detailed plans rarely survive contact with the enemy, probably felt that he was still on course to defeat the Prussians the next day without them being able to receive any support from Wellington.

Chapter 6

Morning, 16 June

Napoleon Plans his Next Move
On the evening of the 15th, Napoleon had retired to Charleroi for the night and had fallen exhausted into bed at 9pm. However, he was up again at midnight as this was the time that Marshal Ney arrived for a conference. If this meeting did not take place, it was still Napoleon's routine to rise at this time, as this was when reports from his subordinates were expected to arrive. Once appraised of the situation facing Grouchy and Ney he could then formulate his plans and issue his orders for the coming day.

It must now have been obvious to the emperor that the Prussian advance guard was withdrawing north-east, across the front of the Anglo-Dutch concentration areas, heading towards Fleurus and Sombreffe. A small Nassau force had been encountered at Frasnes, but this had appeared to withdraw to the north. Not a red uniform had been seen, suggesting that Wellington had been as slow in ordering his own concentration as Napoleon had predicted. The Prussian withdrawal had also opened up the main road towards Brussels, presumably down which Wellington's troops would eventually advance. However, having a reasonable feel for the Anglo-Dutch deployment areas, Napoleon appeared confident that they would require more time to be able to concentrate. The allied armies seemed some way from being able to unite and this left Napoleon increasingly sure that he could now beat them one after the other.

From the varied information he had received, and from the direction of retirement of the Prussian advance guard, Napoleon concluded that their army sought to assemble on the Namur to Nivelles road, as it was by this route that the Anglo-Netherlands army would come to their assistance. Having pushed his advance troops almost as far as Fleurus, he believed Sombreffe was the most likely point for this concentration. However, there was currently no evidence to suggest that the Prussians were actually planning to risk an immediate battle, so Napoleon wanted to push them further away from their allies, down their lines of communication towards either Namur or Liège, before turning on Wellington and beating him, confident in the thought that the Prussians would be in no position to assist him. If the Prussians did choose to stand and fight, then so much the better, as it was clear that Wellington would be incapable of intervening in time and the Prussians could be destroyed first.

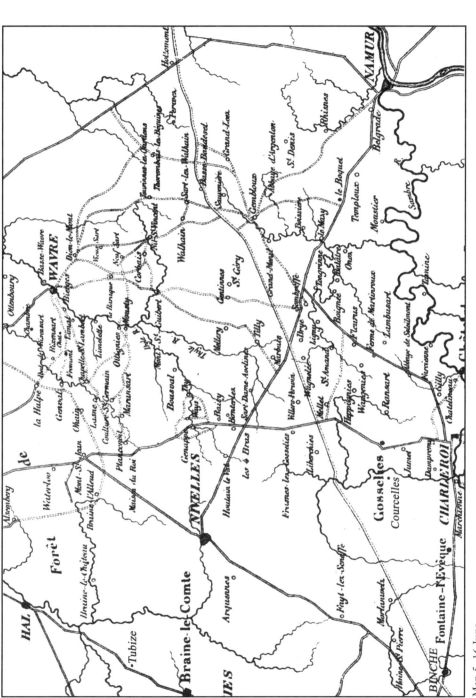

Map 5. 16 June.

Napoleon now finalised his plans. He would accompany Grouchy and the right wing, which would advance against the Prussians, pushing them away to the east. If they chose to stand, then he would attack and destroy them. In the meantime, Ney would concentrate his left wing around Quatre Bras, deploying to hold that crossroads against Wellington if required, or to be able to send some troops down the Nivelles to Namur road to support Napoleon against the Prussians. If the Prussians did not fight then Napoleon would join Ney with the reserve (the Guard and 6th Corps) and this combined force would then march on Brussels, which the emperor believed he could reach at 7am on 17 June.

Napoleon now dictated his orders to Soult, who would then need to fill in the detail and write them out in full; they would also need to be copied. This whole process must inevitably have taken some time and Houssaye estimates that the orders could not have been sent out until between seven and eight in the morning.

Before the orders were sent off, Napoleon received a report from Marshal Grouchy that suggested the Prussians were concentrating a large force in the area of Bry and Saint-Amand; perhaps the Prussians were preparing to make a stand after all. However, Napoleon discounted this prospect for the time being and reiterated the orders he had dictated to Soult by writing his own letters to each of his wing commanders.

The Left Wing
We should remind ourselves of the locations of Ney's troops on the morning of the 16th. Piré's light cavalry division and Bachelu's infantry division were both at Frasnes, 4 kilometres south of Quatre Bras, and with their outposts in contact with those of the allied troops encountered the day before. Foy's and Prince Jérôme's infantry divisions were at Gosselies, about 8 kilometres further south of Frasnes. Girard's infantry division had been sent to the right flank in pursuit of the Prussians that had been encountered the day before at Gosselies and was near Wangenies, about 6 kilometres to the east. Lefebvre-Desnouëttes's division of light cavalry of the Guard bivouacked at Frasnes.

On the evening of the 15th, d'Erlon's divisions were spread from the rear of Gosselies (Durutte's division) all the way through Jumet (Donzelot's Division), Marchienne (Marcognet's Division) to Thuin (Quiot's Division), with a brigade of cavalry right back on the start point of the previous day. During the night he was ordered to call in all his detachments and to close them all up on Gosselies to join Ney. It was therefore imperative for d'Erlon to get his more remote troops on the march as early as possible; after all, most of them had done little except march the previous day. To this end orders were sent out during the night. The chief-of-staff of Marcognet's division, *adjutant-commandant* d'Arsonval, sent the following order to General Nogues, commander of the division's 1st Brigade:

Marchienne-au-Pont, 3am, 16 June.
The intention of the Commanding General is that you set your brigade
off immediately in order to reach Gosselies at 6am or earlier if possible.[1]

Captain Duthilt, who was in the 2nd Brigade of that division, also received
marching orders, 'On the 16th, the 1st Division received the order to move
rapidly to Marchienne-au-Pont, then from there to Gosselies where it only
made a halt, then to meet up with the rest of the Corps ...'[2] However,
Corporal Canler of Quiot's division, the division that had the furthest to
march, claims they did not set off on the 20-kilometre march to Gosselies
until late, 'Our army corps had to leave this town [Thuin] the next morning to
get to Fleurus early; but we only left at midday ...'[3] although he gives us no
reason for this delay.

Heymès claims that efforts were made to bring up the 1st Corps as quickly
as possible:

Due to the shortage of officers in the headquarters, of which the marshal
was in dire need, officers of the chasseurs and lancers of the Guard were
sent to meet the 1st Corps in the direction of Marchienne-au-Pont; they
were ordered to hasten its march towards Frasnes.[4]

Unfortunately, we have no further evidence on the move of d'Erlon's corps,
and if Quiot's division really did set off at midday, it is impossible to imagine
that they would have marched the 20 kilometres to Gosselies before 5pm,
and this was still 5 kilometres short of Frasnes. The other three divisions had
much shorter distances to march and should have been at Gosselies at the
time stipulated to Marcognet's division – 6am.

Ney had spent the night at Gosselies and despite Heymès' claims that at
2am Reille was ordered to move 'as soon as possible', in his own account of
the campaign Reille says:

On the morning of the 16th, the troops of the 2nd Corps were ready to
march. Towards 7am General Reille went to see *M. le Maréchal* Ney,
who had spent the night in Gosselies, to get his orders. This marshal said
to him that he was waiting on the emperor to whom he had reported his
positions, that he was going to Frasnes, and that if in his absence movement orders arrived, he was to execute them immediately and to forward
them to Count d'Erlon, commander of the 1st Corps, who was at Jumet
and further to the rear.[5]

There is no need to return here to the question of whether Ney met
Napoleon during the night, but if he did, it was clear that whatever was discussed still required an executive order and Ney was not prepared to act until
it had been received. Colonel Heymès, Ney's ADC and stand-in chief-of-
staff, gives us this information on Ney's movements on this morning:

On the 16th, at 2am, the marshal returned to Gosselies where he stopped for a few moments to talk to General Reille; he ordered him ... to join him at Frasnes, where the marshal would be moving onto immediately. He then again took the lead of his troops in the presence of the enemy. He received the information that the generals and their other officers had been able to procure. During this time, Colonel Heymès toured the line, visiting each of the regiments. He wrote down the names of the colonels and the strength of each unit. He quickly returned to inform the marshal of the situation.[6]

A little later in the morning, Ney received word of some welcome reinforcements. Although the Guard cavalry of General Lefebvre-Desnouëttes had done useful work the evening before, the fact that he could not commit them to a general engagement made them of dubious value. Now, Napoleon was allocating him a strong force of some of the most feared cavalry in Europe.

Charleroi, 16 June, 8am.

Marshal! The emperor has just ordered Count Valmy, commanding the 3rd Cavalry Corps, to concentrate and head for Gosselies where he will be under your orders.

His Majesty's intention is that the Guard Cavalry, which had been on the road to Brussels, remain behind and rejoin the remainder of the Imperial Guard; but in order that it should not have to make a retrograde movement, you can replace it in the line and leave it a little to the rear and he will send its orders for the day there. Lieutenant General Lefebvre-Desnouëttes will send an officer to pick up the necessary orders.

You will inform me whether the corps has carried out its movement and of the exact position this morning of the 1st and 2nd Corps and of the two cavalry divisions which are attached, informing me what enemy forces are in front of you and what has been learned.

Major Général Duc de Dalmatie[7]

General Kellerman, *Duc de Valmy*, was the son of a Marshal of France, the victor of Valmy (from whom he inherited the title) and, despite a somewhat chequered career, he had an impressive reputation in command of heavy cavalry, founded most famously on his performance at Marengo where, at the head of a heavy cavalry brigade, he was credited with smashing a 6,000-strong column of Austrian grenadiers with just 400 men and saving the battle for Napoleon. He had embraced the return of the Bourbons in 1814 and tried to rally support in the army to oppose Napoleon's return. Indeed, the emperor was reluctant to employ him, but was in desperate need of experienced heavy cavalry commanders and eventually found himself forced into a reconciliation. Kellerman's account of the campaign reflects a reluctance to serve, but his corps was certainly impressive; two regiments of dragoons, four of famed cuirassiers and an élite brigade of carabineers; a total of somewhat over 3,600 men formed in two divisions under the command of the veteran generals l'Héritier and d'Urbal. This addition to Ney's order of battle was formidable.

The total force that Ney now had allocated to him was around 42,000 men, not including Lefebvre-Desnouëttes' division of Guard cavalry and its attendant battery. This included eight infantry divisions (approx. 32,000 men), four each in d'Erlon's and Reille's corps; two light cavalry divisions (approx. 3,000 men in total), one each in corps; Kellerman's heavy cavalry corps (approx. 3,500 men) and just shy of 100 artillery pieces. Unfortunately, these troops were still far from being concentrated and Ney faced Quatre Bras with only Bachelu's infantry and Piré's cavalry divisions immediately available; as Colonel Heymès later wrote:

> Thus, when the whole of the 2nd Corps was concentrated, there were only four regiments of light cavalry, three divisions of infantry and artillery available; in all 17,000 to 18,000 men and not 40,000 that has often been repeated. The light cavalry of the Guard is not included in this total as it will be recalled that the emperor had warned against it getting engaged.[8]

The Allies
During the evening of the 14th, Blücher had ordered the concentration of his army near Sombreffe with the I Corps providing the delaying force that would give them the time required. For reasons we do not need to explain, the IV Corps was unable to reach this point before the battle that was to be fought at Ligny. Wellington, in contrast, and for reasons we have already explored, did not order his own concentration until thirty-six hours later. Blücher should have realised that Wellington's army could not possibly support him for at least another day and a half. It must therefore have been clear to the Prussian commander that if he fought a major battle against Napoleon on the 16th, Wellington would be unlikely to be able to support him with a substantial part of his army.

Sometime between 1.30 and 2am, in a backroom at the Duchess of Richmond's ball in Brussels, Wellington was uttering the famous words, 'Napoleon has humbugged me by God, he has gained twenty-four hours' march on me.' But, as we have discussed, this was almost inevitable if Napoleon attacked through Charleroi. The key now was to get his army concentrated. The first British troops left Brussels at 4am and most of the Brunswick corps at 6am. After a short rest, Wellington himself left at 7.30am. He had decided on Nivelles as the point of concentration and orders were sent out accordingly.

But if Napoleon was unaware of the true situation in front of Ney around Quatre Bras, it seems the allies were also under a misapprehension, for the

Prince of Orange, having just arrived back from a reconnaissance near Frasnes at 7am, wrote to Wellington, '... The French are in possession of Frasnes, near Quatre Bras, with infantry and cavalry, but until now not in force. Our troops are close to this village and, when I arrived, the skirmisher fire was lively. But I ordered our troops to cease fire and since then, that of the French has fallen away ...'[9] The Prince had arrived from Brussels at about 6am and had immediately taken command of all the allied troops at Quatre Bras. By this time the single brigade that had skirmished with Lefebvre-Desnouëttes' cavalry the night before, had, in direct contradiction to Wellington's orders which had the whole division concentrating at Nivelles, been reinforced by most of the second brigade of the same division, so that almost the whole of the 2nd (Netherlands) Division, 6,500 men and sixteen guns, were now concentrated around Quatre Bras. As we have just heard, there was a little skirmishing at this time and even a tour of his outposts gave him no evidence to suggest that there was any significant build-up of French forces to his front. He had been able to cheer his men up by promising them that a force of British troops was on their way to support them. He also sent orders for the rest of the I Corps to start to concentrate between Quatre Bras and Nivelles.

At Quatre Bras, the Prince was concerned that whilst he did not want to provoke a French attack, it might well give the British troops more time to arrive if he was able to convince the French that he was stronger than he actually was. To this end he ordered a skirmish line to advance and push back the French outposts. The French were clearly surprised by this show of temerity and the Dutch troops were able to establish themselves on the line of the Lairalle heights, from where they could see the forward French troops quickly forming up. This initial skirmish seems to have woken the forward French units and Piré's troopers were sent out on patrols to try to fathom Dutch intentions. As they advanced they were engaged by both Nassau skirmishers and Dutch artillery and chose not to press hard. The earlier engagement and the information coming back from Piré's patrols now convinced Ney that Quatre Bras was occupied by more than just advance posts. Consequently, he sent an officer from the guard lancers to warn Napoleon that this was the case.

Other than the despatch of this message, the developing situation seems to have done nothing to spur Ney into any sort of further, more positive, action. Admittedly, he was still awaiting orders from the emperor, but crucially, he had not felt the need to use the time to properly concentrate his troops in order that, whatever Napoleon's decision, he would be well balanced and ready to react to whatever was expected of him. An absence of orders is no excuse for not being ready to execute them promptly when they arrive, especially as they almost inevitably require prompt action when in the presence of the enemy. But Ney does not appear to have had the same strategic overview or intelligence picture as Napoleon, who had a much clearer understanding of where Wellington's troops were and how long they would take to concentrate.

Wellington had expected to concentrate his troops well back from the frontier and then march forward as an army, but Napoleon's lightning strike was forcing him to concentrate forward and this brought the prospect of his troops arriving piecemeal at the front. Napoleon clearly understood this, and it is hard to believe that he had not taken some opportunity to make it absolutely clear to Ney who was to confront the Anglo-Netherlands army. Whilst Napoleon might not yet have made his next move clear to Ney, an officer of such experience was surely trying to second-guess his superior and try to ensure that he was prepared for any eventuality. The eight or so kilometres that separated Bachelu and Piré from the other two available divisions of Reille's corps was too far for immediate support (the best part of a two-hour wait and journey for the rearmost troops), but this was nothing compared to Ney's other corps, d'Erlon's, which was spread over a long distance and would require a considerable time to get forward into a position from which he could support Reille.

Wellington arrived at Quatre Bras at 10am. At the village of Waterloo he had passed some of his breakfasting troops, but had not hastened their march towards Quatre Bras. Indeed, these troops had reached the destination laid down in their movement order and it was only after Wellington had passed and examined the roads from Genappe that they were ordered to continue their march to this latter town. Wellington was keeping his options open; Genappe gave him the option of directing them to Nivelles or Quatre Bras as required. He was still not clear on Napoleon's intentions.

During the morning, with the arrival of most of the 1st Brigade of the 2nd (Netherlands) Division the Prince of Orange had managed to double the number of troops he had available, although he still awaited the final unit of that brigade that was waiting to be relieved at Nivelles before marching to join him. When that arrived he would have about 8,000 men and sixteen guns. Having listened to the Prince of Orange's report and endorsing his deployment, Wellington rode forward onto the Balcan plateau where he could look down on Frasnes. Despite the reports of French deserters that a large French force was present there was little evidence to suggest this, although it appears the French did fire at his party; General Flahaut later wrote that having delivered his letter to Ney:

> I went forward and not far from Quatre Bras I met Général Lefebvre-Desnouëttes with his cavalry. I stayed with him pending the arrival of *Maréchal* Ney's forces, and we then saw opposite us, some way off, some of the English staff who seemed to be taking stock of the position. Général Lefebvre-Desnouëttes ordered a few rounds of artillery to be fired on them, although they were out of range.[10]

Wellington was yet to be convinced that Napoleon was still not attempting to strike towards Brussels through Mons and so he was reluctant to draw more troops to the east.

With little happening to his front and still to be convinced that a major French force was going to march on Quatre Bras, Wellington decided to ride the twelve or so kilometres to meet Field Marshal Blücher near Ligny. From Quatre Bras this was a simple journey straight down the road that led towards Namur and would allow the two commanders an opportunity to discuss their mutual support. Ordering the Prince of Orange to hold on until reinforcements arrived if he should be attacked, he set off.

Ney Receives his Orders
Napoleon's letter to Marshal Ney, carried by General Flahaut, one of the emperor's most experienced and trusted ADCs, must have arrived with him at about 10.30am.

Charleroi, 8am, 16 June.

My cousin,

My aide de camp, General Flahaut, is directed to deliver this letter to you. The *Major Général* should have given you orders, but you will receive mine first because my officers travel faster than his. You will receive the operation orders for the day, but I wish to write to you in detail because it is of the highest importance.

I am sending Marshal Grouchy with the 3rd and 4th Infantry Corps to Sombreffe. I am taking my Guard to Fleurus and I shall be there myself before midday. I shall attack the enemy there if I encounter them and clear the road as far as Gembloux. There, according to circumstances, I shall decide on my course, perhaps at three in the afternoon, perhaps this evening. My intention is that, immediately after I have made up my mind, you will be ready to march on Brussels: I will support you with the Guard which will be at Fleurus or Sombreffe, and I shall expect you to arrive at Brussels tomorrow morning. You will march this evening if I make up my mind early enough for you to be informed of it today, and to accomplish three or four leagues this evening and to be at Brussels at seven o'clock tomorrow morning.

You should dispose your troops in the following manner: the first division at two leagues in advance of Quatre Bras, if there is no hindrance; six divisions of infantry about Quatre Bras, and one division at Marbais, so that I may draw them to me at Sombreffe if I want them. Besides, it will not retard your march.

Count Valmy's [Kellerman's] corps, who has 3,000 cuirassiers, picked troops, should be placed at the crossing of the Roman Road with that of Brussels, so that I can draw it towards me if I want it; as soon as I have with me General Lefebvre-Desnouëttes's division of the Guard and I send you Count de Valmy's two divisions to replace it. But in my actual plan I prefer to place Count de Valmy where I may recall him if I want him, and not cause General Lefebvre-Desnouëttes to make useless marches, since it is probable that I may decide this evening to march on Brussels with the Guard. However, cover Lefebvre-Desnouëttes's division with d'Erlon's and Reille's two cavalry divisions so as to spare the Guard, and because if there is any warm work with the English, it is better done with the line rather than the Guard.

I have adopted for this campaign the following general principle; to divide my army into two wings and a reserve. Your wing will be composed of four divisions of the 1st Corps, four divisions of the 2nd Corps, two divisions of light cavalry and two divisions of Count Valmy's corps. This ought not to fall short of 45 to 50,000 men.

Marshal Grouchy will have almost the same force and will command the right wing.

The Guard will form the reserve, and I shall draw troops from one wing to strengthen my reserve.

You perceive thoroughly the importance attached to the taking of Brussels. From its capture, certain things would happen; for a prompt and sudden move will cut the English off from Mons, Ostend etc.

I desire your dispositions may be made so that your eight divisions can march on Brussels as soon as it is ordered.[11]

It is not clear what time Soult's letter reiterating Napoleon's own instructions arrived with Ney, but as he had hoped, General Reille did get warning of Napoleon's orders before they arrived with the commander of the left wing. Reille says:

It was only at 11am that General Flahaut, ADC to the emperor, passed through Gosselies and informed General Reille of the orders for Marshal Ney to occupy Quatre Bras with the left wing, pushing an advance guard to Genappe. General Reille immediately informed the commander of the 1st Corps, ordering his own divisions to move on Quatre Bras, and rejoined the marshal towards 1pm who, with the cavalry of the Guard was observing the enemy in front of Frasnes.[12]

But Reille must be mistaken in the time that he was shown these orders, or he subsequently slipped the time to try to cover his own inactivity, for we have already seen how Ney must have received them some time prior to this to have enabled him to reply to Soult at 11am, confirming his own plans in the light of the direction he had received.

Frasnes, 11am, 16 June 1815
I have this moment received your instructions for the 1st and 2nd Infantry Corps and for the following cavalry divisions; Piré, light cavalry

of the Guard and the two divisions of the 3rd Corps (Valmy) [he seems to have forgotten the light cavalry division attached to the 1st Corps (Jacquinot's)].

The Emperor's instructions have already reached me.

Here are the dispositions that I have ordered:

The 2nd Corps will place a division in the rear of Genappe, another at Banterlet, and the two others at Quatre Bras.

A division of light cavalry will cover the march of the 2nd Corps.

The 1st Corps will place a division at Marbais and the two others at Frasnes and the light cavalry division will be at Marbais [Ney seems to have forgotten that 1st Corps had four infantry divisions!]. The Count of Valmy's two other cavalry divisions will be placed one at Frasnes and the other at Liberchies.

The two divisions [regiments] of Guard cavalry will remain at Frasnes, where I shall establish my headquarters. All information to hand tends to show that there are 3,000 hostile infantry at Quatre Bras and very few cavalry. I think that the Emperor's arrangements for the advance on Brussels will be carried out without great difficulty.

The Marshal *Prince de la Moskowa*, Ney.

As can be seen from this message, Ney must have received the orders from the *major général* within half an hour of receiving the emperor's letter. As much of the content of Soult's order is similar to Napoleon's, it is not necessary to repeat it. However, it is worth noting one section:

M. le Maréchal, the emperor orders that you are to set off the 2nd and 1st Corps, as well as the 3rd Cavalry Corps which has been put under your orders, and direct them on the road junction called *Trois Bras* ['Three Arms' such is it named on some contemporary maps, as opposed to Quatre Bras 'Four Arms'] where you are to take position and at the same time send reconnaissance patrols on the roads to Brussels and Nivelles, to where it is probable the enemy has retired ...[13]

It certainly seems that Napoleon's initial direction may have lulled Ney into a false sense of security that manifested itself into what was evidently a chronic lack of urgency in getting his advance moving, let alone attacking the small force that he found in front of him; which he estimated as only 3,000 strong.

Ney now sent out his own orders to his subordinates. Given that he must have taken at least forty-five minutes to read the orders, reply to Soult, digest and then decide on his own next steps before committing them to paper, these cannot have been sent off much before 11.45am.

Ney to Reille, Frasnes, 16 June 1815.

Conforming to the Emperor's instructions, the 2nd Corps is to begin its march immediately to take its positions; the 5th Division [Bachelu] in the rear of Genappe, on the heights that dominate this town, the left anchored on the main road. A battalion or two should cover all the approaches towards Brussels. The reserve park and the baggage of this division are to remain in the second line.

The 9th Division [Foy] is to follow the 5th and take a position in the second line on the heights to the left and right of the village of Banterlet [about 1 kilometre north of Quatre Bras]

The 6th and 7th Divisions [Jérôme and Girard] are to be at the junction of Quatre Bras where you are to locate your headquarters. The first three divisions of Count d'Erlon will take position at Frasnes; its right division is to be at Marbais with the second light cavalry division of General Piré; the first is to cover your march and you are to reconnoitre towards Brussels and on both flanks. My headquarters will be at Frasnes.

For Marshal *Prince de la Moskowa*,

Colonel, *premier aide de camp*, Heymès

[PS] Two divisions of Count Valmy are to establish themselves at Frasnes and Liberchies. General Lefebvre-Desnouëttes and Colbert's division of the Guard are to remain in their current position at Frasnes.[14]

Once again we must note that there is little indication that there would be a fight for Quatre Bras, despite the fact that Bachelu's and Piré's men were skirmishing with the Dutch just beyond Frasnes. Ney was with the forward troops at this time and so it is puzzling (at best!) that his orders suggest nothing more than a march forwards. Despite the '3,000 men' in front of him, Ney clearly presumed they would withdraw as he advanced. Heymès' claims that 'The morning of the 16th passed in the reconnaissance of the enemy and the ground over which we were going to fight ...'[15] are rather hollow given the underestimation of his enemy's strength. However, Ney was also expecting Reille's two rear divisions to be on the move, as he had expressly directed Reille, 'that if in his absence movement orders arrived, he was to execute them immediately ...'

Reille's Move Forward

Reille, however, had chosen not to follow this order. Demonstrating the caution and prevarication that seemed to pervade almost the entire French chain-of-command, Reille chose to wait for further orders before moving instead of doing so on his own initiative. The reason for this was a report he received from General Girard, who commanded the division that was covering the right flank. This report Reille forwarded to Ney:

Monsieur le Maréchal,

I have the honour to inform Your Excellency of the report that was made to me verbally by one of General Girard's officers.

The enemy continues to occupy Fleurus with light cavalry with vedettes in front; two enemy masses have been observed on the Namur road, whose head is on the heights of Saint-Amand; they are forming bit by bit, and have reached some ground where they can all concentrate: their strength cannot be judged because of the distance. However, this general thinks that each was of about six battalions in battalion columns. There is also movement to their rear.

General Flahaut has informed me of the content of the orders he is taking to Your Excellence; I have warned Count d'Erlon so that he can follow my own move. I would have started my move on Frasnes as soon as the divisions were under arms; but after the report of General Girard, I will hold the troops ready to march but wait for the orders from Your Excellency, and as you can warn me very quickly, there will be little time lost.

I have sent an officer to the emperor with General Girard's report.

I renew to Your Excellency the assurances of my respectful devotion,

> Commander in Chief of the 2nd Corps
> Count Reille[16]

Reille's reluctance to move forward because of this supposed threat to his right rear has been endorsed by many commentators. However, this Prussian activity, the concentration of its army on Bry and Saint-Amand before Grouchy's troops, was being threatened by Napoleon's proposed move, which had been made clear from the letter carried by General Flahaut, the contents of which had been shown to General Reille. He should therefore have been aware that this was not a force that should concern him. By the time Ney had reiterated the order for Reille to advance to Frasnes, what Reille had said would be 'little time lost' was actually at least two hours. Just when energy and speed were vital to success, each commander seemed to be finding reasons to slow down.

The move forward from Gosselies, which should surely have been anticipated from the earliest hours of the day, did not therefore take place until midday. This is confirmed by a number of officers including General Foy: 'On the 16th June it had been quiet in the morning. Towards midday we started our march to take position at Quatre Bras ...'[17] and Lieutenant Puvis of the 93rd *de ligne*:

> On the 16th, whilst the distribution of rations was taking place in the division and whilst we prepared to move, the corps artillery and the cavalry passed us to take position in front on the Brussels road. At mid-

day we started our march. We had hardly been marching an hour when, to our right, we heard a cannonade which seemed quite close to us.[18]

Perhaps more mysterious is this quote from *Adjutant-Commandant* Trefcon, the chief-of-staff to General Bachelu, whose division was the furthest forward and whose main body was already bivouacked around Frasnes:

> At 5am on the morning of the 16th, we were already mustered and under arms, ready to fight. We remained in this position for three hours. At 8am we received the order to move on Quatre Bras. We headed for this point, but, because of some mistaken movements, we only got to our actual positions towards midday.[19]

What these 'mistaken movements' were is unclear, but Trefcon's account shows that the divisions were ready and expecting to move from relatively early, but apparently lacked any orders.

Napoleon's Second Order

Between nine and ten in the morning, as Napoleon prepared to start off for Fleurus to join Grouchy, the lancer officer that Ney had sent back arrived at headquarters to warn the emperor that there was a force massing at Quatre Bras. For Napoleon, this was the first intimation that Quatre Bras was still occupied by the allies and that Ney would probably have to fight for its possession. Napoleon clearly wanted this vital crossroads in French hands and had Soult send the following message,

> Charleroi, 16 June 1815
>
> *Monsieur le Maréchal*, an officer of lancers has just informed the emperor that the enemy has appeared in force near Quatre Bras. Concentrate the corps of Counts Reille and d'Erlon and that of Count Valmy, who is just marching to join you. With these forces you must engage and destroy all enemy forces that present themselves. Blücher was at Namur yesterday and it is unlikely that he has sent any troops towards Quatre Bras. Thus you will only have to deal with the forces coming from Brussels.
>
> Marshal Grouchy is moving on Sombreffe as I informed you, and the emperor is going to Fleurus. You should address future reports to His Majesty there.
>
> *Major general Duc de Dalmatie*[20]

Whatever uncertainty or lack of clarity there may be in previous orders Ney had received about seizing Quatre Bras, this order cannot be so criticised. It clearly tells Ney what he should have already known and orders him to concentrate his forces and to 'destroy' the enemy forces at the crossroads. But if this order was sent off at about 10am, the time Napoleon left his headquarters for Fleurus, it could not have arrived with Ney until about

11.30am, and we can only estimate that it took one and a half to two hours to travel the 16 or so kilometres of good road that separated Charleroi and Frasnes, and to locate Marshal Ney. The key now was whether Ney was in a position to act immediately on this unequivocal direction.

D'Erlon's Move

We have already seen that at least Marcognet's division, which was at Marchiennes, had been ordered at 3am to move to Gosselies by 6am and, although he may not have made it by that time, d'Erlon was still awaiting orders for his next move. These did not arrive until late morning; d'Erlon himself wrote:

> Towards 11am or midday, *M. le Maréchal* Ney sent me the order for my corps to take up arms and move on Frasnes and Quatre Bras, where I would receive subsequent orders. My corps thus set off immediately after having given the order to the general commanding the head of the column [Durutte], to move quickly. I went ahead to see what was happening at Quatre Bras, where General Reille's corps appeared to be engaged.[21]

But d'Erlon's troops could not pass Gosselies until all of Reille's corps had evacuated it and this did not happen, for all the reasons we have already explored, until sometime after 2pm, and probably at least another half hour later. So, however keen he was to join Ney, d'Erlon was prevented from moving forward because Reille's corps was blocking his path. This wait allowed his rearmost formations, Quiot's division and Gobrecht's brigade of cavalry, to close up. If his lead division left Gosselies at 2.30pm it might well have been able to arrive on the battlefield an hour later and still in plenty of time to make a decisive intervention. Fate was to determine otherwise.

Analysis
The Allies

Having launched his offensive, Napoleon's next move was dependent on the reaction of Wellington and Blücher. It is therefore worth summarising their situation first.

By midday on the 16th, Blücher had succeeded in concentrating three of his four corps around Ligny, although by this time he probably realised that the IV Corps would not reach him that day. Throughout the morning he had remained ignorant of Wellington's location or intentions, and therefore could not rely on receiving any support from him. However, despite these considerable drawbacks, it seems clear that he had set his heart on risking a battle. Thus, Napoleon's estimation of him was turning out to be accurate. Risking a battle in these circumstances can be considered foolhardy in the

extreme, and in other circumstances could well have resulted in the destruction of his army that Napoleon sought.

Wellington was still convinced that Napoleon's major objective was the
capture of Brussels, rather than the destruction of the allied armies followed
by the capture of Brussels. This had resulted in him failing to concentrate
his army early enough to be able to guarantee support to the Prussians; the
fundamental bedrock of their defensive strategy. Although his concerns for a
French offensive via Mons are understandable, it is hard to believe he had no
plan if Napoleon attacked from Charleroi. In this eventuality, he must have
planned to concentrate in depth and then confront the French close to
Brussels; this was always going to compromise his support to Blücher unless
the latter was prepared to fall back to meet Wellington or Napoleon's
advance was so slow that he would have time to concentrate then move forward to meet the Prussians. In the circumstances, what took place should have
been entirely predictable. Once convinced of Napoleon's true axis of attack,
he had little option but to rush his men forward and try to establish a forward
point of concentration that would not expose him to engaging his troops
piecemeal.

Napoleon

The capture of Brussels would have gained Napoleon little if the armies of
both Wellington and Blücher were intact. It was therefore important, if he
was to have the opportunity of destroying at least one of them early, that he
did not scare them off by cutting the communications between them. Under
no circumstances did Napoleon want Wellington and Blücher to concentrate,
as he had little chance of defeating their combined strength.

Napoleon's main aim on this day, therefore, was the destruction of one of
the allied armies, but it was not until mid-morning that there was a real indication that an opportunity might present itself. Wellington had clearly not
concentrated and there was no information as to where he would attempt to
achieve this. However, what was more encouraging was that during the morning the Prussians increasingly showed a willingness to stand and fight, even
though it must have been becoming apparent to them that they would have to
do this without their own IV Corps or Wellington's support.

Napoleon's plans overnight therefore, an advance on Gembloux pushing
the Prussians away from Wellington to the east, followed by an attack on
Wellington's isolated army, turned into an attempt to destroy the Prussian
army. This underlined the importance of Ney holding Quatre Bras in order
to prevent Wellington from interfering, but apart from the orders that the
emperor had sent that morning, which included the option of drawing some
of Ney's force to support the right wing, the situation was still not clear
enough for Napoleon to have fully developed the idea of using them to fall on
the rear of the Prussians.

It is also worth noting that Napoleon's orders of this morning, which arrived with Ney sometime after 10.30am, were the first written orders that he had received which specified the occupation of Quatre Bras.

Ney

The significance of whether Ney's midnight meeting with Napoleon actually took place cannot be overstated; for if it did, Ney's behaviour on the morning of the 16th is difficult to reconcile. Is it possible that in two hours Napoleon and the commander of his left wing did not discuss in detail the options and expectations of the next day? Is it possible that they did not discuss the vital importance of the crossroads of Quatre Bras to the communications between the Anglo-Dutch army and that of the Prussians, and thus its importance to themselves? As we shall see, there is a mystifying lack of reference to Quatre Bras in Napoleon's correspondence with Ney prior to mid-morning of the 16th, and an equally mystifying lack of effort by Ney to occupy it. These failings suggest that, however logical and natural it appears for Ney, particularly in light of his very recent arrival with the army, to have had a long and detailed discussion with Napoleon on his strategy and hopes for the following few days, the incomprehensible events of the 16th cannot but logically suggest that it did not take place. Although Ney's own ADC states that this meeting did occur, it is true that Heymès' account of other events during the morning is riddled with verifiable error and therefore must be considered of doubtful veracity. However, as Heymès wrote to champion Ney's performance it seems inconceivable that he should make this up, as such a meeting is more likely to undermine his case rather than support it. Andrew Uffindell, a respected modern historian, states that it has been proven that this meeting did not take place, but does not explain where this proof lies. Ropes, who wrote in 1892, is convinced that it did take place, but earlier authors, Becke, Chesney, Siborne, Charras and Jomini also accept it as fact, although Houssaye, often the most reliable and objective of French historians, and Clausewitz, make no reference to it at all.

If the meeting did take place, and for me the balance of evidence suggests it did, I can only conclude that Napoleon put some sort of constraint on Ney; such as not to execute the manoeuvre until he received a written order. Such a delay would allow more information on Prussian movements and intentions to come in and allow Napoleon to ensure his plans were still practicable. On the morning of the 16th it is clear that Ney was impatiently awaiting such written orders, although it appears he had done nothing to anticipate them: in particular, ensuring his entire force was concentrated and capable of reacting immediately. If Napoleon had instructed Ney not to advance on Quatre Bras until he received written orders, it was reasonable for him to expect Ney to have prepared his command to react immediately he did so.

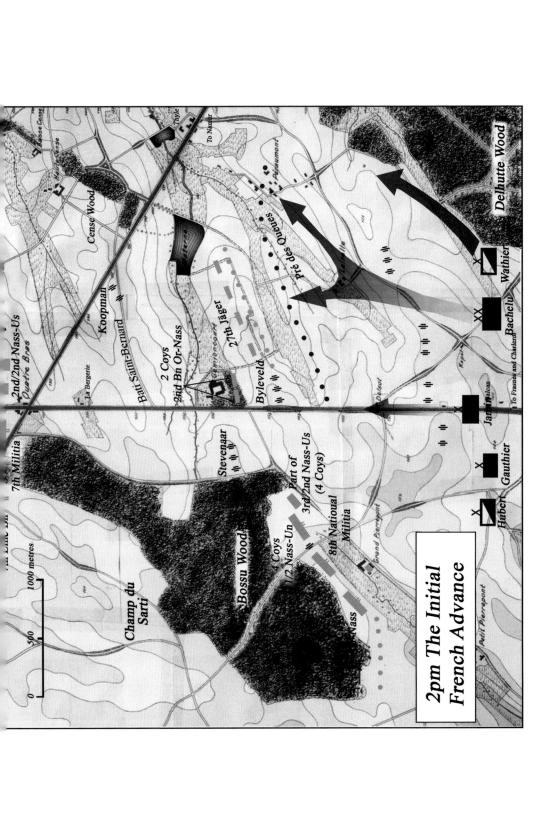

2pm The Initial
French Advance

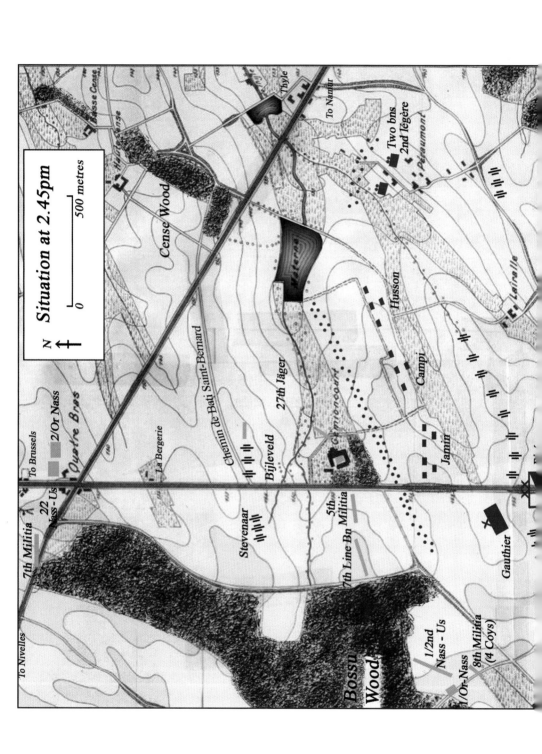

Situation at 2.45pm

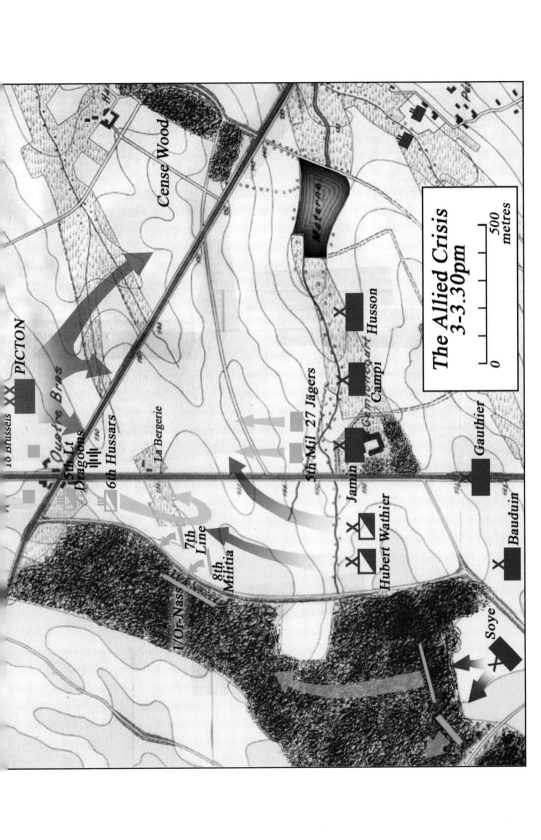

The Allied Crisis
3-3.30pm

0 — 500 metres

Cense Wood

PICTON
XX

To Brussels

Quatre Bras

5th Lt
Dragoons

6th Hussars

La Bergerie

7th
Line

8th.
Militia

1/Or-Nass

5th Mil 27 Jägers

Jamin
X

Gem-Coeur-
Campi

Husson
X

Gauthier

Hubert Wathier
X   X

Bauduin
X

Soye
X

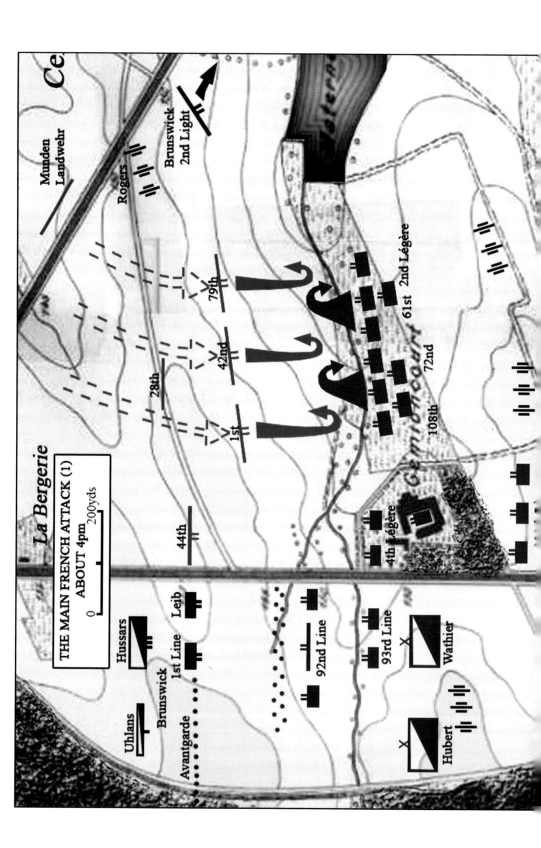

La Bergerie

THE MAIN FRENCH ATTACK (1)
ABOUT 4pm

0   200yds

Munden
Landwehr

Rogers

Brunswick
2nd Light

79th

28th

42nd

1st

44th

61st   2nd Légère

72nd

108th

4th Légère

Uhlans

Brunswick
Avantgarde

Hussars

1st Line

Leib

92nd Line

93rd Line

Wathier

Hubert

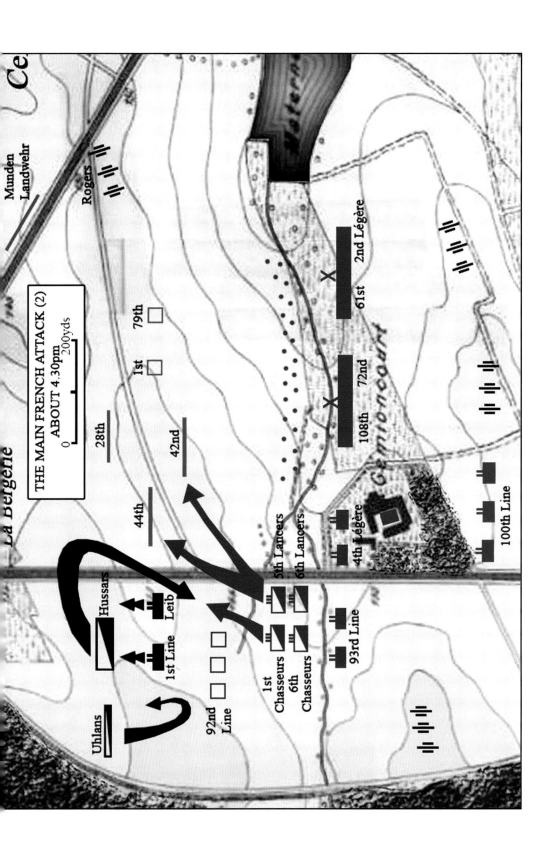

Ce

La Bergère

Munden
Landwehr

Rogers

THE MAIN FRENCH ATTACK (2)
ABOUT 4.30pm
0   200yds

Waterm—

2nd Légère

61st

72nd

108th

Gemioncourt

4th Légère

100th Line

79th

1st

28th

44th

42nd

5th Lancers

6th Lancers

93rd Line

Hussars

Leib

1st Line

1st
Chasseurs

6th
Chasseurs

Uhlans

92nd
Line

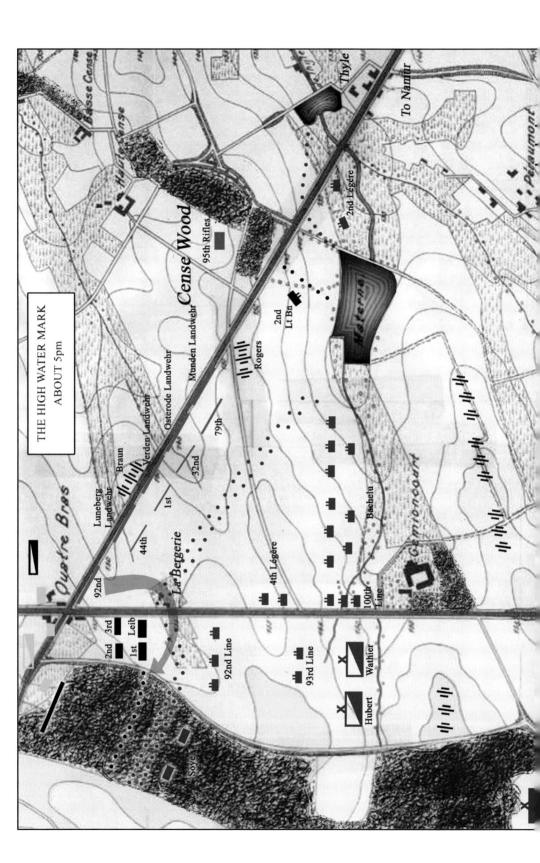

THE HIGH WATER MARK
ABOUT 5pm

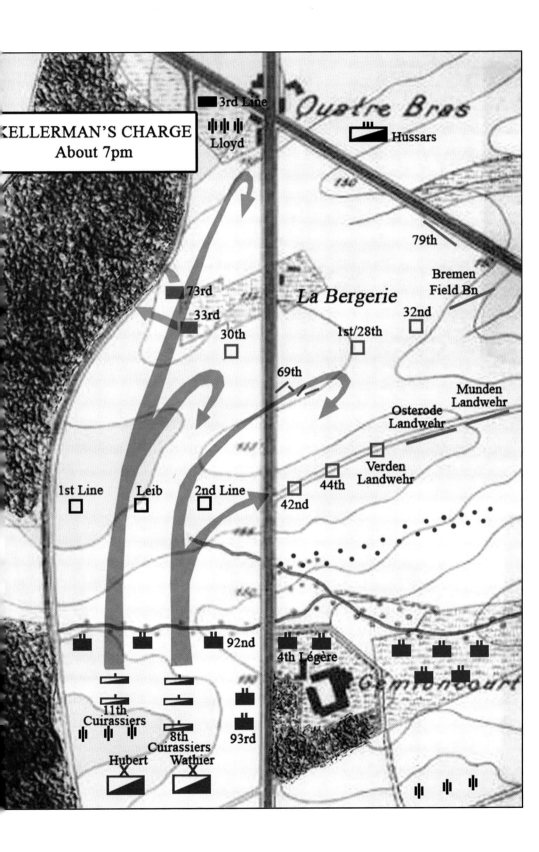

KELLERMAN'S CHARGE
About 7pm

3rd Line

Lloyd

Quatre Bras

Hussars

79th

Bremen
Field Bn

La Bergerie

32nd

73rd

33rd

30th

1st/28th

69th

Munden
Landwehr

Osterode
Landwehr

Verden
Landwehr

44th

1st Line

Leib

2nd Line

42nd

92nd

4th Légère

Gemioncourt

11th
Cuirassiers

8th
Cuirassiers
Wathier

93rd

Hubert

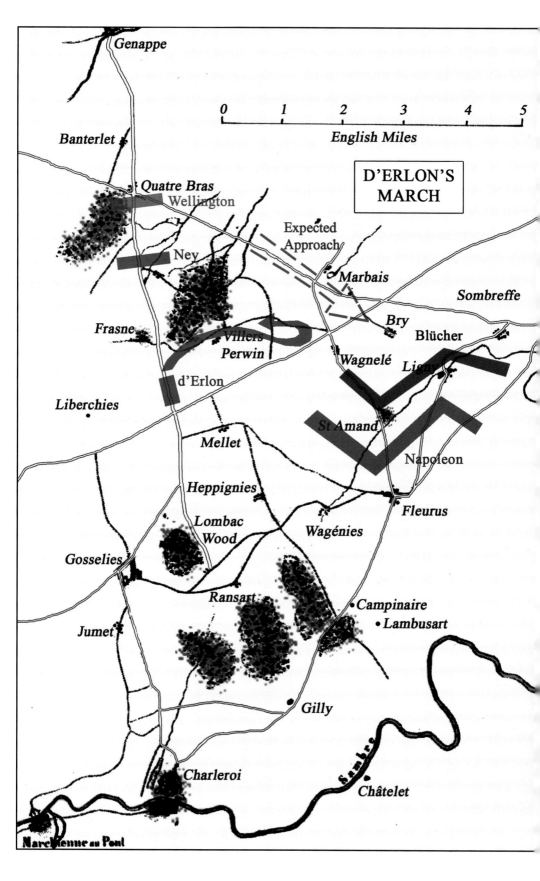

Genappe

Banterlet

0   1   2   3   4   5

English Miles

D'ERLON'S
MARCH

Quatre Bras
Wellington

Expected
Approach

Ney

Marbais

Sombreffe

Frasne

Bry

Blücher

Villers
Perwin

Wagnelé

Ligny

d'Erlon

Liberchies

St Amand

Napoleon

Mellet

Heppignies

Fleurus

Lombac
Wood

Wagénies

Gosselies

Ransart

Campinaire

Lambusart

Jumet

Gilly

Charleroi

Sambre

Châtelet

Marchienne au Pont

It is quite possible that the late hour at which Ney returned from his meeting with Napoleon, the exhausted state of his troops and the apparently weak force that was holding Quatre Bras, might have convinced him that there was time to do what was necessary in the morning. It was also possible that the small force that had been encountered the evening before might well have already withdrawn. Ney may well have expected the order to arrive much earlier than it did.

But if we can excuse Ney for not launching what would have been a night attack on Quatre Bras, it is more difficult to excuse his inactivity on the morning of the 16th. Given the action the previous evening and the Prince of Orange's reconnaissance in force at about 6am, Ney knew that there were allied troops in front of him and that they were prepared to fight. First light was at about 4am and the troops could rightly have been expected to be ready to march at that time. Ney's orders the day before had been to 'push the enemy' along the Brussels road (if not something more robust, as Napoleon claims). And yet throughout the morning, Ney seems to have made little effort to clarify what the situation to his front was, and failed to show any determination to concentrate his command. Although he was not well seconded by Reille in this respect, there was no reason to await Napoleon's orders before concentrating the whole of the 2nd Corps and Kellerman's cavalry corps at Frasnes, thus allowing d'Erlon to concentrate the whole of the 1st Corps at Gosselies as he had been ordered.

Ney's inactivity whilst waiting for orders from Napoleon is frankly inexplicable; especially in a man with such an aggressive and rash reputation. The lack of orders are his excuse, or even the reason, but it is hard to believe that Ney did not see the vital importance of ensuring his entire command was concentrated so he could react immediately to whatever orders he received. The only possible explanation for Ney not having been given a direct order to seize Quatre Bras first thing in the morning is that Napoleon, desperate to destroy the Prussian army, did not want to give it an excuse not to fight; a break in communications with their allies may have encouraged the Prussians to withdraw rather than risk the outcome of a battle that would be fought with absolutely no prospect of Wellington's support. Whilst this argument is quite seductive, it must be remembered that when Napoleon and Ney met, the emperor was still far from sure that he would be confronting the entire Prussian army the next day. Indeed, his letters and orders seem to predict that the Prussians were withdrawing along their communications and that he would personally push them as far as Gembloux before leaving the pursuit to Grouchy's right wing and himself turning back against Wellington with the reserves.

Reille
If we criticise Ney for not concentrating his entire force for whatever next operation Napoleon ordered, then Reille too should be so criticised. It

appears that once Ney was given command of the left wing, Reille, who could be praised for his advance on the 15th, appears to have lapsed into apathy on the 16th. The reasons for this are hard to be clear upon; perhaps losing the responsibility and initiative he had enjoyed on the 15th had irked him? He seems to have been content to await orders to do what should have been taken for granted; like getting his corps well in hand for subsequent operations. Although some critics have praised his caution when Girard warned him of the Prussian concentration on his right, he was also aware, having seen Napoleon's instructions and intentions, that the right wing was confronting this threat, and anyway, this should have encouraged him to concentrate his own corps rather than leave it spread out. If he had started his march one and a half hours earlier it could certainly have had a considerable, if not decisive, impact on the day's outcome.

D'Erlon

In his own analysis of the campaign, Ropes is very critical of d'Erlon's failure to concentrate his corps. However, this seems rather harsh. He was faced with the conflicting orders of covering the left flank of the army, the western crossings over the Sambre and the road to Mons, whilst moving his corps to Gosselies. We have seen that he gave timely orders to get his divisions moving, but given the distance these orders had to travel to reach his furthest division, Quiot's, it is perhaps unsurprising that these struggled to close up. However, d'Erlon's major problem was moving forward from Jumet, where his lead division had spent the night, until the rear divisions of Reille's corps had evacuated Gosselies. It is hard to criticise him for not moving forward earlier, as this proved to be impossible until 2pm when Prince Jérôme's division finally started its own march.

Summary

For the left wing, the morning of the 16th was marked by hesitation and pre-varication. Ney seemed to be in no hurry either to concentrate his forces, or to push along the Brussels road as he had been ordered. He displayed no initiative and was apparently content to await written orders from Napoleon before he did anything. Both Reille and d'Erlon found reasons to delay their marches. Whilst d'Erlon had some excuse, the fact remains that for an offensive to be successful, it requires initiative, energy, determination and audacity; these qualities appear to have been absent in the three most senior commanders of the left wing on this critical day.

Chapter 7

Afternoon, 16 June – Preliminaries

Wellington's Meeting with Blücher

Having left Quatre Bras towards one o'clock, believing there were few French troops on the Brussels road, Wellington joined Blücher on the heights of Bry. En route, he said to his Prussian liaison officer Müffling, 'If, as seems likely, the division of the enemy's forces posted at Frasnes, opposite Quatre Bras, is inconsiderable, and only intended to mask the English army, I can employ my whole strength in support of the Field Marshal [Blücher], and will gladly execute all his wishes in regard to joint operations.'[1] On arrival, Wellington and Blücher climbed up the mill of Bussy from which there was an excellent view of the surrounding area. From here they were not only able to see a very large French force assembling, but also, with their telescopes, Napoleon himself, surrounded by a numerous staff. They concluded that they had before them the entire imperial army. The discussion then turned to how Wellington was going to support his allies, supposing that he had only a small holding force in front of him at Quatre Bras.

Two options were discussed. Wellington's preference was to brush aside the force in front of him and march on Gosselies, thus threatening the French left rear and their lines of communication. This appealed to Wellington as it preserved his own independence of command and freedom of action. The Prussians, led by Blücher's chief-of-staff, Gneisenau, who had a lingering suspicion about Wellington's dependability, argued for the Anglo-Dutch army to march straight down the road from Quatre Bras towards Namur, which would bring them in behind the Prussian right and into reserve, where they would be well placed and available for use wherever they were required. Wellington opposed this option as he foresaw his men being drip-fed into battle, and because he would therefore lose centralised command of them. A consensus was not reached and Wellington reportedly ended the discussion with the words, 'Very well! I will come, if I am not attacked myself.'

It seems that Blücher, by concentrating his army around Ligny during the morning, had already determined on fighting a battle without any assurance from Wellington that he would be directly supported by his allies. Wellington's visit, although a final plan had not definitively been agreed, would no doubt have reassured him that he was to get some substantial help which, given Bülow's failure to move sufficiently quickly to join him, would still give him a superiority in numbers. As the Prussian deployment left their right flank very much 'in the air', we can assume that Blücher felt that if this was exploited by Napoleon, Wellington's troops would be closest to this flank to come to his support.

But did Wellington really believe he could concentrate enough of his own troops and then march them to Ligny in sufficient time to make a decisive impact? We do not know what size force Wellington envisaged, but he must have realised that he would need to keep some troops at Quatre Bras to contain the 'division' he calculated the French had there, and given the locations of his troops and the forced marches they were already making in order to concentrate, it is reasonable to predict that it would be late afternoon at the earliest before he could bring even a modest force to support the Prussians. Whether Wellington deliberately misled his allies has been hotly debated in recent years, but whether or not it was deliberate, it does indeed seem that he misled them, even given the 'let out clause' he finished with, and not all those present at the discussion agree that this was what he said. We shall return to this issue later.

At 2pm Wellington left the Prussian commander-in-chief to return to Quatre Bras.

Napoleon's Plans

It is important to understand how Napoleon's mind was working as the situation before him became clear. He had informed Ney that he planned to push the Prussians down their lines of communication and away from their Anglo-Dutch allies so that he could then turn and attack Wellington, destroy him and then march on Brussels. This supposed that Blücher was not planning to make a stand and risk a battle, which would probably be without Wellington's support. However, as the hours passed, it became increasingly evident that Blücher was indeed planning to make a stand. As Wellington and Blücher met at the Bussy windmill, Napoleon was carrying out a reconnaissance of the Prussian position and identified that its right wing was 'in the air'; that is, not anchored on a strong feature that would prevent it being outflanked. As we have heard, we can only suppose, since this was the western flank, that Blücher was relying on Wellington to arrive to support this wing of his army.

At two o'clock, it was clear that there was going to be a major battle at Ligny and it is only at this point that Napoleon finally developed his idea of fixing the Prussian army in place by a strong frontal attack, and then enveloping their right wing by drawing troops from Marshal Ney, whom he expected to have occupied the vital crossroads of Quatre Bras and to have deployed his troops as he had directed in his orders sent that morning. Napoleon gave the necessary orders to the right wing and reserve for the attack and had Soult write an order to Ney informing him of the need to send a force onto the Prussian right flank. We will note the detail of this order and its arrival with Ney later, but at this point Ney was unaware that Napoleon had the majority of the Prussian army in front of him and was about to attack it. But equally, the emperor was unclear on the situation facing his left wing commander. This breakdown of communications and the failure of each of these two key commanders to understand the true situation that faced the other, was to have catastrophic consequences.

The Battlefield of Quatre Bras

To a modern visitor the area around the crossroads and small hamlet of Quatre Bras has little to recommend it as a defensive position, and it certainly did not offer the true reverse slope position that Wellington was so renowned for. The hamlet of Quatre Bras consisted of only a large farm, named for the hamlet, an inn (apparently named *Trois Bras*, which may also account for Marshal Soult referring to the crossroads by this name) and a few other buildings associated with farming.

The field of action was an undulating plain which was delineated by the heights of Quatre Bras to the north and Balcan to the south. From the relative high ground of Quatre Bras, the ground fell gently away towards the farm of La Bergerie; an open area which would have offered a clear killing ground for the defenders if the crops had not been so high as to partially obscure their sight. Unfortunately it is impossible to really understand how this lack of visibility affected the view for those in the area of the crossroads, but it certainly commanded the undulations of the ground immediately in front of it towards the Barti Saint-Bernard ridge. This ridge blocked all further observation into the shallow valleys beyond and only the crests of the Gémioncourt ridge and the Balcan heights could be seen beyond it.

A little over a mile to the south, the Balcan ridgeline acted for the French as Quatre Bras did for the allies; giving a good, wide view of the battlefield, but no line of sight into the shallow valleys. However, it offered an excellent gunline for the artillery to support the initial deployment and advance. The Delhutte wood, to the east of Frasnes, formed something of a chicane with that village, which needed to be negotiated by the French before they had sufficient open ground to deploy their entire line of battle. Once clear of this choke point, Reille's divisions could shake out into their prescribed formation.

From the Balcan heights, named after the inn that once stood there, the French had three approaches they could use to seize the crossroads.

The right (eastern) approach would require them to secure the farm of Lairalle, then the farm and hamlet of Piraumont, followed by the small hamlet of Thyle that lay on the main Namur to Nivelles road, before advancing up this road towards Quatre Bras. Close to Quatre Bras itself, the Namur road had quite high banks which made it a natural defensive position facing south and south-west, but offered no protection against anyone marching up the road from the south-east. This approach had the advantage of cutting the main road between Quatre Bras and the Prussian position at Ligny, but risked having Prussian troops moving up it towards their allies and on to the French right rear. The relatively small, but significant lake called the Étang Materne, and the Gémioncourt stream that fed it, would also rather isolate this approach from the rest of the battlefield.

The second approach was a central approach using the main Brussels road as an axis. To the right of the road, this would take the attackers up and over a number of low ridges with shallow valleys in between. The two biggest of these shallow valleys had small streams running along the bottom; from the south, these were the Pré des Queues and then the Gémioncourt stream. The latter in particular was a serious obstacle, described as:

> ... bordered by hedges impassable for mounted troops, and through which infantry could only move in single file. The ground inside the two hedges is from three to five feet lower than that outside, and this added to the difficulty of passing through them.[2]

Along the main road lay the farms of Gémioncourt and La Bergerie; the former lay in a hollow beside the main road and was particularly strongly built, with high walls joining the farm house and outbuildings making it almost a fortress. La Bergerie was a relatively small, two-storey building, surrounded by a hedge. Across the road was a small garden, also surrounded by a hedge. The shallow valleys offered protection from artillery fire and the ridges above them made a series of ideal artillery positions. This part of the battlefield was widely cultivated and was described by one British soldier as, 'being covered with rye, and of an extraordinary height, some of it measuring seven feet'.[3] This made orientation and coordinated movement difficult, and largely hid from view the troops moving through it, making identification equally tricky. One of the main constraints of this approach was that the main Namur road to the east, and the Bossu wood to the west, funnelled any advance towards the crossroads on an ever-decreasing frontage.

To the west of the main road the ground was more undulating and irregular, with a number of hollows and heights, although suitable for both infantry and cavalry to manoeuvre in cover. The heights to the west of the main road that can be clearly identified on the map offered more dominating artillery positions. An advance along this left-hand (western) approach would first need to clear Petit and Grand Pierrepont, two large farms that could be easily fortified and which were surrounded by orchards and gardens. Unfortunately for the defence, the latter was built in a dip, without fields of fire, and was therefore of little tactical importance. The open ground was relatively flat and good for both infantry and cavalry, although a number of sunken tracks offered cover for defenders and obstacles for attackers.

The third approach was through the wood of Bossu. This was a relatively long, thin wood (long since cut down); about 2,500 metres long and between

500 and 1,000 metres wide, it offered a covered approach right up to within 150 yards of Quatre Bras itself. Orientated south-west to north-east it had a sunken track running north to south and another east to west about two-thirds of the way down its length. Level with Gémioncourt, the edge of the wood was 500 metres from the main road, forming, with that farm, a relatively narrow bottleneck through which, given the difficulty of the stream to the east of Gémioncourt, all French cavalry would have to pass. Contemporary accounts give the impression that within the wood there were areas of dense undergrowth where movement, observation and command and control were very difficult, and more open areas where the trees were thicker and there was little undergrowth. Indeed, one author claims that cavalry could pass through in 'extended order' and even that the French deployed two batteries within it.[4] The edges of the wood were lined with thick vegetation, giving the impression of a hedge, and making the ordered entry and exit of the wood difficult except on the few tracks. The wood provided good cover to those who occupied it and wished to shoot out across the open ground, but it would be as difficult to defend as to attack due to the difficulty of maintaining cohesion and control.

The Allied Deployment

At 2pm when the French attack began, the Prince of Orange had available 8,000 infantry and sixteen guns. In fact, the two battalions of the Orange-Nassau Regiment had no more than ten rounds in their ammunition pouches; a shocking failure of logistics given that these troops had not yet been seriously engaged in the campaign. To make ammunition resupply even more challenging, the two volunteer chasseur companies had four different calibres of firearms! Significantly, apart from fifty stray Prussian hussars that left soon after the outpost skirmishing early in the morning, there were no allied cavalry at Quatre Bras until sometime after 3pm.

Across his whole front the Prince of Orange had deployed a line of skirmishers, but the main line of defence was heavily weighted to the west of the main road. Here he had a line of four battalions and a company of volunteer jäger, orientated along the edge of the Bossu wood. These were supported by a battery of artillery (Stevenaar's), deployed just to the west of the main road on one of the low ridges where it had a good field of fire covering that road. The Prince of Orange clearly felt that the Bossu wood offered good cover for his outnumbered troops and, by making it something of a bastion, he would protect the Nivelles road along which he expected his earliest reinforcement to come.

To the east of the road, the line between Gémioncourt and the Étang Materne was held by a single battalion; the 27th Jägers, although the farm itself was occupied by two companies of the Orange-Nassau Regiment. This flank did, however, also have the support of a battery of artillery; two sections were deployed on the heights just forward of Gémioncourt with the other section covering down the main road towards Namur.

In reserve were a further four battalions, including the 7th Line Battalion, the final unit of the 2nd (Netherlands) Division which rejoined just before the battle started. These were deployed either side of the Quatre Bras crossroads, but rather too far back to give the front line any immediate support.

The Netherlands defence line was therefore very much based on the natural defence line of the Bossu wood, protecting the Nivelles road. The Prince had given no thought to trying to keep the Namur road open, along which the Prussians were expecting allied support; he clearly felt he had insufficient troops to do both.

The French Deployment
At 2pm, Ney still had only the divisions of Bachelu, Foy and Piré immediately available; a total of about 10,000 infantry, 2,000 cavalry and thirty guns, although he did have Lefebvre-Desnoüettes' 2,400 Guard cavalry and its two horse batteries available in an emergency. Having concentrated these divisions around Frasnes, they first had to advance and skirt around the Delhutte wood on the high ground above the village from which allied officers, including Wellington himself at one time, had been observing them throughout the morning. Reille describes the initial deployment:

> The 5th [Bachelu] and 9th [Foy] Divisions and the cavalry division [Piré] formed up, starting the attack towards 2pm. The 5th Division marched in columns *par bataillon*, to the right of the road and the 9th Division had a brigade on the road and one in reserve.
>
> Piré's cavalry division flanked the right, while the marshal was on the main road with the Guard cavalry division and a body of heavy cavalry commanded by the Count de Valmy which had just arrived, deployed to the left.
>
> The 6th Infantry Division [Jérôme] was still spread out behind and the commander of the 7th [Girard] sent word that at that moment the emperor had met him at Wagnée [in fact it was Wangenies] just as he was setting off for Quatre Bras and had taken him off with him to Saint-Amand.[5]

So even before the battle started, Ney had been deprived of one of Reille's divisions. Girard's troops were destined to take a leading part in the battle of Ligny and Girard himself was to find a glorious death there at the head of his soldiers during the desperate fighting.

Wathier's lancer brigade had led Bachelu's division into position towards the right, but it soon became clear that the ground here was unsuitable for cavalry action and they were promptly recalled to join Hubert's brigade near the main road. The artillery unlimbered along the ridgeline, giving them an

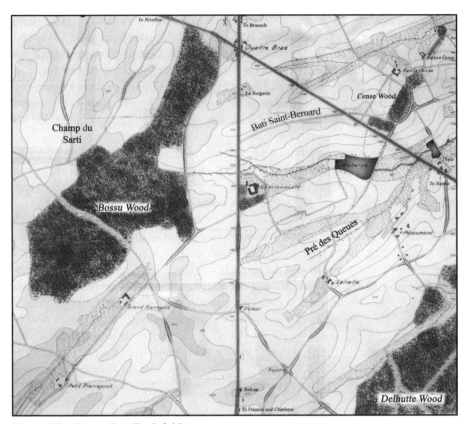

Map 6. The Quatre Bras Battlefield.

excellent field of fire towards Quatre Bras about 2 kilometres to the north. Having skirted the wood, Bachelu's battalions wheeled to the left to face north, except for the lead regiment, which had been ordered to seize the farm and hamlet of Piraumont and to cut the Namur road. This deployment was conducted in full view of the relatively inexperienced Dutch and Nassau troops and must have been an impressive and intimidating sight.

French formations deployed with the senior regiments taking the position of honour on the right, and we must presume that this was the case at Quatre Bras. In the case of Bachelu's division, therefore, we would expect the 2nd *légère* to have been the first to move forward and to have been tasked with the seizing of Piraumont; a mission well suited to a light infantry regiment. However, this regiment was particularly strong, having four battalions, and it seems that one or two of its battalions were used to strengthen the skirmisher line which preceded the main attack on the centre. The remaining line regiments, in battalion columns, would therefore have been, from the right, the 61st, the 72nd and the 108th. As we have no eyewitness confirmation, we must also assume that in line with standard operating procedure, those regiments consisting of two battalions (the 61st and 72nd) would have advanced with their battalions side by side, whilst the 108th Line with three battalions would have advanced two battalions forward, with the third in reserve in a second line. Each battalion would have deployed its light (*voltigeur*) company into a thick skirmish line forward of the columns. The columns *par bataillon* (see Figure 1) would have had a frontage of about fifty men shoulder to shoulder; 40 or so metres.

Foy's brigades were deployed separately; his first brigade, that of Jamin, consisting of the 4th *légère* and the 100th Line (each of three battalions), were in column astride the main road. Gauthier's brigade (92nd and 93rd Line) was designated as the reserve and was deployed to the left of the main road, facing the wood of Bossu.[6]

Hubert's brigade of Piré's division was initially deployed to the left of the main road. The lie of the land suggested that it would only have an unobstructed advance along and to the left of this road. French cavalry rarely charged in line and it is safe to assume that his regiments were deployed in columns by squadron; each squadron deployed in line of two files (giving a frontage of about 60 metres), with one squadron behind the other.

Lefebvre-Desnouëttes' guard cavalry were kept out of sight behind the ridge to the right of the main road in line with Napoleon's direction. These

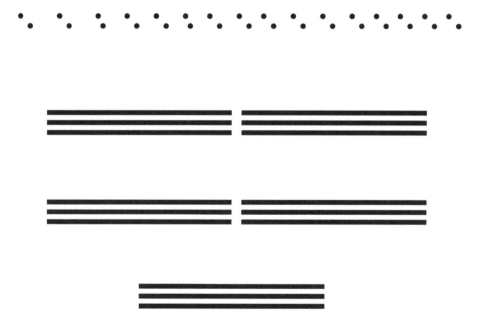

Figure 1. A French Battalion Assault Column.

were later joined (at about 2.30pm) by Guiton's brigade of cuirassiers, consisting of the 8th and 11th Cuirassiers, accompanied by Kellerman himself. They took position to the left of the main road, level with the guard cavalry. The other three brigades of Kellerman's corps were kept at Liberchies, about 5 kilometres south-west of Frasnes, in line with the orders of Marshal Ney. It remains a mystery why Ney left such a potent force so far away as to prevent it being available for the battle he was about to fight. It has been suggested that Ney sent them there because Napoleon had warned that he might call on them himself, but the emperor's orders were based on the belief that Ney would not be involved in any serious fighting that might require their involvement. Napoleon made clear however, that they were under Ney's orders and we might feel that it was Ney's tendency to forget troops that were not immediately under his eye that actually accounts for their absence from Quatre Bras.

From this deployment, Ney's initial plan for the assault on Quatre Bras becomes evident. The 2nd *légère* was to seize Piraumont and, from there, to threaten the main road to Namur, along which any Anglo-Dutch troops would have to march if they were to offer any support to the Prussians fighting at Ligny. It is unclear if they were ordered to cut that road, although their later actions suggest that they were. The main effort would be an overwhelming infantry attack, supported by cavalry and artillery, to the right of the main road, aimed at seizing the crossroads at Quatre Bras. The Bossu wood would be covered by Gauthier's brigade, which would also serve as Ney's reserve.

*   *   *

Whilst Wellington was visiting Blücher and Ney was wasting time at Frasnes, Napoleon was using the time it was taking for Gérard's troops to come forward to develop his plans and to try and get things moving. It is evident that he was becoming very frustrated at the time everything was taking; he had always understood the importance of time, and had prided himself on the celerity of his strategic manoeuvres. Unfortunately for him, this campaign was blighted by indecision, hesitation and a lack of energy and urgency amongst his subordinates, although many historians have also laid this charge at his own door.

Having ordered Ney to 'engage and destroy all enemy forces that present themselves ...' at 10am, and having received no reports and heard no artillery fire from the west, Napoleon wrote to Ney again at one o'clock:

Monsieur le Prince de la Moskowa, I am surprised at your great delay in executing my orders – there is no more time to waste. Attack everything in front of you with the greatest impetuosity. The fate of France is in your hands.
    Napoleon[7]

Whilst this message could not have arrived with Ney before he finally opened his attack on Quatre Bras, Napoleon's growing frustration is evident.

Due to the delays we have already explored, Reille's corps was not complete north of Frasnes even at 2pm. Foy, Bachelu and Piré had all deployed, but Jérôme's division, the strongest in Reille's corps at about 7,000 men, was still on the march and required another hour before its foremost units had reached the battlefield.

As for d'Erlon's corps, we have already established that they had been ordered to reach Gosselies by 6am, even though it was unlikely that Quiot's division, which had furthest to march and had clearly set off very late (if Corporal Canler is to be believed), would reach there much before 5pm. But all this suggests that a large proportion of the corps could have been at Frasnes, and available to Ney, by 8am at the latest. However, this was reliant on Reille's own move forward; d'Erlon could not move until 2nd Corps had cleared the road. In fact, Jérôme did not clear Gosselies until after 2pm, so it was impossible for d'Erlon to move until then.

Despite the Prince of Orange pushing back his outposts earlier in the morning, it is only at about 2pm that we have some firm evidence that Ney was attempting to gather some intelligence on his enemy. Lieutenant Henckens of the 6th Chasseurs à Cheval of Piré's division wrote in his memoirs:

> It was ... towards 2pm, we were half a league from Quatre Bras when I received the order from Colonel Faudoas to make a reconnaissance with my platoon against the enemy to the right of the main Charleroi to Brussels road ... It was the first time the colonel had seen me on operations. As we were already exposed to the enemy's artillery fire, it was thus under canister fire that I gave my orders to the platoon, of which the front rank were all legionnaires [recipients of the *Legion d'Honneur*], Colonel de Talhouët [the previous commanding officer] having chosen ... the best men for the *compagnie d'élite*. These chasseurs all understood my intention; it appears that the calm with which I acted on this occasion made such an impression on the colonel, that he approached me at the gallop and shook my hand in front of the whole regiment; this was for me a mark of esteem that I have remembered all my life.
>
> The reconnaissance made, with the support of the whole company, which was ordered to follow me, my impression was that the force that we had in front of us was minimal, that the enemy only wanted to impose on us and that with a bit of daring a great success was possible. The regiment, to complete the reconnaissance, started to engage a battalion close to the farm that we later learnt to be the farm of Gémioncourt; but because of a lack of support we could not complete this success.

Later in the day, reinforcements came continually for the enemy, but at the time of the reconnaissance I believed there was a total absence of cavalry, but there soon arrived hussars, dragoons and horse artillery.[8]

Henckens' assessment was clearly accurate (but may have been coloured by hindsight) and we must presume that patrols from the other regiments of Piré's division would have carried out similar missions across the whole of Ney's front. But Ney does seem to have been complacent about what he was facing, and his statement that there would be 'but a handful of Germans to deal with, who were cut to pieces yesterday',[9] and the lack of any suggestion in his movement orders that there was likely to be any fighting before occupying Quatre Bras, suggests this was indeed the case.

Despite his lack of aggression and initiative during the late morning, it seems Ney was convinced that the enemy before him was not in great strength, and once Reille's troops were deployed Foy reports:

> He [Ney] said that there were not many men in the Bossu wood and that it was necessary to take it immediately. Reille thought that this might well be like a battle in Spain, where the English troops would only show themselves when it was the right time and that it was necessary to wait and only start the attack when everyone was concentrated and massed on the ground. The Marshal, impatient and without thinking, appeared to believe that the companies of skirmishers were sufficient to take this position.[10]

There is no evidence to suggest that Reille's caution retarded Ney's determination to attack; after all, Napoleon's messages were becoming ever more urgent and prescriptive, and he may well have just received the emperor's latest order. But it must be said that Ney, Reille and Foy had all fought the British in the Peninsula, were aware of Wellington's rear slope tactics and had developed a healthy respect for the fighting qualities of his troops. Unsure whether there might be some British troops hidden away somewhere in a fold in the ground or behind one of the woods, they were most likely to advance with some caution.

It is also surprising that Foy tells us that Ney was convinced that the Bossu wood was not strongly held, and 'it was necessary to take it immediately'. His initial deployment displays no intention of occupying the wood, nor does he appear to have given any orders to attack it to any of the troops he had on hand. We must therefore assume that despite this wood providing an excellent covered approach right up to Quatre Bras itself, Ney's concern that it might be occupied by British troops that had remained out of sight convinced him that it was better not to get committed into a wood where it would prove almost impossible to keep informed or be able to control what was going on there. Seizing Quatre Bras by a more direct approach would outflank a garrison of the wood and force it to withdraw. He decided he would concern himself with taking the wood when he had more troops available.

Much of Ney's artillery was now deployed on the heights around Balcan and Lairalle; well served and in overwhelming numbers compared to what was facing them, the advance would have excellent fire support. As the columns advanced across the shallow valleys that ran across their front, the guns would be able to fire over their heads at the enemy's infantry and artillery.

Analysis

We shall examine the tactical handling of the battle later. But first we need to take a quick look at the promise of support, or otherwise, that Wellington gave to Blücher. Although the evidence suggests that Blücher had probably decided to risk a battle irrespective of support from his allies, not all the Prussian witnesses agree. Indeed, most Prussian officers that were present at the meeting state that it was only once Wellington had promised support that Blücher made his final decision, and they all suggest Wellington gave unequivocal promises of help. However, most of them wrote their accounts long after the event and some at least may have wished to shift some of the blame for their defeat. Clausewitz quotes Wellington as saying, 'At four o'clock, I will be here', but Clausewitz was not present and does not name the source of his own quote. The conditional commitment given in my own narrative comes from Müffling, Wellington's Prussian liaison officer, whom even Hofschröer has little confidence in. Perhaps the most objective witness is Thurn und Taxis, the Bavarian liaison officer to the Prussian army, who kept a diary and therefore was more likely to be accurate. He wrote, 'The Duke promised to send 20,000 men from his army by 3 o'clock.'[11] Of the two British witnesses present, Wellington himself and his own liaison officer to the Prussian headquarters, Hardinge, neither mentions any support whatsoever being promised.

Neither of the two allies could be confident of beating Napoleon on their own, and there was fundamental agreement at Thirlemont that mutual support was vital to their defensive strategy. It is hard to believe that Wellington did not fully intend to support Blücher and that Blücher was ambivalent about Wellington's support. However, the duke should have understood that given the lack of concentration of his own army, and aware of where most of his troops from Brussels currently were, that he may not have been capable of delivering that support and therefore could not make a solid commitment. Equally, although he probably realised that Bülow's IV Corps would not reach him in time, Blücher may well have been overconfident in his belief that he could beat Napoleon without Wellington's support, and thus his naturally aggressive temperament and hatred of the French drove him to an ill-advised confrontation with his old enemy.

We have looked in detail at Ney's failure to concentrate his troops prior to the battle and ascribed this partly to his own lack of initiative and foresight, and partly to over-caution and a lack of initiative in his key subordinates. The result of this was a failure to concentrate sufficient force to overwhelm the defence. With Napoleon's orders to 'engage and destroy' any enemy at Quatre Bras, at 2pm Ney still had only about 15,000 men, of his total command of over 40,000, immediately available to oppose a force of whose strength he was unsure. Although this just emphasises his failure to use the morning and his light cavalry to best effect, it is also true that the rolling ground, the high crops and the Bossu wood made identifying the exact strength of his opponents difficult. Given his experiences of fighting the British in Spain, it is unsurprising if he was somewhat cautious, but this situation was one of his own making, and if he had only done what common military practice demanded of him he must have been better placed to carry out his orders promptly and successfully.

Chapter 8

The Initial French Attack

The battle opened at close to 2pm, marked by a heavy artillery barrage and the advance along the whole front of a thick line of skirmishers. Writing in the third person, General Reille later wrote:

> Only the 5th and 9th Infantry Divisions of the 2nd Corps, led by General Reille, started their attack over difficult ground. A brigade of the 9th Division [Foy] occupied the Gémioncourt farm, whilst the 5th Division [Bachelu] crossed the two shallow valleys under the protection of the artillery ...[1]

In the light of the relatively few allied troops that could be seen on the edges of the woods, the sunken tracks, high crops and in the folds of the ground, the French artillery fire seems to have been concentrated against the line of Dutch guns on the heights of Gémioncourt. The experienced French artillerymen soon found their range and the Dutch battery started to take casualties in both manpower and horses. Such was the effectiveness of the French fire that both Dutch batteries were ordered to retire to the shallow ridgeline closer to Quatre Bras marked by the Bati-Saint-Bernard track. Two guns required immediate repair.

Freed from the threat of enemy artillery fire, the whole French front line began their advance. General Foy described the initial move.

> Bachelu marched in the direction of a small lake [the Étang Materne] that was near Gémioncourt; I followed him supporting his left with my first brigade, and whilst my second finished forming up, my last regiment waited at the farm in front of Frasnes until it had been relieved by the troops of the following division.
>
> Having received the order, Bachelu and I, being the head of the column to the left, took the direction towards the northern point of the Bossu wood. The enemy showed many men outside the wood, around the houses of Quatre Bras and on the Namur road. Four guns fired on us; our numerous horse artillery returned fire.[2]

On the right flank, the 2nd *légère* advanced on Lairalle, the tentative move of their skirmishers suggesting that they expected to have to fight for the farm. However, finding that they did not come under fire, the tirailleurs rushed forward and after a quick search found it was deserted.

In the centre, the French skirmishers made rapid progress against their equivalents of the 27th Jägers. The latter were quickly pushed back across the Pré des Queues stream towards their supports by the veteran French tirailleurs, who appeared particularly adept at picking off officers and NCOs. The infantry columns, which had initially skirted around the edge of the Delhutte wood, now wheeled to their left so that they formed a long line from the Étang Materne to the main road, with other columns following them up in reserve. Although the Dutch skirmishers had been ordered to concentrate their fire on the more vulnerable columns, this was almost impossible due to the need to protect themselves from the pressing French tirailleurs. It quickly became apparent that their fire did little to deter the French advance.

However, whilst the skirmishers were able to choose their routes and use available cover to the best advantage, this was not true of the columns. As the skirmish line crept forward towards the low ridge of the Gémioncourt heights in pursuit of the withdrawing jägers, the following columns were not able to maintain the pace of their advance. As they met the line of the Pré des Queues stream, the boggy ground, hedges and undergrowth forced them to slow down and they had to take a far more structured and controlled approach to their movement. This was complicated by the inconsistent difficulty of the obstacles and some battalions were able to negotiate them more easily than others. Those units that had moved through relatively unhindered were then forced to hold and wait for the other battalions to catch up to avoid losing the order and integrity of the advance. Although the opposition was relatively weak, the bulk and lack of manoeuvrability of the columns across difficult ground made their advance painfully slow.

The slow French advance gave the Prince of Orange the time to take action to meet the developing attack: the Dutch 5th National Militia and Belgian 7th Line Battalion were moved forward to support the front line. Their advance to a position about 450 metres behind the Gémioncourt farm was made under artillery fire that caused their first casualties. The 5th Militia advanced astride the main road, heading for Gémioncourt, with the 7th Line moving through the Bossu wood and then taking position parallel to their right. Meanwhile, the 27th Jägers were in danger of being overwhelmed by the mass of advancing French skirmishers and at about 2.30pm they rallied and started their withdrawal in column back towards Gémioncourt. As they approached this farm, two companies were sent forward to occupy the buildings.

The French continued their advance towards the farm. The heat of the day was already beginning to be felt; an officer in Bachelu's division wrote, 'We continued our march in the direction of Gémioncourt. The rapidity of our movement, along with the extreme heat, made this advance very tiresome.'[3]

As the advance of the French infantry columns freed up space on the Balcan heights, so more French artillery was able to deploy. These guns quickly came into action and once again, with a paucity of infantry targets, the Dutch artillery became the focus of attention. With the Dutch guns concentrating their fire on the vulnerable French infantry columns, the French artillery returned their fire free from harassment. Very soon Bijleveld's troop was being pounded by the French guns at a range of just 600 metres. The limbers and caissons, with their large teams of horses, made relatively easy targets and soon so many horses were falling that the point was approaching when the guns would be stranded. If this were to happen, the battery would surely be destroyed and so it was ordered to fall back towards the crossroads. Once again, just as the pressure was mounting on the forward infantry, they were losing their precious artillery support.

With the withdrawal of Bijleveld's troop, the French artillery turned all its attention to the guns of Stevenaar. Within only a short time, crews, horses and equipment were all suffering from the heavy fire. Two guns were damaged and had to be withdrawn for repair. To stay was to invite annihilation and the Prince of Orange ordered that this battery too was to withdraw. The French artillery was having a devastating effect. Both batteries made their way back and re-established a line along the heights along which ran the *chemin de* Bati-Saint-Bernard. Stevenaar's howitzer became separated on this latest move and, now reduced to a total of just six guns and one howitzer, the two batteries were courageously trying to support their hard-pressed infantry, but were being over-whelmed by the power and accuracy of their opponents.

On the right of the French advance, Colonel Maigrot's 2nd *légère* now continued their advance towards the farm and hamlet of Piraumont, a far more daunting-looking position than Lairalle. However, once again this farm and cluster of buildings was found to be undefended and they consolidated their gains. A strong skirmish line was pushed forward towards the Namur road and the following columns drew up waiting for the next move. It appears that it was at this point that the 2nd *légère* was split; it was well suited to a flank protection task, but its specialist skirmishing role also required it to support the main advance. It seems that two battalions were designated to the extreme right flank around Piraumont and towards Thyle, whilst the other two battalions provided some of the thick skirmisher screen ahead of the rest of the division's advance that was to cause the allies such trouble throughout the rest of the day.

On the French left there had been little activity, although a number of allied sources describe a charge by the Red Lancers of the Guard. However, given Napoleon's strict instructions that Ney was not to use them, it seems inconceivable that he would have engaged them so early in the battle: no French sources mention their use. However, some French artillery was active on this flank and caused casualties to members of the 2nd Nassau-Usingen Regiment who, unable to retaliate, were pulled back into the cover of the trees.

Most of the significant action was therefore now taking place in the centre, where the bulk of the French infantry, cavalry and artillery were deployed. The suffering Dutch artillery were given no respite by their opposite numbers and no sooner had they come into action in their new position than they began taking another hammering. So many of the Dutch and Nassau troops were either in the cover of the woods or fighting in open order that it seems there were few other worthwhile targets. Crewmen and horses were again beginning to fall, a limber was destroyed and Stevenaar himself was struck down and killed. Having occupied the buildings of Gémioncourt, the rest of the 27th Jäger formed a skirmish line in the hedges and bushes that lined the stream as it ran down towards the Étang Materne. However, this had to be done under fire as the French skirmishers followed up the retreating Dutchmen closely and maintained the pressure on them. Significantly, a continuing number of Dutch officers were falling and control of the battalion, spread as it was in skirmish order, was beginning to suffer. Hiding in the crops on the heights of Gémioncourt, the tirailleurs shot down on to the sweating, green-clad troops. However, they were soon to get some support; the 5th Militia were ordered to move forward down the main road to link up with this battalion and continue its line to the west. Its two élite companies occupied the orchard and gardens forward of the farm and the centre companies straddled the road. However, they soon came under increasingly accurate and annoying fire from the ubiquitous French skirmishers. In an effort to push these back, a company was sent forward in open order, but they were soon overwhelmed by fire and, with the French manoeuvring to cut them off, they lost all cohesion and rushed back to the main body of the battalion having suffered heavy casualties.

Up to this point the clouds of French skirmishers had proved particularly effective and had generated a slow but inexorable forward momentum. No need had yet been identified for the long line of battalion columns following them up. They had been left free to tackle the difficulty of negotiating the Pré des Queues stream and the hedges lining it, and as long as the skirmish line was not being held up by a well-formed and effective defence line, the French infantry commanders were clearly content to let them have their head. The heat was intense.

The 27th Jägers and 5th Militia were in great danger of being overwhelmed. Although still only engaged by skirmishers, the French fire had proved to be particularly effective and the Dutch troops had struggled to contain the open order infantry hidden amongst the high crops who were expertly picking off the officers that were trying to organise and galvanise the defence. However, as things began to look precarious, the 7th Line Battalion emerged from the Bossu wood and formed in line between the wood and the road.

The Dutch and Belgian troops had now established a defence line anchored on Gémioncourt and, although it was somewhat brittle, they appeared determined to hold and the French skirmishers did not have the power to break it alone. However, it was not the line of infantry columns that moved forward to test the strength of this line, but Piré's cavalry. Advancing north along the western side of the main road, one of his regiments, no doubt believing that the Dutch line was close to breaking, fell on the 5th Militia. The militia, however, had sufficient time to form square, and displaying an admirable steadiness, awaited the French attack. The battalion broke the cohesion of the first squadron with their fire. The succeeding squadrons, despite the urging of their riders, were unable to goad their horses into the hedge of bayonets and none of the following squadrons were able to threaten the steadiness of the square. Trying to re-establish order after their failed charge, and now taking casualties from both the square and the Dutch guns to the north, the cavalry broke off the attack and returned to their own lines to rally. The Belgian 7th Line chose not to form square but retired to the safety of the woods before any cavalry gave chase. Once the cavalry had withdrawn, the 5th Militia and 7th Line retook their original positions in line with Gémioncourt.

On the French left, the situation remained relatively quiet: an artillery battery was bombarding the allied troops who were deployed just forward of the Bossu wood and the entrances to it. Still lacking the men to do any more, Ney was content to keep any ambition the allied troops here might have had in check with this artillery fire. Little did he know, however, that the effect of this fire, the inexperience of the units placed there and the unsettling effect of hearing the fighting taking place in the centre, but being unable to see what was happening, was having an adverse effect on their morale. So jumpy were the battalion of Orange-Nassau that they were panicked by the appearance of a small group of horsemen and began a disordered withdrawal back towards the imagined security of the wood. The horsemen turned out to be none other than the Prince of Orange and his staff and the battalion was halted and brought back under the control of its officers. However, as a precaution, both this battalion and the 8th National Militia were pulled back into the Pierrepont wood to give them some shelter from the French artillery fire. Shortly afterwards these two battalions were ordered to withdraw north and take a new position in the Bossu wood. This would bring them more into line with the battalions defending the position around Gemioncourt. Exposed once more to the French artillery, they again took casualties which caused some confusion in the ranks. The allied troops on this flank were showing poor morale even before they had been seriously engaged; if Ney had only had the whole of Reille's corps available, a determined attack on this flank might well have succeeded.

Indeed, the whole allied line appeared close to breaking point and it seemed that all that was required was a determined advance by the infantry columns straight towards Quatre Bras itself. Although until Prince Jérôme's division came up Ney did not enjoy an overwhelming superiority of numbers, his troops were well concentrated and in hand; in contrast, the Prince of Orange's men were spread in a long, thin arc trying to defend all points of an extended front. Consequently, he now made an effort to strengthen and consolidate his line with the troops he had available and pulled back his southernmost battalions to reduce his front. If Ney could quickly shake himself out of his apparent lethargy and caution, victory was beckoning; his battering ram was aimed at the very centre of a crumbling allied line. It was 3 o'clock.

Chapter 9

The Allied Crisis

During most of the journey back from Ligny, Wellington had become more and more concerned as the sounds of firing from the direction of Quatre Bras had increased in intensity. With a small cavalry escort, he travelled along the Namur road and must have been spotted by some of the 2nd *légère* in the area of Piraumont. Having secured this hamlet some time before, a little more adventure shown by the commander here could well have made Wellington's return to the crossroads rather more problematic; however, whoever it was, he had been content with consolidating his position there and made no effort to control access along the main road, and it was only after the passage of Wellington and his staff that the French skirmish line advanced and appeared to want to occupy the wood (Bois des Censes) which was to the north of the main road.

Wellington approached Quatre Bras at about three o'clock. A quick examination of the battlefield was sufficient for him to judge that the situation was close to desperate. He later said:

> By God if I had come up five minutes later the battle was lost; I found the Prince of Orange just after twenty French had made a spirt [sic] at two of our guns and he said, 'it is all over, they are driven back.' 'Over! But what are those in that wood?' 'They are Belgians.' 'No by God, but they are French – and the wood is full of them and they will be on you directly – aye, and the emperor is there too', for I heard them just then shout, '*Vive l'empereur*!' – but I was wrong, he was not there. But I just had time to save it ...[1]

Things were about to get worse before they got better. There were virtually no fresh troops in reserve at Quatre Bras, but Wellington was well aware that the first British units were marching south from Genappe as he had passed them earlier in the morning. He clearly felt that his only chance of salvation was the arrival of these fresh troops, so despite the desperate situation he personally set off up the road to hasten their arrival.

It was at about this time that heavy gunfire was heard from the direction of Sombreffe. Napoleon had finally concentrated the right wing and had begun his attack on the Prussians. The heavy and constant cannonade from the east should have served to remind both the commanders at Quatre Bras that their action was only a sideshow to the main event that was being fought elsewhere, and that they both had a potentially vital part to play in the outcome of the day.

Wellington was not the only commander waiting for reinforcements. Ney too was anxiously awaiting Prince Jérôme's infantry division; at over 7,000 men it was the strongest in the *Armée du Nord*. Jérôme had a mixed career as a formation commander, and was not highly regarded by his fellow generals. No doubt aware of this, Napoleon allocated General Guilleminot to the division to second his brother. To many senior officers, Guilleminot was the real commander. It was at about 3pm that this division approached the battlefield. Ney immediately ordered the emperor's brother to advance on the left flank towards the Bossu wood. Jérôme sent Soye's brigade (1st and 2nd Line) forward, leaving Bauduin's (1st *légère* and 3rd Line) back in reserve. This seems a strange choice, as Bauduin's brigade contained the divisional light infantry regiment, which was perfectly suited to the type of fighting inevitable in such close country; small groups of determined men fighting in close contact with the enemy under loose control and having to use their own initiative.

The deployment of Jérôme's division freed up Gauthier's brigade of Foy's division, who had been covering this flank as the reserve, and they were able to march forward and join the rest of their division, extending the French line to the west of the main road. Lieutenant Puvis of the 93rd Line wrote:

> At 3 o'clock we deployed our masses and our whole line moved off, covered by our skirmishers. We marched thus into the middle of some rye which, because of its height, hid us from the enemy that was in front of us, but whose balls did not slacken, just as ours did not let up firing back.[2]

Ney now had almost 20,000 infantry, over 2,500 cavalry (4,500 including the guard) and fifty pieces of artillery (including the guard's) available; with this latest reinforcement surely nothing could stop him securing the vital crossroads. Until reinforcements arrived, Wellington had no cavalry at all and only the exhausted remains of Perponcher's 8,000 or so infantrymen and sixteen guns (of which only eleven were still in action) to oppose them.

It was only with Jérôme's arrival, and coincidentally in Wellington's temporary absence, that Ney felt strong enough to mount an attack in earnest. He decided to push his columns forward across the Gémioncourt stream and break through the thin and crumbling allied line. On the left, Jérôme's division would clear the Bossu wood, and on the right, the 2nd *légère* would advance and cross the main road, finally cutting communications between the two allied armies. Once again the columns started their advance with the usual cloud of tirailleurs preceding them, and with Piré's cavalry following up, poised and waiting for an opportunity to charge. This was a well co-ordinated attack of all arms. The shaken allied battalions had no chance of stopping the French juggernaut and immediately began their withdrawal covered by the guns on the heights above and behind them, pressed by the French skirmishers. The farm of Gémioncourt, although very strong, had not been prepared for defence and thus, although it was difficult to get into, there were very few positions inside to fire from and thus beat back an assault. As the French skirmishers pushed their opposite numbers back, Jamin's brigade of Foy's division advanced against the farm. There appears to have been little resistance; the companies of the 5th Militia and 27th Jägers that were defending it quickly retired to join the main bodies of their units.

Once this retirement had begun and the heights just to the south of Gémioncourt were secure, the French artillery was brought forward to this new position from which they could reach further towards the crossroads. Coming quickly into action they began to bring the retreating allied troops under increasingly accurate fire.

Once again the Dutch artillery began to feel the power of their rivals and as their own infantry withdrew towards them another limber was destroyed. It was soon time for them to hook up their own guns and once more fall back to another position in depth. However, with its limber destroyed, one of the remaining two howitzers had to be abandoned to the French as there was no means of moving it. The hard-pressed batteries withdrew with difficulty and took up a new position just 200 metres south of the crossroads; another retro-grade move and the position of Quatre Bras would be lost.

On the French left, Prince Jérôme advanced Soye's brigade against the Bossu wood. It quickly became evident that the Nassau troops which occupied this flank were not going dispute the ownership of the twin farms of Petit and Grand Pierrepont. Covered by a strong force of skirmishers and with supporting fire from the divisional artillery battery, the battalion columns approached the wood itself to loud cries of '*Vive l'empereur!*' The allied skirmishers fell back offering little opposition, but as the French skirmishers entered the wood they were met by several well coordinated and disciplined volleys from the two Nassau-Usingen battalions deployed amongst the trees.

However, the fire was insufficient to stop the momentum of the French columns, which now burst into the wood and began to push the Nassauers back. But the thick undergrowth did not allow movement in closely packed columns, and the fight was continued between two strong forces of skir-mishers fed from the main battalion bodies held further back on the edge of the woods. This was a fight almost impossible to coordinate, follow or control and officers relied on the individual initiative and experience of their NCOs and troops to maintain pressure on the enemy.

With the situation in the Bossu wood hidden by the trees, the Prince of Orange was more concerned by the situation in the centre. He could not afford for the French to reach the crossroads and it was evident that if the withdrawal of his infantry continued there would be insufficient time to establish a viable line of defence before the French were on them. He therefore took the courageous decision to call on the battered troops of the 5th Militia and three companies of the 27th Jägers, and to lead them in a desperate counter-attack against Gémioncourt.

By the time he had organised the attack, the French skirmishers were well established in the orchards and gardens and behind the hedges that surrounded them. With the buildings also occupied by French troops it would prove a formidable objective for the already exhausted and weakened Dutch troops. Advancing with apparent enthusiasm, they were met by a withering fire and quickly brought to a standstill. Although some of the more determined troops reached the hedges held by the French, they could get no further. It had been a brave but futile attempt, although it had bought a little more time for allied reinforcements to arrive. Suffering a constant trickle of casualties and with one eye on the columns of infantry and cavalry formed up beyond the farm, they hesitated and then started to fall back in some confusion. This was the opportunity Piré had been waiting for; two weak battalions falling back in disorder across open ground.

The Prince of Orange, however, had also realised how vulnerable the retiring infantry were and at last some vital reinforcements had arrived; the Dutch cavalry brigade of General van Merlen, a very experienced ex-officer of the French imperial guard. Although they had not had time to prepare for battle, the Prince ordered the 6th (North Netherlands) Hussars to charge the threatening French cavalry that were forming up astride the main road. Despite not being fully deployed, the hussars charged forward. The charge was spirited but, having insufficient time to get properly organised, it lacked the cohesion and order that might have brought success. The French counter-charge broke up the already splintered Dutch formation and in a short time the hussars were fighting for their lives against better-organised and more disciplined troops. The combat was short lived; the Dutch hussars were broken and turned to flee.

It appears that it was Hubert's chasseur brigade (the 1st and 6th Regiments) that met and broke the charge of the hussars forward of Gémioncourt and just to the west of the *chaussée*; Wathier's lancers had initially been held back in reserve. Seeing the Dutch cavalry in disordered flight, they now launched their own charge against the fleeing Dutch infantry. These troops had no chance; lacking the cohesion to be able to form square and individually focussed on saving themselves, they were easy prey to the French lancers who were ideally armed for such a fight. Smashing into the running men, many were struck down, incapable of putting up any resistance. Others were rounded up and sent to the rear as prisoners. The 5th Militia and 27th Jägers had effectively been destroyed as a fighting force and were to take no further part in the fighting. Two companies of the 8th Militia also dispersed into the woods.

The disaster was not yet complete: beyond the scattered battalions, Stevenaart's artillery had advanced to support the Dutch hussars and been left exposed. Seeing the vulnerable guns, Wathier's lancers charged forward and attacked the crews that tried desperately to protect them. Beyond the guns was the 7th Belgian Line, who hurriedly tried to form square. The gunners were overwhelmed, and those that did not escape were cut down or captured; the four guns were left in the possession of the victorious lancers. The following lancer squadrons continued the charge against the Belgian infantry who, having witnessed the merciless and ruthlessly efficient destruction of the forward battalions, and faced now by the terrifying sight of charging lancers, spontaneously disintegrated and ran. Some formed a rallying square, a small cluster of determined men who stood back to back with their bayonets presented to the victorious cavalry, but the lancers were not interested in those who wanted to resist; they concentrated their efforts against the defenceless men who had discarded their muskets in order to reach the safety of the Bossu wood unhindered. The battalion was scattered and crippled; it would take the rest of the day to rally the survivors and get them back into some sort of order.

The Prince of Orange, who had moved forward to organise and motivate the original counter-attack, now found himself isolated in the middle of the disorder. Lieutenant Henckens takes up the story:

> Piré's division, with the 6th Chasseurs at its head, threw itself on the enemy cavalry which was broken and put to rout, whilst the gunners of the cannon that had been deployed were largely killed and the caissons and the horse attendants followed the cavalry in rout; the guns remained in place and were not secured, probably because the means were lacking. It was at the end of this attack that Captain Estève and I saw on a height an isolated group of officers that our instinct told us was the enemy's commanders which rushed off at great speed, leaving us with an officer's horse which we took with us. At that moment, being exposed to musket fire from a square that was in position behind a hedge, the division was called to rally.[3]

The captured horse belonged to Major Count Van Limburg Stirum, ADC to the Prince of Orange. In the confusion he had been obliged to abandon his wounded horse and found himself surrounded by a group of French horsemen who mercilessly cut him down as one of them shouted: 'Kill him, it's the Prince!' Van Limburg Stirum suffered serious wounds and remained on the battlefield until he was found in the evening.[4]

Piré's troopers found one last target. A half battery of Dutch artillery had arrived on the battlefield with van Merlen's cavalry and this now also found itself vulnerable to the victorious French cavalry. Although their momentum had been lost, some individuals attacked the guns and caused some disorder and casualties before turning bridle and rallying with their units. Piré's cavalry had scored a notable success; the 6th Hussars, Stevenaart's battery and three Dutch-Belgian battalions had been put *hors de combat*.

Some French infantry from Campi's brigade of Bachelu's division followed up the cavalry and, seeing the abandoned Dutch guns, ran forward to secure them. The citation for *Sous-lieutenant* Chapuzot of the 72nd Line relates:

> *Sous-lieutenant* Chapuzot, with three soldiers of his regiment, under fire from two enemy battalions, captured an ammunition caisson, harnessed with two horses and took it back to the divisional artillery park. This action, in which this intrepid officer received two wounds, was close to the farm of Quatre Bras, and has remained without reward.[5]

Up to four guns were also captured – the number varies with different sources – but it appears that at least two were brought back to the French lines, whilst others were taken but then recaptured by a rush forward by the Dutch gunners. This small counter-attack also retrieved other guns that had been abandoned during the cavalry combat.

Much of the French cavalry were now over-extended and their horses were tired; they too were vulnerable to a well-timed counter-attack and could not maintain themselves so far forward. The Prince of Orange had one uncommitted cavalry regiment available: the Belgian 5th Light Dragoons. This regiment had a number of very experienced officers who had fought in the French army, including two who had served in the imperial guard. Nearly a quarter of the men had also served with the French army. Although tired from their march they were no doubt keen to avenge the humiliation of the 6th Hussars. Having had time to properly organise themselves they were better placed to deliver a well-formed and controlled charge.

The two chasseur regiments of Hubert's brigade were quickly rallying when the 5th Light Dragoons bore down on them. Despite the tiredness of their horses, the chasseurs met the charge, which quickly deteriorated into a mass of individual combats. The Belgians held their own for a considerable time and it appears there were a number of charges and counter-charges. The fight was marked by the number of combatants from each side that personally knew the men they were fighting against, since a number of the Belgian dragoons had served in the 6th *Chasseurs-à-Cheval* in the previous years and they had again met each other several times during picket duty at the border in the previous months. The uniforms were not that different either, both being green with yellow facings. Old comrades in arms recognised each other and the French appealed to the Belgians to join them once more, while they lowered their sabres to indicate that they weren't enemies, crying out, '*À nous,*

Belges, à nous' ['To us, Belgians, to us!']. It appears that no one accepted the invitation and old friends exchanged blows.[6]

> Captain Delienne found himself face to face with Devielle, his old brother-in-arms in France, Captain Van Remoortere* received a sabre blow to the stomach from one of his old NCOs and Senior Sergeant Beauce fought with one of the senior sergeants of his old squadron.[7]

The fighting was fierce and the advantage swung from one side to the other until the intervention of the 5th Lancers, which finally broke the Belgian resistance. Colonel de Mercx was seriously wounded and the light dragoons rushed towards the perceived safety of their own lines. Intoxicated by their success, the French chasseurs pursued their beaten opponents, but were stopped by a shattering volley from a Scottish regiment (the 92nd) deployed on the Namur road. This regiment had mistaken the fleeing Belgians for Frenchmen and, believing themselves threatened, had opened fire. The accuracy of their fire caused considerable casualties amongst their allies; the 5th Light Dragoons lost forty men to this single volley.

The 92nd had come up with General Picton's 5th British Division that had arrived under cover of the chaotic fighting that was taking place between Gémioncourt and Quatre Bras. There seems little doubt that without this timely reinforcement, Quatre Bras would have fallen to the French. Isolated, tired and facing steady infantry, the French cavalry turned bridle and moved back towards Gémioncourt to rally.

The effect of the French cavalry actions was not limited to those involved in the fighting; a senior British officer recorded:

> The French cavalry charged the Belgian Cavalry and dispersed them – they went to the rear. The carts, etc coming up along the highroad from Brussels took the alarm, turned round and went back with followers etc in the greatest confusion. Many of the Belgic cavalry went to Brussels and spread the alarm. The Duke and Lord Fitzroy Somerset were in front when the French cavalry charged the Belgic cavalry and with difficulty got back to the 92nd, posted at Quatre Bras. The Duke leaped a bank and ditch, and on a worse horse he might not have escaped.[8]

Piré's cavalry had effectively destroyed the Dutch-Belgian cavalry as a fighting force and come close to killing or capturing Wellington himself. As the French cavalry withdrew, the tirailleurs continued their own advance and continued the pressure on the very centre of the allied line.

In the Bossu wood, things had also been going well for the French. Although the advance was slow, the Nassau battalions seemed reluctant to

---

*Van Remoortere had joined the French chasseurs in 1805, had made eight campaigns from Austerlitz to that of 1814 and had twice been decorated with the *Legion d'Honneur*. He died in 1847 as a general.

come to close quarters. In a French infantry battalion, a company of about 100 men had only three officers; a ridiculously small number to exert any control over small groups of men who could see only a few metres to each side. It is impossible to follow what happened with any accuracy during this fighting, but slowly the overwhelming numbers of French infantry, more experienced and motivated than their opponents, gradually gained ground. In places the undergrowth was so dense that swords and bayonets had to be used to penetrate it. Small groups of men found themselves cut off and surrounded; no doubt individuals, separated from their friends, quietly made their way out of the wood and the fighting, whilst others, in small groups, fired at point-blank range at those hidden amongst the trees and fought hand-to-hand.

Combat at such short ranges almost always results in the most desperate fighting as the instinct for survival motivates each individual. Best use was inevitably made of the trees and bushes for cover and observation was no doubt further impaired by the thick smoke that built up below the roof of foliage. All control must have been lost and the best that could be hoped for was to maintain a thick line of skirmishers advancing almost like beaters on a game shoot. The battle here swung one way and then the next as one side and then the other committed fresh troops or was able to infiltrate behind their adversaries. Slowly, but surely, Jérôme's men pushed the allied troops back and the Nassauer battalions were finally forced out of the western edge of the wood onto the Champ du Sarti from where they began to fall back to the north.

Ney must have felt everything was going to plan. Up to this point, he had only engaged his skirmishers, artillery and cavalry; apart from Soye's brigade in the Bossu wood, the main body of his infantry had still not been committed and had suffered negligible casualties. Perponcher's division were taking a battering, the Dutch-Belgian cavalry had been crushed and a high proportion of the Dutch artillery had been destroyed or captured. The Namur road, along which he was to march to the emperor's support, was not secure, but this must be only a matter of time. All that was required was a resolute march on Quatre Bras itself and surely victory would be his. Little did the marshal know was that things were about to take a dramatic turn for the worse.

Chapter 10

The First Allied
Reinforcements Arrive

The sacrifice of Perponcher's division and van Merlen's cavalry had not been entirely in vain; they had held up the French sufficiently for desperately needed reinforcements to arrive and save the day for Wellington. These reinforcements were to counter the numerical superiority that Ney had enjoyed until this point and the advantage was about to swing in favour of the allies.

The first to arrive after van Merlen's cavalry had been two brigades of Picton's 5th British Division; over 3,500 excellent British infantry and two batteries of guns, led by a battalion of the famous 95th Rifles. Wellington had met the commanding officer on the Brussels road and personally briefed him on his mission to keep open the Namur road to leave the British commander the option of sending troops to support Blücher. The 95th set off at their quick march round the crossroads towards the allied left flank. The remainder of the division were sent directly down the Brussels road to Quatre Bras, turning left to line the Namur road, linking the Rifles to the centre of the position and leaving Perponcher's remaining brigade to contest the Bossu wood. Their deployment had been courageously covered by the sacrifice of van Merlen's cavalry.

With the deployment of Picton's men complete, it is now worth reviewing the situation facing Marshal Ney at about 3.30pm. On the left flank, Jérôme's division had cleared the southern half of the Bossu wood and were now trying to clear north against determined opposition, fighting in very close and difficult terrain. The fighting was fierce, fought at point-blank range, often hand-to-hand and lacking tight control; the pace of the advance was slow and dearly bought.

In the centre, Foy's and Bachelu's divisions had established a long line of infantry columns, so far virtually untouched by the fighting, that stretched along the line of the Gémioncourt stream, from the Étang Materne, to the Gémioncourt farm, across the *chaussée*, and almost to the Bossu wood. The strong skirmisher screen, which had done the majority of the fighting so far, had occupied a line on La Bergerie, and ran down parallel to the Namur road along which the allied reinforcements were deploying. From here they were able to engage the main allied line, albeit at long range, and in places obscured by the very tall crops that covered this part of the battlefield. They were being particularly troublesome to the crews of the remaining Dutch artillery who continued to take casualties.

On the right, troops of the 2nd *légère* had firm control of the farm and hamlet of Piraumont and its skirmisher screen was advancing to try to cut communications between the allied armies by occupying the Bois des Censes to the north of the Namur road.

Ney was no doubt aware of the arrival of British reinforcements, placed as he always was well to the front, but he had made sufficient progress to be content with the situation and was well balanced to make a strong and well-coordinated attack on Quatre Bras. Whilst he no doubt understood that his numerical superiority was being chipped away, he was expecting that d'Erlon's entire corps, some 20,000 men of all arms, would soon come up, and with this reinforcement he was confident that he could secure a victory.

*   *   *

Whilst the battle had raged in the centre, the 2nd *légère* had had a quiet time watching the right flank. Their skirmish line overlooked the Namur road and after Wellington had been left free to travel back along it, it was ordered forward so it would be able to fire on anyone else who attempted to pass. As they waited, the artillery behind them opened fire on a line of green-clad riflemen who were advancing towards the Bois des Censes. As the riflemen approached the road the *tirailleurs* also opened fire and a lively skirmish started up. The allied line extended to the east as more men arrived and the hamlet of Thyle was occupied. Any attempt by the French skirmishers to advance was quickly held up by accurate rifle fire. The French right had the support of a battery of guns which engaged the fresh allied troops that were arriving on this flank. Soon after a British battery (Roger's) moved down the Namur road and opened fire on the 2nd *légère*. This battery was also engaged by French artillery and the light infantry unit sent some skirmishers to engage the crews; these soon started to cause casualties among the sweating gunners and were unopposed for the time being.

On the left flank, the fighting in the Bossu wood was inevitably going slowly, but because of his numerical superiority, Jérôme's lead brigade had been making progress. The southern half of the wood was now in his possession and his troops were working their way north through the trees, engaging the allied troops that opposed them and that lined the eastern edges, slowly pushing them back towards Quatre Bras. Eventually, the first French skirmishers reached the Nivelles road just a short distance from the crossroads.

Near Quatre Bras, Wellington was in discussion with the Prince of Orange. Having just been informed that the Bossu wood was held by Nassau troops, a force of French skirmishers spilled out onto the road. The Prince was forced to deploy the last two unused battalions of Perponcher's division to push the French back into the wood. The situation was saved by the arrival of more reinforcements; part of the Brunswick corps had followed Picton's division, bringing another 4,500 infantry and 900 cavalry to Wellington's support. They were tired from their long march, but fresh to the fight. The Brunswick specialist light troops, the Gelernte-Jäger companies, were immediately thrown into the Bossu wood. Once again, the timely arrival of reinforcements had frustrated Ney and started to tip the balance of numbers in Wellington's favour.

A battalion of Brunswick light troops (the 2nd Light Battalion) were sent to reinforce the extreme allied left flank. The 1st Line and Leib battalions moved through Quatre Bras and filled the void between the Bossu wood and the Brussels road, whilst the rest provided a reserve. Foy's division, which occupied Gémioncourt and extended beyond the Brussels road towards the Bossu wood, watched the two black-uniformed battalions take position in front of them. The French *tirailleurs* moved forward to engage them and were soon causing casualties. What was not apparent to the French was that the inexperienced and poorly-trained Brunswick conscripts lacked the cohesion and morale to deploy into line, and their Duke felt he had no option but to leave them in column, which gave them a greater feeling of security despite the casualties they were suffering. Such a choice target did not go unnoticed by the French artillery, which also began to make furrows through the densely-packed men. The Brunswickers' own artillery was still some way in the rear and unable to come to their support. With almost no defence against the galling fire that was directed against them, these battalions must have felt exposed and unsupported until the Brunswick Hussar Regiment formed up in their rear.

Still further reinforcements were arriving for Wellington. Picton's infantry brigades of Best and Halkett arrived and were moved to support the allied left flank. This gave him the opportunity to drive back the troublesome French skirmishers and establish some vital depth in his position. Content that his right flank had been stabilised, Wellington now turned his attention to the French skirmish line that was causing so much damage to his artillery. To the east of the Brussels road, the French *tirailleurs* saw a solid red wall of infantry (the 1st, 32nd and 79th Line) advancing towards them. To try to hold would have been suicidal, and so they began their withdrawal using fire and man-oeuvre to keep their assailants under fire, helped by the height and density of the crops. Eventually they found themselves back on the line of the Gémion-court stream. Taking advantage of the cover this afforded, and supported by the main line of infantry columns on the southern slopes of the Gémioncourt heights and the artillery above them, they held this line.

Where was d'Erlon?

Whilst the seemingly constant arrival of allied reinforcements threatened to wrest the initiative from Ney, Napoleon was about to force his hand.

Chapter 11

The Main French Attack

Napoleon's First Message

To his immense frustration, Napoleon was not able to open the battle of Ligny as early as he had hoped. Gérard's 4th Corps was slow in coming up and the emperor would not be able to start his attack until towards three o'clock. However, as he studied the developing Prussian deployment, he identified the fact that the Prussian right flank, although anchored on the villages of Saint-Amand and Bry, was still 'in the air'. He thus now further developed the idea he had had early in the morning of drawing some of Ney's troops, which he had already ordered to take position at Quatre Bras, down the Nivelles to Namur highway and straight on to the right rear of the Prussian army, enveloping its entire right wing. But it is important to understand that, at this moment, Napoleon was still not clear that he had virtually the whole of the Prussian army in front of him. Consequently, just as the battle at Quatre Bras was starting, Napoleon had Soult write to Ney:

> 'In front of Fleurus', 16 June, 2pm.
> Marshal! The emperor has directed me to inform you that the enemy has gathered a body ['*corps*'] of troops between Sombreffe and Bry, and that at two thirty Marshal Grouchy will attack it with the 3rd and 4th Corps. His Majesty's intent is that you should attack all that is in front of you, and that, after having vigorously pushed it back, you should advance towards us to assist in enveloping the force I have just mentioned. If this force has already been beaten, His Majesty will manoeuvre towards you to speed up your operation in turn. Immediately inform the emperor of your dispositions and what is happening to your front.
> *Major Général, Maréchal de l'empire, Duc de Dalmatie*[1]

This message should certainly have reached Ney by 3.30pm, just as he was about to launch his main attack. This was the first time that Ney was ordered to send a force towards the emperor; in the orders he had received in the morning he had been directed to place a division at Marbais (almost exactly halfway between Quatre Bras and Ligny) so they could be called on to support the emperor, but at that time Napoleon did not envisage fighting a major battle against the Prussians. Soult had also failed to make it clear that the Prussian force they faced was almost the entire Prussian army and had given this cooperation only secondary importance by placing it after the capture of Quatre Bras.

There is no record of Ney's reaction when he received this order, but it is not too hard to guess. He was no doubt frustrated by the time it had taken for him to get his initial attack underway; piqued also by the message the emperor had previously sent him censuring him for not having attacked earlier. The almost continuous stream of allied reinforcements arriving emphasised the cost of that failure. But also, he was ready to launch his attack; his troops had not yet suffered appreciable casualties and although perhaps slow, his advance had captured ground, scored some notable successes and Foy and Bachelu were poised to make the decisive assault. Although the allies were now much stronger, he too had considerable reinforcements (d'Erlon's 1st Corps) on the way. Soult had not suggested that the right wing were facing the whole of the Prussian army or that the situation was in any way serious. The chances are that Ney felt he was being ordered to do exactly what he was on the point of executing and, should Wellington prove too strong, Soult had declared that the emperor was planning to move to his support after destroying the Prussians in front of him. He was probably quite satisfied with the situation he found himself in, if a little annoyed at not having already seized Quatre Bras.

However, it is also worth noting that there is no record of Ney complying with the last line of the message; he did not inform Napoleon of his dispositions, plans or 'what was happening to his front' as he was ordered. Thus the emperor remained ignorant of the situation around Quatre Bras and was unable to make well-informed strategic decisions. Given the direction Ney had received, in light of the allied reinforcements and the fact that he was still some way short of capturing the vital crossroads, it was surely his duty to inform the emperor of this. If Napoleon had had a better strategic overview, it is possible that things might have turned out differently for the French.

The French infantry columns, largely spectators up to this point, were keen to advance and Wellington seemed to know what was coming next:

> At that moment loud cries of '*Vive l'empereur!*' were heard, taken up in succession by brigades, and a loud voice could be heard distinctly crying – '*L'empereur recompensera celui qui s'avancera!*' [The emperor will reward all those who advance.] 'That', observed the Duke, 'must be Ney going down the line. I know what that means; we shall be attacked in five minutes.'[2]

The whole of the French centre, composed of Foy's and Bachelu's infantry, started their advance to the north from the forward slopes of the Gémion-court heights. Whilst Foy found his advance relatively unobstructed, the same was not true for Bachelu's division. They soon had to cross the thick and tangled hedges that lined the course of the Gémioncourt stream, which, as we have already heard, formed a substantial obstacle to close order troops. Sergeant Mauduit described the advance of this division across the hedge line:

The 108th Line, commanded by Colonel Higonet, took a glorious part in this first attack ... This regiment, three battalions strong and of 1,340 bayonets, found itself deployed at the rear left of Bachelu's division. The enemy, after a lively and murderous fight, retired in the direction of Quatre Bras, crossing a shallow valley of meadows and took position on the higher ground in the fields of corn, having to its front a natural defence composed of a long hedge of sharp thorns.

The first three regiments of the division were able to cross this hedge, having found it cut down to two or three feet from the ground, although not without difficulty. However, the piece of hedge that covered the front of the 108th had not been cut down, forming an impenetrable barrier 1 metre thick and 2–3 metres high. Colonel Higonet, in the midst of enemy fire, ordered a large gap to be made by a platoon made up of his sappers and grenadiers, so that this obstacle could be crossed by his three battalions which formed a column 'at full distance' during this operation. When the opening was practicable, the first battalion passed through and formed in line in front to conform with the 72nd which was to its right. But before this manoeuvre could be executed, a volcano of fire erupted along the line from the very feet of our soldiers. This unexpected fire, from point blank range, came from several English regiments hidden in the high corn. The fire made cruel ravages in our ranks and caused a retrograde movement in the other three regiments, who, returning to the hedge, were unable to cross it without confusion. The English launched a charge to profit from this disorder. A witness of the confusion, from which the 108th suffered little, Colonel Higonet hastened to make an about turn with his first battalion so that it could re-cross the hedge and to mass it behind the other two that he formed at the same time by a turn to the right in line, commanded them to raise their muskets and give a defensive fire on his word of command. When the 72nd, energetically pursued by the English up to the bayonets of the 108th, having cleared its front, opened a terrible fire bringing death into the already confused ranks of the enemy. Colonel Higonet immediately charged them with the bayonet. The English who survived the musketry, wanting to re-cross the hedge, but closely pursued in their turn; the carnage was terrible. Captain Arnaud, son of a member of the Institute, whose sword was broken in the mêlée, seized a musket with a bayonet and put nine Englishmen *hors de combat*. At the view of the success of the 108th, the three other regiments of the division, which had rallied, retook the offensive and threw the enemy back to their first position. During this struggle, the 108th had 400 men [out of an initial strength of 1,340], including twenty one officers, *hors de combat*. But it must be said that there were many acts of courage and devotion on both sides.[3]

The devastating volleys that had struck Bachelu's division had come from the British 1st (the Royals), 32nd (the Cornwalls) and 79th (the Cameron Highlanders) Regiments that had been sent forward by Wellington to push back the French skirmishers and establish a forward line parallel with the Brunswickers to the west of the main road. As they advanced through the high corn on the heights of Bati-Saint-Bernard they had suddenly found themselves confronted by Bachelu's advance and been first to react. *Adjutant-Commandant* Trefcon, the chief-of-staff of Bachelu's division, also described the advance:

> As we moved across a shallow valley close to the Namur road, we were struck by an extremely violent fire. It came from the English who, hidden in the very tall corn, shot down on us.
>
> As we could not see where this fire was coming from at first, there was a slight hesitation in the column. The English took advantage of this by charging us vigorously. They fell on us with terrible cries and in a moment we were all stupefied.
>
> Before the suddenness and violence of this attack, we were forced to retire. We formed again in front of Piraumont. It was now our turn to open a violent fire, supported by that of our artillery which had remained in position at Piraumont ... it was the English in their turn who attempted to regain their positions. They executed this retrograde move in an order that filled us with admiration! It was a good struggle with honour to both sides.[4]

The attack by these three British battalions had thrown back almost the whole of Bachelu's division. However, the French artillery, and the battalions that rallied quickly, ensured that they did not have it all their own way. The 79th (the Cameron Highlanders), who were on the extreme left of the line, pursued the French through the hedge line and found themselves isolated:

> While the combat was going on at the hedge, the French seeing our regiment alone and at a considerable distance in front of our main body, advanced against us in great numbers, and made an attempt to surround us, to make us prisoners, shouting to us, 'Prisoners! Prisoners!' Our commanding officer, seeing this, called on us to, 'Run like devils – the French shall not make us prisoners.' ... The French directed their fire at us as we were crowding to get through the hedge and killed and wounded many of us in our retreat to our station in a field of rye.[5]

Astride the Brussels road, Foy's division did not have the same obstacle to cross and was not directly involved in the mishap met by Bachelu. Appearing to claim some of the credit for stopping the British attack, Foy wrote:

Having received the order, Bachelu and I, being the head of the column to the left, headed towards the northern point of the Bossu wood, around the houses of Quatre Bras and the Namur road. Four guns fired on us; our numerous horse artillery returned fire. Four English and Scots battalions formed in line by battalion mass, on the place where the plateau above Gémioncourt is crossed by the Namur road, fell on the 5th Division as it climbed this plateau. The 2nd *légère*, forming Bachelu's head of column, did not wait for the enemy and took flight; the rest of the division was put into disorder and, not content with abandoning its ground, did not even stop on the ridge behind Gémioncourt. I then crossed the stream close to this house with my first brigade; I ordered General Jamin, a brave and good officer, very devoted, to continue with the 4th *légère*; I brought back and formed up the 100th, a dependable regiment, onto the ridge behind Gémioncourt. The 100th held well; the enemy column which pursued the 5th Division was stopped by the firm countenance of our regiment and by the difficulty of the terrain. The rest of my division formed on the ridge ahead of the Lerat house [Lairalle]; the 5th Division rallied between Lerat and the village of Piermont [*sic*]. The first prisoners that we took announced that Lord Wellington was there, that eight English brigades were coming from Enghien and Brussels, that other troops, including artillery, were going to continue to arrive, that there was already a considerable body of Belgians, Dutch and Germans.[6]

The whole of Bachelu's division had been pushed back to its start line having suffered heavy casualties. Here they were able to rally as the British advance had brought them under short-range fire from the powerful French artillery and the 108th that quickly drove them back behind the ridge of Bati-Saint-Bernard after causing considerable casualties. Seeing the British battalions withdraw, the French skirmishers immediately pursued them; the effectiveness of their fire being remarked upon in all the allied eyewitness accounts of this battle. The *tirailleurs* were such a nuisance that several times the British line advanced to push them away; their own skirmish line apparently ineffective in achieving this alone.

Once again, the power of the French artillery is evident. Whilst the initial encounter was beyond the range of their batteries, the British advance brought them once more into the French sights and it was perhaps this, more than the reformed French infantry line, that forced the British infantry to once more drop back out of range, as General Reille inferred in his report:

> ... the 5th Division crossed the two shallow valleys under the protection of the artillery; but this protection was lacking for the high ground where Quatre Bras lay and it was unable to counter the charge of a line of English infantry that had the advantage of order over the troops who had

crossed two ravines. The English forced us to recross them, but were themselves obliged to return to their ridge to escape our fire.[7]

It had been a brief but savage encounter that had brought into close contact former adversaries from Spain and the south of France. Despite their ultimate repulse, the British units appear to have re-established their moral superiority over their opponents and the caution of the French columns thereafter suggests a reluctance to come to grips with British infantry against whom they never appeared as effective as they were against other troops. It seems this encounter also rekindled that mutual respect between the soldiers of these two nations. Mauduit again:

> Here is a story that does honour to the English. In the retrograde movement of the 1st Battalion of the 108th in the middle of the corn, the *fourrier* of the grenadiers had his leg broken by a ball and fell without anybody noticing. During the time that passed from then until when the regiment retook the offensive, this poor young man had been discovered by English soldiers who had bandaged him and laid him on a bed of the woollen tunics of their dead comrades and laid at his side a tin of grog, some biscuit and bacon. This act of humanity in such circumstances profoundly touched the whole regiment which, despite the sad losses that it had just suffered, treated all the English wounded or prisoners as good and brave comrades.[8]

The British, however, did not feel the French reciprocated; Private Vallence of the 79th complained:

> Our passion of rage and fury had risen to such a height that we were like madmen all the time we were engaged; yet we always kept our rage and fury within proper bounds; none of us were ever so base and cruel as to hurt or insult our fallen foes. The French, on the other hand, cruelly tortured and stabbed to death our wounded men whenever they found them.[9]

On the French left, the battle for the Bossu wood continued unabated; the advantage swinging to one side and then the other, the forward line invisible amongst the trees and thick undergrowth. Foy's chief-of-staff commented, 'The Bossu wood was taken and retaken three times with enormous loss . . .'[10] Prince Jérôme set an example to his troops during this intense, close-range fighting; his ADC, Captain Bourdon de Vatry, wrote:

> Prince Jérôme was struck by a ball on the hip. Happily for him, the projectile first struck the heavy gold hilt of his sword, could not penetrate it, and caused only a large bruise which made him pale. Overcoming his pain, the prince remained on horseback at the head of his division, giving

everyone an example of courage and self-sacrifice. His *sang-froid* produced the best effect.[11]

On the right flank the French were also able to make some headway. Even though the Rifles had been reinforced by a Brunswick battalion (the 2nd Light), the latter appeared reluctant to commit themselves to the fighting and the French skirmishers, supported once more by accurate artillery fire, were able to push forward. The veteran British and French skirmishers knew instinctively how to make best use of cover and fire and manoeuvre, whilst the younger recruits, inexperienced in such tactics, inevitably seemed to be the first to fall. For a time the Rifles were forced to withdraw towards the Bois des Censes, leaving the French in possession of the hamlet of Thyle and in control of the vital Namur road. The British established a new line in the rear of the wood, at right angles to the main road; the Rifles and Brunswick light battalion were now *en potence* to the main allied line. There was a real danger that if a significant French force exploited this gain, they could advance up the road and roll up Wellington's flank.

However, this part of the battlefield was somewhat isolated from the main French forces by the Étang Materne, and given the forces allocated to him, the local French commander had probably been ordered just to observe and contain this flank. Lacking the forces to make a breakthrough and apparently cut off from the main action in the centre, the opportunity was missed. Either way, the commanding officer of the Rifles, understanding the importance of holding the flank and keeping communications open with the Prussians, launched a counter-attack, pushing the French back across the main road but unable to progress any further. The French right flank had settled down into a stalemate.

Back in the centre, Foy's 1st Brigade, Gauthier's, facing the Brunswickers to the west of the road, had been unaffected by the combat forward of Gémioncourt. The skirmishers of this brigade were giving the Germans a fairly torrid time, whilst most of their own skirmishers were deployed inside the Bossu wood or continuing the line from the wood to the two stationary columns. French artillery, deployed just to the west of Gémioncourt on the low but dominating height, was also causing increasing casualties to which they could not reply. It was evident that these troops, despite the example set by their Duke who sat coolly on his horse in front them, were suffering severe casualties and beginning to look unsteady and vulnerable. Gauthier's brigade moved forward supported by Piré's troopers, who had now recovered from their earlier charges.

Advancing with loud cries of '*Vive l'empereur!*', the French troops were no doubt encouraged by the Brunswick Hussars moving away from them to the east of the main road. In the gap between the Leib and 1st Line battalions and the Bossu wood, the two light infantry companies of the Avantegarde

Battalion fell back through the ranks of the uhlan squadron behind them. In order to relieve the pressure on his infantry this single squadron was ordered to charge the French infantry. With plenty of warning of the charge, the French infantry coolly formed square and met the charge with its fire. Disordered by the fire and their charge, the uhlans were now vulnerable to a counter-attack and the French chasseurs moved forward.

Seeing what was coming, the uhlans started their withdrawal in as much order as they could manage while the two infantry battalions behind them formed square. Hubert's chasseurs charged after the uhlans, but were met by a ragged fire from the two infantry squares. Insufficient to drive off the chasseurs, the French cavalry bypassed the Brunswick infantry and charged on after the fleeing Brunswick cavalry. The chasseurs reached as far as the cross-roads, and forced Wellington to rush to the protection of the 92nd (the Gordon Highlanders) to avoid being captured or killed. Indeed, one account[12] claims an officer of the chasseurs actually attacked the Duke, who was only saved by the fire of some soldiers who just turned round in time. At Quatre Bras the tired French cavalry came under an intense fire from the Brunswick reserve and British battalions that had been held back to protect the crossroads. Without infantry support the chasseurs were forced to make a hasty retreat. Lieutenant Henckens described this action:

> Towards 4.30, our infantry, that we had followed after rallying and who had much difficulty in approaching Quatre Bras, was stopped by an attack of [Brunswick] uhlans; our divisional commander, seeing that this attack was serious and that it was necessary to disengage the infantry, we were not content to break the enemy cavalry, but reached Quatre Bras itself, where we endeavoured to maintain ourselves. But our infantry advanced only slowly, whilst we observed the continuous arrival of enemy rein-forcements, so that we were once again forced to rally behind our infantry.[13]

However, the trials of the two forward Brunswick battalions were not over. With the chasseurs behind them forcing them to remain in square and under fire from the advancing French skirmishers with Foy's battalions again advancing, they found themselves in an impossible position. Coming under a heavy fire from a battalion formed in line, and looking increasingly shaky, the two battalions started to move away towards the main road. However, at this moment Wathier's lancers moved forward and the very threat of these imposing cavalry caused them to break and rush towards Quatre Bras in a mob. Attempting to rally these troops the Duke of Brunswick was struck by a musket ball and mortally wounded. In an effort to hold up the French advance, the Brunswick Hussars, who had formed up to the east of the main road, charged towards the advancing French infantry. They immediately came under a flanking fire from the most advanced units and as they closed with those following up they came under an increasingly heavy fire from all directions. Unable to maintain their order or cohesion, the charge broke up before closing and the black-uniformed hussars streamed back the way they had come before striking a blow.

The dramatic collapse of the Brunswick front line had left the British troops to the east of the Brussels road with their right flank very much 'in the air'. As Wathier's advancing lancers saw the Brunswick Hussars break and run, they too were quick to spot the exposed and vulnerable British lines on their right-hand side. Quickly and efficiently wheeling to the right, the two lancer regiments bore down on the British battalions closest to the main road. Nearest to them was the 42nd and beyond them the 44th. Although both these battalions were aware of cavalry to their flank, at first they believed it to be allied and were slow in reacting.

The 6th Lancers fell on the 42nd, who, suddenly realising that they were French, desperately attempted to form square. The light company that was on the battalion's right was ridden down, but by the time the lancers had reached the main body it had formed a square of sorts and, although some Frenchmen got inside the square before it was fully formed, the side was closed and the unfortunate, if courageous, men were despatched. Having escaped a controlled volley on the run in, the French cavalry was able to close in good order and set about the highlanders with their deadly lances. In the space of just a few minutes the commanding officer and two of his successors were struck down, but despite the havoc that surrounded them, the discipline and morale of the Scotsmen held and after a few, bloody minutes of close combat the lancers were driven off. The price had been high and most of those that had not reached the sanctuary of the square were killed; 284 men of the 42nd had become casualties. Colonel Galbois, who commanded the 6th Lancers, was shot in the chest but remained on horseback and led his regiment again at Waterloo two days later.

The 5th Lancers, meanwhile, had targeted the 44th Regiment who were also formed in line. However, believing it was too late to form square, their rear rank was quickly ordered to turn about and receive the lancers with a volley. Although the regiment's skirmishers were ridden down, the volley was effective and broke the impetus of the charge. Some of the lancers closed on the thin ranks and a savage battle took place for possession of the regiment's colours. One grey-haired old lancer severely wounded Ensign Christie, who carried one of the colours, driving his lance through his left eye to the lower jaw. He then endeavoured to seize the colour, but Christie fell on it, leaving the lancer with only a small part of it that he had torn off. The brave lancer was eventually bayoneted by some nearby soldiers.

Other lancer squadrons continued the rush along the rear of the forward line of British units and attacked other battalions, but all had managed to form square and easily repulsed the charging cavalrymen. However, one squadron did succeed in catching the skirmish line of the Verden Landwehr Battalion out in the open and destroyed it before being repulsed by the fire of the Lüneberg Landwehr Battalion. One by one the squadrons rallied and, their momentum spent, turned back towards their own lines.

Like a wave breaking on the beach, the cavalry charges had reached their own high-water mark and then swept back into the safety of deeper water. But the respite given by the retreat of the cavalry was not to last long. As soon as they had disappeared, they were replaced by the ubiquitous French skirmishers. Once again their fire began to claim the lives of officers and the allied light infantry proved ineffective in keeping them back out of range of the vulnerable close-ordered main bodies. Unwilling to waste ammunition in an ineffective volley against open order troops, several times units advanced to drive off these elusive fellows; but as the range decreased, so casualties increased and the skirmishers would fade away at the last moment, only to reappear once the attackers had resumed their place in line.

A kink had been driven into Wellington's line, but it had not been broken. To the east of the main road, Picton's division firmly held a line along the Bati-Saint-Bernard heights, although some of his units had suffered heavy casualties and all were exhausted and running short of ammunition. But he had been strengthened by the arrival of Best's 2,500 Hanoverian landwehr, who had formed up in his rear along the Namur road. The French *tirailleurs*, although continuing to annoy them with their accurate shooting, did not have the strength to seriously threaten the integrity of the British line, whilst the infantry columns that might have done so were still suffering from the bloody nose they had received earlier in the afternoon. Best's arrival had boosted Wellington's infantry strength to about 20,000 men; although he was considerably weaker in cavalry and artillery he now had parity in infantry, and although many battalions were incapable of further effort, Ney had almost no fresh infantry available.

Where was d'Erlon?

To the west of the road, Foy's attack had been held, but the rout of the first line of Brunswick troops had pushed the front line closer to Quatre Bras and the original line had not been re-established. The French skirmishers had even occupied the La Bergerie farm to the east of the main road in the right rear of Picton's troops, establishing themselves in the buildings and behind the hedges and supported by two columns. These were probably from Foy's light regiment, the 4th *légère*. This position was now something of a dagger pointed at the heart of Wellington's position and it was unlikely that he would allow the farm to remain in French possession for long.

It was just a short time later that these French troops saw a kilted Scottish regiment (the 92nd) advancing in line towards them. These were immediately brought under fire and one of the officers carrying the regimental colours was killed, the flag falling to the ground. One of the lieutenants of the regiment recorded that it was the heaviest fire of musketry he had ever witnessed. Despite this heavy fire the Scottish regiment continued its advance, realising the futility of returning fire against a fleeting and well-protected enemy. With a final rush, those directly opposite the garden broke through the hedges and engaged the defenders in hand-to-hand combat whilst the rest of the regiment passed either side of the garden. The fighting in and around the buildings was fierce; men are less inclined to avoid close combat by running from cover than if they are deployed in the open. It took considerable effort to overcome the Frenchmen that had barricaded themselves into the house itself and they sold their lives dearly.

However, only the French skirmishers had occupied the farm, and beyond it lay two formed battalion columns of the 92nd Line which would be rather less simple to defeat. The highlanders continued their advance, but immediately came under a heavy fire from one of the columns. The other started to retire, but suddenly stopped, the rear ranks turned about and also opened fire. The commanding officer of the Gordons fell mortally wounded. The Scots were forced to stop and return fire; although outnumbered, their two-deep line meant that they were able to bring at least as many muskets to bear as the French columns. Eventually, the French columns continued their retreat, no doubt encouraged by the sight of Brunswick columns moving forward in support of the highlanders. Although the Scots had defeated their opposite numbers, they now came under a heavy artillery fire. Lacking the order in their rapidly thinning ranks to attempt to rush the guns, and having lost four commanding officers in as many minutes, the battalion made for the comparative safety of the Bossu wood. Whilst traversing this towards the west they had several encounters with French troops and when they finally made their way back to their own lines they had suffered casualties of twenty-eight officers and 270 men, killed, wounded and missing.

Chef de bataillon Jean-Baptiste Jolyet commanded the 1st Battalion of the 1st *légère*, part of Bauduin's brigade of Prince Jérôme's division. His regiment was held back in reserve as first Soye's brigade and then the other regiment of his own brigade, the 3rd Line, were sent into the Bossu wood. He was particularly frustrated by the lack of orders and information that was being sent to him, but finally his time came:

> Towards 4 o'clock, our 2nd Battalion advanced into the wood and, after searching through it, moved back to its edge from where it harassed the enemy regiments. I remained in the rear until towards 6pm awaiting orders. Finally, one of General Guilleminot's ADCs came to give me the order to move onto the road and to march against the English. I found myself under artillery fire the moment I moved off in column to support the skirmishers of the 4th *légère* [Jamin's brigade of Foy's division] who

were pushing the English back. I had my horse killed under me and I lost many men in a short time. The skirmishers of the 4th *légère* were to my right and I found myself alone with my battalion in the middle of a large plain, having before us the English in considerable masses.[14]

Jolyet clearly felt unsupported and unable to advance alone. In fact, apart from the constant bickering of the skirmish lines, there was now a lull in the fighting as each side licked its wounds and prepared for the next move. On the right flank fresh troops had allowed the allied forces to hold the line of the Namur road, whilst the battalions of the 2nd *légère* had been fighting all afternoon with no respite. Although they had held, they were coming under increasing pressure as the recently arrived allied troops began to make their presence felt. In the Bossu wood, Jérôme had cleared almost to the Nivelles road, but fresh allied troops had prevented him from deploying out of the wood and into a position to threaten Quatre Bras. The desperate fighting and the intense heat had exhausted his troops.

Ney's main attack had failed to break the allied line and he had insufficient fresh troops to be able to mount a new effort. But despite the arriving reinforcements, Wellington's situation was also quite desperate; hardly any of Perponcher's division remained in the fight and Picton's division was exhausted, almost out of ammunition and had suffered significant casualties. Although some of the Brunswickers had hardly been committed, two of its battalions and all its cavalry were almost *hors de combat*; the whole corps seemed decidedly shaky and their combat value was questionable. No fresh cavalry were available, and the remains of the Dutch-Belgian and Brunswick cavalry had been so roughly handled that they could only have been called upon in an emergency. But the forward elements of General Alten's division were now arriving with their two valuable artillery batteries, and Wellington just needed sufficient respite to be able to get them up and deployed before he considered any offensive action. He seemed to give no thought to sending any support to the Prussians.

Despite the pause, at the front line French skirmishers continued to be active, picking off officers and causing considerable annoyance: just prior to the latest cavalry attack they had succeeded in capturing over sixty men of the Verden Landwehr Battalion who had pushed their own skirmish screen out too far. The timidity of the French infantry columns marks a striking contrast to the activity and effectiveness of their light troops, although this probably reflects the caution of their senior commanders rather than the enthusiasm or courage of the troops themselves. But all Ney's available troops had been engaged; he had no fresh reserves to hand with which to make a new effort apart from Kellerman's cuirassiers, and for now these troops must remain as an emergency reserve. He waited impatiently for the heads of d'Erlon's columns to appear from the direction of Frasnes.

The battle had become something of a stalemate; even with the arrival of Alten's division, Wellington still felt he lacked sufficient strength to launch a counter-offensive. Indeed, the allied situation was still quite desperate and there was some confusion over where Alten's men were best deployed. Ney lacked the resources to make another assault. The key to success would be determined by which side received reinforcements first.

Where was d'Erlon?

Chapter 12

'Like a Pack of Hungry Wolves' – Kellerman's Charge

But see, the haughty Cuirassiers advance,
The dread of Europe and the pride of France!

Once the whole of Alten's division had deployed, Wellington would have about 25,500 infantry, 2,000 cavalry and thirty-six guns, less casualties, on the battlefield. This gave him a slight superiority in infantry and, whilst Ney had virtually no uncommitted troops, Alten's division of 5,500 men were still deploying and had not yet fired a shot. One of his brigades had moved to support the Brunswickers to the west of the Brussels road and the other, Picton's 'much crippled'[1] division to the east. The two batteries were particularly welcome, but once again, as they deployed they attracted the attention of the French gunners and soon after, one of the batteries (Lloyd's) had to abandon two guns as there were insufficient uninjured horses to move them.

As Wellington was beginning to feel the advantage was finally swinging in his favour, Marshal Ney was no doubt contemplating the same thing. It is hard to believe that he had not sent a stream of officers back down the Charleroi road to hasten d'Erlon's march and then to report back on their progress, but there is no evidence to support this. Perhaps his lack of a proper headquarters meant his few available officers were already overstretched, or in the heat of the battle he had just not thought of it.

But as Ney was reflecting on the fact that he was facing a deteriorating situation, he received an order from Marshal Soult, carried by Colonel Laurent:

'In front of Fleurus', 16 June, 3.15pm

Marshal! I wrote to you an hour ago that the emperor would attack the enemy at two thirty in the position he has taken between Saint-Amand and Bry. At this moment the engagement is very fierce. His Majesty has directed me to tell you that you must manoeuvre onto the field in such a manner as to envelop the enemy's right and to fall with full force on his rear. The enemy army will be lost if you act vigorously. The fate of France is in your hands. Therefore, do not hesitate an instant to move as the emperor has ordered, and head toward the heights of Bry and Saint-Amand to co-operate in a victory that should be decisive. The enemy has been caught *en flagrant délit* while trying to unite with the English.

Major Général, Maréchal de l'empire, Duc de Dalmatie[2]

As if this was not bad enough, and before Ney had the time to decide how he should act in the light of this order, General Delcambre, d'Erlon's chief-of-staff, rode up and informed him that the emperor had ordered the 1st Corps to march towards the Ligny battlefield and that the movement had already begun. General d'Erlon, unsure whether Ney was aware of the situation, had despatched his chief-of-staff to confirm that he was. At Ligny, Napoleon's attack on Blücher was in full swing and the intense artillery bombardment could be clearly heard at Quatre Bras. It was only after the emperor's first message was sent off, and the Prussian deployment became clear, that Napoleon realised he had the main Prussian army before him. In fact, Blücher had concentrated his 1st, 2nd and 3rd Corps, but by this time had realised that his 4th, under General Bülow, would not be able to join him in time for the battle. However, with the support he expected from Wellington, the Prussian general was determined to fight a major battle against his inveterate foe.

Thus, as Ney had been impatiently awaiting d'Erlon's arrival at Quatre Bras, Napoleon had been further developing his own scheme of manoeuvre to destroy Blücher's army. After all, in Napoleon's eyes, Ney's command was just a wing of the main army that he commanded; it was not an independent army with a completely separate task, it was intrinsically linked to the emperor's operations. Ney's mission was subordinate to that of destroying the Prussians, but supported that end result by denying Blücher any support from Wellington and directly manoeuvring at least some of his own troops to ensure that destruction. Merely defeating Wellington was insufficient in itself in supporting Napoleon's intent.

Committed now to a major battle against the main body of Blücher's army, whose right flank was clearly vulnerable, Napoleon had developed his idea of the march of Ney's troops on the Prussian right rear. About this time he received a letter from Lobau, commander of the 6th Corps, telling him that Ney had only 20,000 of Wellington's troops in front of him. Lobau, allocated as the army's reserve, had wisely sent his deputy chief-of-staff forward to Quatre Bras to bring back information that might be useful to him should he be deployed to this flank, and he had forwarded this information on to Napoleon. This had helped the emperor determine what his next step should be; he now aimed to use Ney to hold Wellington's relatively weak force in check, whilst he annihilated the Prussians. In order to achieve this, Ney would only require Reille's corps and Kellerman's cuirassiers, leaving Napoleon free to use d'Erlon's corps to support his main effort.

For Ney, whilst the urgency of Napoleon's order is clear, what is less so is the description of what was happening 10 kilometres away on Ney's rear right. Soult fails to inform the marshal that the emperor is engaged with the main body of the Prussian army, a significant piece of information in itself and one that should put all other activity into perspective. The message also lacks sufficient information for Ney to clearly understand that the action at Quatre Bras is very much of secondary importance should the Prussian army be destroyed. In modern military parlance, destroying the Prussian army was the main effort and all other activity and even sacrifices should be directed to ensure its success. Napoleon was clear in his own mind that Ney should keep the smallest possible force at Quatre Bras and send, and possibly lead, as many troops as possible to ensure a decisive victory at Ligny. But Soult's order fails to make this clear.

Just as Ney received this unequivocal direction, he was at the point in the day when he was least able to execute it. We cannot be sure exactly what time this order arrived with Marshal Ney and estimates vary depending on the route that the carrier travelled and how good his horse was. We can confidently say that on a journey that was about 13 kilometres as the crow flies, or up to twice as far using a route that was better going and safer, should not have taken more than two hours. In his time as *major génèral*, Berthier would have sent a messenger on each route; Soult sent only one and appears to have left the route selection up to the messenger. We shall see some implications of this approach again later.

By the time the order had been written, despatched and put in the hand of Ney, it seems reasonable to estimate that the marshal received it at approximately 5.15pm. This was just the moment that he probably saw Alten's division deploying onto the battlefield and realised that his chances of victory were slipping through his hands, as there was still no sign of d'Erlon's troops. His frustration can be imagined; without the occupation of the Quatre Bras crossroads he clearly felt he could not execute the emperor's demands and the chances of that happening were fading. Without d'Erlon, the task would be impossible. However, if he was now unable to seize Quatre Bras, he could at least support the emperor by facilitating the 1st Corps's march on Ligny. True, he could not march it down the Namur road onto the Prussian rear, but as it had already started its march to the east it still had an opportunity to fall on the Prussian right flank.

However, Ney was furious, and even if he had understood the full importance of Napoleon's orders it no doubt rankled that he had lost his own chance of gaining a victory. Up in the line of fire as usual, he was heard to exclaim, 'Ah! These English shells; I wish they would all bury themselves in my body!'[3] In a rage, he turned to General Delcambre and ordered him to return to d'Erlon and demand that he turn his troops about and return to Quatre Bras. In his anger, not only did he ignore the fact that d'Erlon was executing the emperor's orders and he would be risking the outcome of the battle at Ligny, but he also clearly did not consider how long it would take d'Erlon to retrace his steps and reach Quatre Bras. If he had been thinking clearly he would have quickly realised that d'Erlon would not reach his own battlefield until night had brought an end to the fighting, and thus his recall would be useless.

'The fate of France is in your hands!' – the words must have echoed around in Ney's head; the imperative was clear. The problem was how to seize the crossroads and still have time to intervene decisively at Ligny. As desperate times call for desperate measures, Ney called on the only fresh troops he had available. No doubt he reflected on his earlier decision to have only a single brigade of Kellerman's powerful corps immediately under his hand; the remainder were too far away to call on in this emergency. He called Kellerman forward.

Arriving with the marshal, Kellerman, writing in the third person and referring to himself as Count Valmy, takes up the story:

> ... the marshal called Count Valmy, commander of the cuirassier reserve, and repeating to him the emperor's words, he said to him, 'My dear general, we must save France, we need an extraordinary effort; take your cavalry, throw yourself into the middle of the English army, crush it, trample it underfoot etc'
>
> It was the hottest moment of the day, it was 6 or 7 o'clock. This order, like those of the emperor, was easier to give than to execute. Count Valmy objected to Marshal Ney that he only had a single brigade of cuirassiers with him, that the remainder of his corps had remained, in accordance with the Marshal's orders, two leagues in the rear at Frasnes, and that he did not therefore have a sufficient force for such a mission.
>
> 'It's not important' he replied, 'charge with what you have, destroy the English army, trample it underfoot, the salvation of France is in your hands, go!'[4]

Kellerman put himself at the head of Guiton's brigade, which consisted of the 8th and 11th Cuirassiers. The 11th were distinguishable by their lack of cuirasses; there were insufficient to equip all the regiments and this explains why some of the allied accounts refer to dragoons, for without a cuirass, the two were very similar in appearance. The 8th numbered 452 in three squadrons and the 11th, 325 men in two. Thus fewer than 800 men were about to charge well over 20,000! The two regiments rode forward in squadron columns with each squadron separated by an interval double its own front. Kellerman led them onto the high ground to the west of the road opposite Balcan, wanting to avoid the close and difficult country to the east, and formed them up with the 8th on the right and the 11th to their left. Whilst this move was being completed, the artillery, who had previously reduced their rate of fire, increased it again in an effort to prepare the way for the coming charge. This sudden increase in intensity made the allies suspect that the French were about to make a new assault.

Once the cuirassiers were in position and aware that his men might baulk at what was being asked of them, Kellerman gave them no time to reflect:

Count Valmy launched himself, like a devoted servant of Death, at the head of 600 cuirassiers, and, without giving them time to realise and reflect on the extent of the danger, led them, lost men, into a gulf of fire.[5]

The French cavalry rarely charged at more than the trot, putting more emphasis on order than on speed. However, on this occasion the order was given, 'Charge, at full gallop, forward, charge!'[6]

Their move over the high ground was spotted and the order to form square had been given before the cuirassiers got close. The 2/69th (the South Lincolns), however, positioned just to the east of the main road, having been told there was no cavalry threat by the Prince of Orange, were in the middle of deploying back into line when the foremost squadron of the 8th Cuirassiers spotted them. Veering to their right the wall of heavy cavalry rushed towards the panic-stricken red coats caught in the middle of their manoeuvre.

A young British officer later described what it was like to face these celebrated warriors:

No words can convey the sensation we felt on seeing these heavily-armed bodies advancing at full gallop against us, flourishing their sabres in the air, striking their armour with the handles, the sun gleaming on the steel. The long horse hair [of their helmets], dishevelled by the wind, bore an appearance confounding to the senses to an astonishing disorder ... Nothing could equal the splendour and terror of the scene ... The clashing of swords, the clattering of musketry, the hissing of balls, and shouts and clamours produced a sound, jarring and confounding the senses, as if hell and the Devil were in evil contention.[7]

Unsurprisingly, the volley of the 69th was hurried and ragged; insufficient to stop the charging cavalry:

This regiment [the 69th] fired at thirty paces, but without being stopped, the cuirassiers trampled it under foot, destroyed it completely and overthrew everything they found in their path.[8]

The 69th were quickly dispersed and a fierce struggle started for possession of their colours. One fell out of sight beneath the bodies of an ensign and a colour sergeant, but the other eventually fell into the hands of the victorious cuirassiers and was carried off in triumph.

Having ridden down the 69th, the squadron rode on and confronted the square made up of the remains of the 42nd and 44th, but despite these regiments being much weakened they remained steady and, when called upon to surrender, replied with a disciplined volley that sent the cuirassiers scurrying off back towards the main road.

On the left, the 11th Cuirassiers did not fare quite so well. Despite their previously flaky morale, the Brunswickers' squares remained solid and the cuirassiers rode round them, enduring their fire and looking for easier targets. The front squadron charged a square of the 30th (the Cambridge) Regiment; they again suffered casualties without making any impression. However, the second squadron wheeled left towards the 33rd (1st Yorkshire) Regiment that was in line between the Brunswickers and the Bossu wood. This newly arrived and inexperienced regiment had formed square with the rest, but had subsequently suffered severely from two French batteries that had been moved forward. One of their officers wrote, 'Two French batteries, which had stealthily advanced to point blank distance, opened fire simultaneously on our helpless square, cutting down the men like hay before the scythe of the mower.'[9] Eventually, fearing the square might break, the commanding officer ordered the regiment to re-form line to try to reduce casualties. One of its privates recalled:

> The cannon shot from the enemy broke down our square faster than we could form it. Killing nine and ten men every shot, the balls falling down amongst us …[10]

In this shaken state, a shout of 'cavalry' was enough to panic the battalion, and its line broke up as it became a mob that rushed for the perceived safety of the Bossu wood. Unfortunately for the French, the cuirassiers were not well formed and most of the battalion made it into the trees before they were ridden down. The slower members were sabred or taken prisoner and one member of the unit claimed that one of their colours was in the possession of a cuirassier before he was shot down. Such was the level of officer casualties in the 33rd that in the closeness of the wood no order could be re-established and the men were ordered to move out of the wood to the north, where the regiment was eventually reassembled. Over a hundred men were unaccounted for.

This squadron of the 11th continued their forward move and although they bypassed the 73rd (Highlanders) that stood in the third line behind the 33rd, a number of this regiment too broke ranks to run to the safety of the wood. One of its soldiers reported '… a large body of the enemy's cuirassiers … coming so unexpectedly upon us, threw us in the utmost confusion. Having no time to form square, we were compelled to retire, or rather run, to the wood …',[11] but the majority stood their ground and the integrity of the battalion was not compromised. These troopers of the 11th Cuirassiers, joining those of the 8th Regiment, found themselves at Quatre Bras itself, having charged through the entire allied army. But now their horses were blown, they had lost all order and they began to come under heavy fire from the allied reserves posted in the buildings and fields around the crossroads.

Kellerman reported:

> Some of them even penetrated as far as the Quatre Bras farm and were killed there. Lord Wellington only just had time to jump onto his horse and slip out of the way of this furious charge.
>
> It had completely succeeded, against all probability. A large breach had been made, the enemy army was shaken, but no cavalry was there to support it; the English lines were wavering, uncertain, in the expectation of what was going to happen next. The least support of our reserve cavalry engaged on our right would have completed the success; nothing had shaken it, this formidable cavalry was left on its own, unsupported, dispersed, disorganised by the very impetuosity of its charge.
>
> No longer under control of its leaders, it was struck by the fire of the enemy, who were recovering from their surprise and fear. It abandoned the battlefield as it had taken it, without being pursued by enemy cavalry, for it had not arrived. Count Valmy himself, knocked from his horse which had been killed by a musket shot, returned on foot from the middle of the English and finally met, close to the point from where he had started off, Piré's division, which moved off slowly and only made fruitless attacks that were too late against an enemy that had recovered from its terror.[12]

Now was the temerity of this charge exposed. All the momentum and order of the charge had been lost and it was now that the disorganised cuirassiers required support. In fact, the survivors were able to repulse a counter-charge by the shattered remains of the Dutch-Belgian light cavalry, causing them 'great loss',[13] but they were unable to maintain themselves at the crossroads without support. Kellerman later reflected on the failure to keep his whole corps concentrated:

> The distance of the other three brigades of Count Valmy's corps was a great disaster for the army, for France. If they had been under his hand, ready to profit from this great temerity, to throw themselves into the middle of the English army like hungry wolves in the middle of a distressed herd, perhaps, in less than an hour, this is what the English army would have become. It would have disappeared under the horses hooves or under the merciless iron of the cavalrymen and this day would have become one of those actions that decide the destiny of empires.[14]

Kellerman, his horse killed under him and on foot near the crossroads, was not in a position to appreciate the lancers' efforts and later rather unjustly complained:

> The most complete success would have been assured if the lancers had followed us; but the cuirassiers, riddled by musket fire, were not able to

profit by the advantages obtained by one of the most resolute and daring charges, against an infantry that did not allow itself to be intimidated and fired with the greatest sang-froid as on an exercise. We have taken the colour of the 69th Regiment, which was captured by cuirassiers Volgny and Hourise.

The brigade suffered an enormous loss and, seeing itself unsupported, retired in the disorder that is normal in such circumstances. My horse was killed by two shots and it was only with difficulty that I was able to escape. General Guiton, Colonel Juravapes were dismounted as well as a number of other officers and cuirassiers. I have had my knee and foot trampled, but nevertheless I will be back on horseback tomorrow ...[15]

A number of French accounts claim that Kellerman was saved by hanging onto the bridles of two of his cuirassiers.

In fact Piré's regiments did move forward to try to support the cuirassiers, but their horses were tired from their previous efforts; cavalry were rarely called upon to make more than one all-out charge in a battle and they had already conducted two. Their charge was carried out with less enthusiasm and they were driven back by the fire of the steady allied squares before they could reach the high-water mark of the cuirassiers' charge. Lieutenant Henckens wrote:

As Marshal Ney was determined to become master of Quatre Bras, and as d'Erlon's corps were not available, Kellerman's cuirassiers were ordered to capture it with us in support. The cuirassiers' charge began at 7pm and was admirable; but it did not have the success that Ney had hoped for; it was repeated by us, with the same courage but with the same lack of success, notwithstanding our great persistence. At the first charge we were received by Scottish infantry; an admirable troop. It was like a hail of balls that was fired at us; my beautiful horse, good and expensive, received seven of them. I mounted another horse to charge and charge again, but with the same result ... In these final charges we had suffered heavy casualties. Captain Estève was killed, comrades dismounted and wounded, and when I gathered together the *compagnie d'élite*, there were only 25 men left mounted; the others remained on the ground over which we had charged, killed, wounded or dismounted.[16]

Noteworthy in this attack was the French cavalry response to finding the allied squares that were hidden by the tall rye; individual lancers would ride within fifty yards of a square and, having located it, would stick their lance into the ground as a point for the following squadrons to aim at.

The infantry too seemed disinclined to second the cuirassiers. A swift and resolute advance by Reille's infantry might have been able to exploit the initial disorder and anxiety that Kellerman's charge had caused. However, Bachelu's infantry apparently made no forward move, suggesting that no order had been given or that they now lacked the determination for offensive action.

Colonel Heymès blames the lack of fresh infantry for the failure:

> If the 1st Corps, or even a single one of its divisions had arrived at this time, the day would have been one of the most glorious for our arms; it needed infantry to secure the prize that the cavalry had taken, but the marshal had none available, all three divisions of the 2nd Corps were entirely committed.[17]

Some allied accounts claim that the cuirassiers made two charges, but this must be a mistake. Kellerman would surely have mentioned it if it was true and, given the circumstances, for the cuirassiers to have fallen back through the allied squares, rally and then charge again, seems fanciful. More likely is that allied units were charged by two different squadrons at different times; the whole aim of attacking in echelon being to strike the enemy with successive blows.

It will be noted that Kellerman described the withdrawal of the cuirassiers as taking place 'in the disorder that is normal in such circumstances'. However, almost surrounded, disorganised and under heavy fire, the surviving cuirassiers now thought only of saving themselves; they wheeled round and in small disorderly groups fled back towards their own lines.

One serving French cavalry officer (who was not present at Quatre Bras), clearly basing his account on a conversation with someone who was there, blamed the rout on one of the cuirassier officers:

> A small number of troopers went from retreat into flight, causing trouble in the rear amongst some baggage which was pillaged. This flight, said M. Giraud, was attributed to the poor conduct of a *chef d'escadron* who lost his head, or more likely his willingness, and who fled at top speed, striking all those he encountered in his path, causing disorder far and wide by shouting 'SAUVE QUI PEUT!' [save yourselves][18]

Nothing could stop this panicked flight, not even reaching the rear of their own gun lines, and the panic spread throughout the rear areas. One account blames the panic in the 1st Corps baggage train on the cuirassiers displaying the captured colour and the drivers thinking they were the enemy:

> At this moment, the cuirassiers that had come from overthrowing a Scottish square [he means the 69th], and whose colour had been captured during a vigorous charge, appeared on the crest on the main road in front, carrying in the middle of them the Scottish colour that they had captured flying in the wind; the first wagon drivers at the head of the

column, suddenly seeing this cavalry moving towards them, thought they were the enemy and, seized by a sudden terror, they quickly turned their horses to get away and rapidly got into disorder on the sides of the route, dragging with them the wagons in the centre until the road and both sides of it was absolutely blocked by vehicles.

The drivers then cut their traces and took off across the fields without looking back, leaving their wagons abandoned, the baggage scattered and losing all the division's stores, fleeing as far as Charleroi where they spread panic.[19]

However, this seems to be finding an excuse for the cuirassiers, as other accounts make it clear that the cavalrymen themselves spread the panic:

A brigade of cuirassiers ... fled in disorder as far as Frasnes and more than half a league in the rear, encountering and bowling over the artillery reserves and baggage which were coming from Gosselies, pillaged the baggage and spread terror everywhere.[20]

Chef d'escadron Levavasseur was one of Marshal Ney's ADCs. He was moving forward to join the marshal when he was a witness to this panic, which reached much further back than many others claimed:

On the 16th ... I moved to Charleroi; fighting was in progress. I entered a house to rest my horses. I was at table, the cannon roared. Suddenly, a great commotion could be heard in the town; everyone was fleeing. The road was blocked with vehicles, cavalrymen, infantrymen who were running. 'We are lost!' I said to my host, 'the enemy is here.' I ran to the stable and, in the alley there, I met a naked man fleeing on one of my horses. I threw him off, mounted, and, not wanting to run without having seen the enemy, I rode forward; but coming out onto the plain, I only noticed a few dragoons, who told me of a cavalry charge in the distance. It was a false alarm which spread its terror all the way back into France.[21]

The charge, glorious at first, had finished in ignominy. But the brave survivors, having rallied and rejoined the rest of their corps, were to take part in the great cavalry charges at Waterloo just two days later.

The casualties for Guiton's brigade are recorded as 300 killed and wounded out of a strength of 777.[22] There is even disagreement on who captured the colour of the 69th. As we have seen, Kellerman credits cuirassiers Volgny and Hourise, but *maréchal de camp* Berton (a brigade commander not present at the battle) wrote in his account of the campaign:

Cuirassier Lami, of the 5th company of this regiment [the 8th], captured an enemy colour. The General-in-Chief, in complementing Colonel

Garavaque on the courage displayed by this regiment, awarded Cuirassier Lami 100 Louis as a reward.[23]

The charge, though glorious, had been futile and doomed to failure; General Foy described it as 'featherbrained.'[24] Ney must surely have realised that fewer than 800 cuirassiers had no chance of turning the day around, and the fact that he ordered the charge is more indicative of his state of mind than it was a tactical miscalculation. It was a sign of his desperation and impotence.

Chapter 13

'We felt abandoned . . .' – The Allied Counter-Attack

There was an almost inevitable lull in the battle after the desperate charge of the cuirassiers and its aftermath. On the allied side, casualties had been high and a number of regiments had been forced to join with others to ensure a viable fighting force. Many of the remaining troops were almost out of ammunition and were driven to search the pouches of the dead to try and replenish their own. This was particularly true for those light troops who had been facing the ubiquitous *tirailleurs*; many of the allied skirmishers had completely run out of ammunition and were forced to rejoin the main body of their regiments, leaving them exposed to the fire of the French. Many felt the battle was on the point of being lost and silently awaited the inevitable knock-out blow.

After the charge, General Halkett, fearing the battle was nearly lost, wrote a note to his wife and advised another officer to tell his own wife to move to Brussels.[1] Other officers were not convinced they were winning the battle; Major Jessop of the Quarter Master General's department, meeting the 1st Foot Guards as they arrived on the battlefield, urged them on as 'the action was going badly.'[2]

At about six o'clock Cooke's British Guards division and its two batteries arrived after a 40-kilometre march from Enghien. This was a vital reinforcement for Wellington as he had now concentrated sufficient troops to contemplate a counter-attack. He had no doubt noticed that Ney had no fresh troops available and the enthusiasm and élan of the French troops was waning as they became increasingly exhausted after hours of desperate fighting in stifling heat. It is hard to believe that the allied commander could have contemplated such an offensive without this reinforcement, but once again he had the initiative of a junior commander to thank, rather than his own planning, for Cooke, in the absence of any orders on arrival at Braine-le-Comte, had taken the decision to continue his march. The necessary orders did not reach him until an hour later; if he had waited for them it is unlikely that his 4,500 men and twelve guns would have arrived in time to contribute to the fighting.

Cooke's arrival was quickly followed by the two batteries of Brunswick artillery and two Brunswick infantry battalions that had marched south from

Brussels; the tide had finally tipped irrevocably against Marshal Ney, who no doubt realised that the 1st Corps was unlikely to return in time to seize the crossroads. Wellington had now established a line along the heights of Bati-Saint-Bernard; with the main bodies of the units on this line able to shelter behind the crest, they were able to get some respite from the heavy and accurate French artillery and skirmisher fire.

As Wellington contemplated a counter-attack, a Prussian staff officer arrived from Ligny. This officer informed him that Blücher's army had suffered heavy casualties and that the best that could be hoped for was that it could maintain its position on the battlefield until last light. He finished by requesting that Wellington launch a strong offensive that might deter Napoleon from launching a final, decisive attack.

Whilst Bachelu's and Foy's columns seemed reluctant to advance, for Prince Jérôme's troops in the Bossu wood success must have felt very close. Since their commitment into the wood they had fought hard in the close and claustrophobic terrain, where order and cohesion were almost impossible to maintain. The fighting had been confused as troops of different nations entered and left the wood at different points and from different directions. Now operating in small groups, often without supervision or orders, they had been fighting against troops in uniforms of green, blue, grey and red, and been able to push them back to the very northern edge of the wood where it met the Nivelles road. But now, just as it seemed that they would push them out of the trees altogether, Cooke's guardsmen were launched into the wood. Although exhausted from their long march they were eager to enter the fight and did so with enthusiasm and full ammunition pouches. Committed in growing strength and being well disciplined, they slowly began to force the *tirailleurs* back. Experienced and determined troops, the French skirmishers were able to cause considerable casualties on the advancing guardsmen and they were able to deliver a considerable check where the Gémioncourt stream cut through the wood and offered an obstacle covered by thick undergrowth. Step by step they disputed their withdrawal, giving up their previous gains reluctantly.

Outside the wood, astride the main road, the allied line also began a cautious advance. This was no grand advance against a demoralised and broken enemy like that which would be seen at Waterloo two days later. General Foy's chief-of-staff wrote:

> His considerable numerical superiority gave him a great advantage. Happily, his habitual caution did not desert him ... Lord Wellington took the offensive, but quite timidly.[3]

The French, exhausted by their efforts and short of ammunition, gave up their ground reluctantly, drawing back slowly and maintaining their fire. But Ney had no fresh reserves with which to oppose the allied advance; all his men had been committed and at the very moment that he needed them most, he had learnt that the 1st Corps had been denied him. Like their compatriots in the wood, Bachelu's and Foy's men fell back slowly; the allied units in the centre were too exhausted and lacking in ammunition to be able to push them hard. It appears that there was little fighting here; the French falling back as the allied troops advanced. Colonel Jolyet reported:

> Two regiments of cavalry (one of cuirassiers and one of lancers) then appeared and made several charges on the English squares; but, as they were unsuccessful, they retired. Seeing myself alone and not wanting to lose all my men, I moved towards a large farm [Grand Pierrepont] which would serve as a strongpoint, and two companies from the third battalion came and joined me. We were followed by a cloud of English skirmishers, supported by artillery and columns of infantry. Nevertheless, we were able to hold on to the farm until night.[4]

On the French right things were a little different. Here the Rifles and Brunswick light troops had been significantly reinforced by Hanoverian troops, tasked with pushing the French back and clearing the Namur road. In the face of their advance, the 2nd *légère* had no option but to drop back and soon Piraumont was back in allied hands. General Foy wrote:

> ... the English, no doubt fearing that they would be pressed along the Namur road where they deployed without interruption, approached Piermont [Piraumont] and, despite our artillery fire which caused them considerable loss, captured the village and reached the neighbouring wood [Delhutte]. This situation forced us to extend and withdraw our right.[5]

Colonel Trefcon, the chief-of-staff to Bachelu, was on this part of the field:

> Our retreat on Piraumont was almost fatal for me. As I had remained a little in the rear to rally the soldiers and to hold them in position, my horse, getting excited, got itself caught up in the wheat or in I know not what and kicked, refusing to advance. I sensed the English on my heels and, worried that I would be taken, threw myself to the ground, when suddenly my horse decided to gallop off. I took off in fear, for the English were already very close to me ... We were forced to abandon Piraumont and to reoccupy the positions from which we had started the action.[6]

On the French left, two strong battalions of British guardsmen had deployed into the Bossu wood. Unfortunately, there is no French account of the fighting here, but we get a good feel from an officer of the 1st Foot Guards:

> The men gave a cheer, and rushing in drove everything before them to the end of the wood, but the thickness of the underwood soon upset all

order, and the French artillery made the place so hot that it was thought advisable to draw back to the stream, which was rather more out of range. A great many men were killed and wounded by the heads of the trees falling on them as cut off by cannon shot.[7]

Prince Jérôme's men were eventually pushed out of the wood, but formed up to its south and disputed with determination the exit of the guards who tried to deploy in the open ground. However, suffering casualties from the French fire and threatened by cavalry, in a scene reminiscent of earlier in the day the two guards battalions broke and dashed for the safety of the trees and the hollow way which ran along its edge. Piré's troopers failed to catch them and suffered severely from their fire and that of a Brunswick square which stood in the open ground. Cooke's men, faced by the determined resistance and the strongpoint of Pierrepont held by Jolyet's men, advanced no further; the skirmisher fire continued until darkness fell.

As the light failed the French found themselves on the ground where they had started the attack in the morning. Wellington appeared content with how the battle finished; Quatre Bras remained in his hands and that crossroads, and the Namur road, was no longer under French fire. His communications with the Prussians had been restored. The French troops were sullen and felt defeated; Colonel Jolyet reported:

> I have recounted these moments in detail to show what disarray reigned in the headquarters. One never knew who commanded; from our arrival on the battlefield we did not see a single general. It was only a junior staff officer who gave me, on the move and without detail, the order to advance. When the English appeared to be shaken, no fresh troops were sent that could have completed the enemy's rout. Our regiments fought well; there were some brilliant actions, guns taken from the enemy, but there was no co-ordination, no direction! We felt abandoned ...[8]

Chapter 14

Order, Counter-Order, Disorder

We must now retrace our steps and examine d'Erlon's activity on the 16th. We have already seen that he had issued orders during the night of the 15th/16th with the aim of concentrating his command and moving on Gosselies in order to support Marshal Ney. However, despite his best intentions, Quiot's division was still some way behind and would require time to close up. Houssaye only tells us that the 1st Corps was concentrated at Jumet (2 kilometres south of Gosselies) 'in the morning' and that any forward movement was held up by the fact that Reille's troops still occupied Gosselies itself. Thus, any charge of tardiness against d'Erlon has to be balanced against the fact that he could not move until Reille had done the same, and we have already seen how the latter had been slow to move forward despite Ney's orders.

Some time before noon, d'Erlon received Ney's order to advance, but as we have heard, he was forced to delay his march because of Reille's inactivity. In particular, Prince Jérôme's division, which had bivouacked on the south of the Lombac wood (which lay east of Gosselies), did not start its move until between 1.30 and 2pm, preventing d'Erlon from starting his own march as long as he planned to use the main road rather than some of the poor quality cross roads. D'Erlon was then held up even further by reports that he was threatened by a substantial allied force to his west, and it was only after he had satisfied himself that this was not the case (in fact it was van Merlen's cavalry moving to Quatre Bras) that he finally began his own move at about 3pm. The march from Jumet to Frasnes was only about 8 kilometres, but given the length of the marching column it would take up to three hours for all his troops to complete the march and deploy.

A little time after four o'clock, the first two divisions had passed the Roman way when d'Erlon was joined by Colonel Forbin-Janson, a staff officer from Imperial headquarters. He carried an order from Napoleon ordering Marshal Ney to send d'Erlon's corps to the east and attack Ligny from the heights of Saint-Amand, in line with the emperor's new strategic design. The order was written in pencil and was almost illegible. Unfortunately, Forbin-Janson was unable to offer either clarification or elaboration, exhibiting a gross lack of military understanding. In fact, he had been promoted straight to colonel after the campaign in France the previous year in recognition of his exploits in commanding a band of partisans against the invading allies. Whilst no doubt this was praiseworthy, it hardly qualified him for such an important mission. What's more, whilst it was to his credit he had taken a more direct route than Colonel Laurent, the carrier of Soult's 3.15pm order to Ney, and had thus arrived earlier, inevitably much of the context and imperative of Soult's order was lost. Forbin-Janson also informed d'Erlon that in passing his troops on the road he had already, in the name of the emperor, directed them off towards Ligny in line with the emperor's intent.

To make matters worse, the inexperienced officer, perhaps overwhelmed by the enormity of what was going on, and having informed d'Erlon of Napoleon's order, forgot to continue his mission and deliver it to Marshal Ney! Thus Ney was not only unaware of the order, but also of the fact that d'Erlon's troops were already marching east. Forbin-Janson hastily returned to imperial headquarters where this error was identified and he was sent back to complete his task. D'Erlon had immediately departed to join his troops, but wisely took the precaution of despatching his chief-of-staff, General Delcambre, to inform Marshal Ney of what was happening.

Unfortunately, the message carried by Forbin-Janson has been lost, so we are unable to examine its exact wording. However, we shall see a little later that General Deselles, commander of the 1st Corps artillery, quotes the message in his own account of what happened. Even if we do not know the exact wording, it was clearly an order direct from the emperor, putting Napoleon's own stamp on the importance of the order written by Soult and carried by Colonel Laurent in much the same way that Napoleon had sent a reiteration of his orders in the morning of the 15th, using his own personal staff officers to send duplicates of the formal orders sent by the *major général*. He was to use this method throughout the campaign and it was his own way of ensuring the orders got to the right place, often more quickly than through the established process. It is therefore not surprising that on this occasion too Napoleon's own order reached d'Erlon before that of Soult, which had to go via Ney.

Perhaps most importantly from Napoleon's perspective, was that d'Erlon was much further south than the emperor expected; with no information on Ney's dispositions or the delays of his subordinates, Napoleon was expecting the 1st Corps to march down the Namur road from Quatre Bras, where he had directed Ney to take position earlier in the morning. Instead, d'Erlon's troops turned east at Frasnes and approached the Ligny battlefield from the direction of Villars-Perwin. Far from supporting Napoleon's final, decisive attack, his unexpected appearance on the left rear of Vandamme's 3rd Corps caused considerable anxiety that they had been outflanked by Wellington, and it appears that some troops were on the point of panic. The final assault was delayed for an hour and a half before d'Erlon's troops were identified as such and the attack could go ahead. At this point in the battle, this time gave the

Prussians a vital respite in which they could re-establish some order in their wavering troops.

With Forbin-Janson having forgotten to continue his mission to inform Marshal Ney of Napoleon's order to d'Erlon, it was by Soult's written order that the marshal first learnt of the 1st Corps's march towards Ligny. Colonel Heymès, Ney's ADC/chief-of-staff, wrote:

> It was at this time that Colonel Laurent, sent from Imperial Head-quarters, came to inform the marshal that the 1st Corps, by the emperor's order, which had already been given to General d'Erlon, had left the Brussels road instead of following it, and was moving in the direction of Saint Amand. General d'Elcambre [Delcambre], the chief-of-staff of this corps, arrived soon after to announce the action it was taking.
>
> The enemy now had 50,000 men at Quatre Bras. He was pushing us back; and the marshal, a great captain, now judged success impossible. He rallied his troops that were fully engaged and made good dispositions in order to defend Frasnes, waiting and sleeping there, whilst the enemy, although three times the strength, made no attempt to prevent us.[1]

This order would have arrived at approximately 5.15pm. By this time, the 1st Corps had been marching towards Ligny for over an hour.

General d'Erlon wrote two accounts of the sequence of events; the first was his response to an enquiry from Ney's son which appeared in *Documents inédits sur la campagne de 1815 publiés par le Duc d'Elchingen*, and the second in his own book *Le Maréchal Drouet, Comte d'Erlon Vie militaire ecrit par luimême*.

In the first of these he wrote:

> Towards 11 o'clock or midday, M. le Maréchal Ney sent me the order for my corps to take up arms and to move on Frasnes and Quatre Bras, where I would receive further orders. Thus my corps started its move imme-diately. After having given the commander of the head of the column the order to take the necessary precautions, I went ahead to see what was happening at Quatre Bras, where General Reille's corps appeared to be engaged. Beyond Frasnes, I stopped with generals of the guard [presum-ably of Lefebvre-Desnouëttes's light cavalry] where I was joined by General Labédoyère [one of Napoleon's ADCs], who showed me a note in crayon which he carried to Marshal Ney, which ordered this marshal to send my corps to Ligny. General Labédoyère warned me that he had already given the order for this movement, having changed the direc-tion of march of my column, and indicated to me where I could rejoin it. I immediately took this route and sent my chief-of-staff, General Delcambre, to the marshal, to warn him of my new destination. Marshal Ney sent him back to me with definitive orders to return to Quatre Bras, where he was hard pressed and counting on the co-operation of my

corps. I thus decided that I was urgently required there, since the marshal took it upon himself to recall me, despite having received the note of which I spoke above.

I therefore ordered the column to make a counter-march; but, despite all the effort that I put into this movement, my column only arrived at Quatre Bras as it got dark.

Was General Labédoyère authorised to change the direction of my column before having seen the marshal? I do not think so; but in any case, this single circumstance was the cause of all the marches and counter-marches which paralysed my corps throughout the 16th.

D. *comte* d'Erlon
Paris, 9 February 1829[2]

His second account, in his autobiography, gives the same information and thus does not need to be repeated.

We must first note that this letter was written fourteen years after the events it describes and thus it is possible that a few mistakes have crept in. For example, d'Erlon names General Labédoyère as the officer that carried the message, though we can be quite sure that it was Colonel Forbin-Janson. Indeed, in his second account, he does not name the officer. It can also be seen that d'Erlon presumed that the message had been forwarded to Marshal Ney as it was intended. More interestingly, d'Erlon claims that he had moved forwards towards Quatre Bras and was not with his troops when the message arrived with him, informing us that the column had already been turned towards Ligny by the time he learnt of the emperor's order; this does not appear in any other accounts. We shall examine why he might have claimed this later, but as far as the sequence of events is concerned, it is of little importance.

Another useful account comes from General Deselles, who, as the commander of the 1st Corps artillery, would always be found close to the corps commander. He later wrote:

As we slowly closed up on the 2nd Corps, a *sous-officier* of the Guard arrived with a letter from the emperor which directed,

'*Monsieur le comte* d'Erlon, the enemy has fallen headlong into the trap that I have set for him. Move immediately with your four infantry divisions, your cavalry division, all your artillery and the two divisions of heavy cavalry that I put under your command and move, as I say, with all these forces to the area of Ligny and fall on Saint-Amand. M. *le comte* d'Erlon, you will save France and cover yourself in glory.'

It is well known that the generals of artillery and engineers do not leave their commander-in-chief; I can thus give precise information on these events which had such disastrous consequences for us.

e Emperor Napoleon.

Marshal Soult. He proved a poor substitute for Napoleon's previous iconic chief of staff, Marshal Berthier.

arshal Ney. Commander of the Left Wing of e French army. Napoleon heaped much of e blame for the failure of the campaign on y's shoulders.

Lieutenant Général Jean-Baptiste Drouet, *Comte* d'Erlon. Commander of the 1st Corps.

Lieutenant Général Honoré Charles Reille.
Commander of the 2nd Corps.

Lieutenant Général Prince Jérôme Bonaparte.
Napoleon's brother and commander of the
6th Infantry Division.

Lieutenant Général Comte Gilbert Désiré Josep[h]
Bachelu. Commander of the 5th Infantry
Division.

Lieutenant Général Comte Maximilien Sebastie[n]
Foy. Commander of the 9th Infantry Divisio[n]

Lieutenant Général François Etienne Kellerman, Comte de Valmy. Commander of the 3rd Reserve Cavalry Corps.

The Quatre Bras farmhouse. Sadly due for demolition, it is claimed that some of the French cavalrymen actually penetrated the courtyard.

The Namur road looking south-east from Quatre Bras. This road had banks on both sides and provided good cover for many of Wellington's infantry.

A view from the Quatre Bras crossroads showing how Wellington could not see further than the Bati-Saint-Bernard ridge. In the centre of the photograph, the sun can be seen shining off the roof of Gémioncourt farm.

The farm of La Bergerie as it looks today.

The Gémioncourt farm from the south; the direction from which the French attacked. The Bati-Saint-Bernard ridge rises beyond the buildings.

The entrance to the
Gémioncourt farm looking
east from the main road.

The memorial to the Duke
Brunswick that stands nex'
the main road in the centre
the battlefield and close to
where he fell.

The 42nd are caught by French lancers before they were able to complete their square.

The colour of the 2/69th is captured by a trooper of the 8th Cuirassiers.

In execution of the imperial order, all the nominated forces directed their march across the plain towards Ligny (or Saint-Amand).

With a weak escort we went ahead of the marching columns, when we suddenly saw General Delcambre, the chief-of-staff of our corps, sent by Marshal Ney to demand our support.

Count d'Erlon was unsure and hesitated; he needed advice. General of Engineers Garbé and I thought that the emperor's order was the one that was definitely more pressing, that if executed we would later be able to take the English in the flank and thus disengage the marshal. But General Delcambre insisted. The Count d'Erlon took a middle course which upset all the plans of the General-in-Chief. He sent Durutte's division, which was the lead division, Jacquinot's cavalry division and two batteries, to the heights of Ligny. With the rest, he moved to the support of Marshal Ney ...[3]

In a footnote to this account, Deselles added, 'Not having a map of Belgium in front of me, it is possible that I have got the names of these two villages the wrong way round. I believe it was Saint-Amand to fall on Ligny ...' However, as we have already seen, the 1st Corps was approaching Ligny from a different direction to the one that Napoleon was expecting and thus this uncertainty is probably of little consequence. A number of historians have discussed the implications of where d'Erlon understood he was to march to, and what effect he would have had at various places, but the fact remains that this is speculation; d'Erlon did not arrive with his whole corps on the battlefield and it is the reasons why not that need to be understood.

Deselles also claims that it was a '*sous-officier* of the Guard' who delivered this message and this seems to contradict d'Erlon, Heymès and Houssaye. However, whilst one or more may have had a lapse of memory, it is equally possible that Napoleon sent a succession of officers to ensure this important order got to Ney and d'Erlon. To support this theory, Colonel Crabbé, attached to Imperial Headquarters, but later to serve as Ney's ADC at Waterloo, wrote:

I am exhausted. I have been on horseback for eighteen hours. Three times I have been sent to Marshal Ney to tell him to seize Quatre Bras at any cost and to arrive before the English who did not cease to send their columns there.[4]

It is also worthy of note that Deselles claims that both he, and the general of engineers, Garbé, advised d'Erlon to comply with the emperor's order rather than return to Ney. However, it is wise to be wary of such claims in accounts written with the benefit of hindsight.

D'Erlon's dilemma can be well understood; on one side, he had the emperor's order to march to the Ligny battlefield in order to take a key role in the destruction of the Prussian army; on the other, he had his immediate superior demanding his return to Quatre Bras where the left wing was in danger of being overwhelmed. The dilemma should have been settled by a simple appreciation of the situation; although he was not approaching the Ligny battlefield from the direction Napoleon expected, he had a substantial force close enough (3 kilometres) to be able to make a significant contribution to the combat taking place there. On the other hand, he was 12 kilometres from Quatre Bras (about a three to four-hour march for a complete corps) and it was now too late to make a counter-march and arrive in time to have any significant influence on the outcome of the fighting there. Furthermore, he had received a direct order from the emperor himself. The decision should not have been a hard one and yet d'Erlon took a middle course that was to influence neither battle.

Ney seems to have been so absorbed in his own battle that he was incapable of understanding that Napoleon was trying to achieve an infinitely more important strategic outcome. But the succession of orders from the emperor and imperial headquarters should have convinced him that there was now a greater good than the simple seizure of Quatre Bras and that his own battle was now nothing more than a sideshow. However, for whatever reason, the previous messages and orders had either failed to make this clear to him or he had deliberately chosen to ignore them. Napoleon now made a final effort to make Ney understand the importance of carrying out his orders. Colonel Baudus, Soult's ADC, explains:

> At the moment when the affair [Ligny] was closely engaged along the whole line, Napoleon called me and said, 'I have sent Count d'Erlon the order to move with his entire corps onto the rear of the Prussian army's right; you go and take a duplicate of this order to Marshal Ney which has to be communicated to him. *You are to tell him that, whatever the situation he is facing, it is absolutely necessary that this direction is executed; that I attach no great importance to what happens on his flank today; that the key is what happens where I am, because I need to finish off the Prussian army. As for him, he should, if he cannot do better, to be content with containing the English army.* [My italics]
>
> When the emperor had finished giving me these instructions, the *major général* recommended me, in the most energetic terms to insist with equal force that nothing should hinder the execution of the movement prescribed to Count d'Erlon.[5]

This message should have made the situation clear to Ney, but we cannot be sure from Baudus's account exactly what time he was despatched or what time he reached Marshal Ney. However, Baudus continues his narrative thus:

> The journey was long, but I went quickly. Hardly had I rejoined the main road between Charleroi and Brussels than I saw it far off covered by a

large body of cuirassiers that were retiring in the greatest disorder; it was the brigade consisting of the 8th and 11th Regiments of this arm. This corps had been so badly affected by the fire of some English infantry which occupied the wood of Bossu, that after delivering some beautiful charges they had finished by taking flight, taking several colours that they had taken from the Anglo-Belgian army. I quickly took a different route so that I would not be dragged along by this mass, and soon I found Marshal Ney at the point of most danger in the middle of a terrible fire. I gave him the emperor's orders, but he was so agitated that I felt at first that he was unlikely to execute them. In fact, he had good reason to be highly irritated, for, in his attack on Quatre Bras, he had not hesitated to commit the three divisions of the 2nd Corps commanded by General Reille, because he was counting on the co-operation of the 1st Corps, under the orders of Count d'Erlon, who was, after the instructions of the marshal placed in the second line at Frasnes. But, when he wanted it to advance, it could not be found because Count d'Erlon, having received the direct order of the emperor, which directed him to move against the rear of the Prussian army, had set off immediately to conform with his orders of which the marshal had not been warned; at least he formally assured me that he had received no other official advice of this order other than that which I had brought him. The words of this illustrious marshal convinced me that this was indeed the truth of the matter, even though the anger that he suffered seeing himself compromised by this manoeuvre was evident. In fairness to the Count d'Erlon, to whom I spoke some years after these events, he confirmed to me that he had warned his superior of the new direction his troops had been given by the emperor. The officer charged with this mission was probably wounded or killed before arriving at his destination. The marshal, desperate at having no reinforcements to support the divisions that had only been committed because he thought he had 20,000 men in reserve, came, when I joined him, to have Count d'Erlon strictly ordered to return to the position that had been assigned to him. I insisted with the greatest force to the marshal not to oppose the emperor's intentions; I thought I had succeeded; but after the events of the day I saw, as I returned to the rear with him, that Count d'Erlon had returned with his troops ...[6]

Given that Baudus met the fleeing cuirassiers on the road, he cannot have reached Ney until after 7pm at the earliest. Ney's statement to him that this was the first time he had heard of d'Erlon's flank march cannot be true; either Baudus or Ney having made a mistake, as if he had only recalled d'Erlon at this late hour the 1st Corps could not have arrived until very much later than they actually did.

We must now return to General d'Erlon. Having received the peremptory command from his immediate superior to return to Quatre Bras and the advice of his key headquarters staff to continue towards Ligny, he decided on the compromise outlined by General Deselles: the 4th Division (commanded by General Durutte), three of the four regiments of cavalry from the corps cavalry division (commanded by General Jacquinot) and two batteries were to continue towards Wagnelé, whilst the remaining three infantry divisions and cavalry regiment would turn and march on Quatre Bras. Clausewitz claims that the time now was 8pm; like Ney, d'Erlon seems not to have calculated that his arrival there would be too late to have any significant impact.

General Durutte has left his own account of what happened:

On the 16th, towards 10am, he [General d'Erlon] received the order to set off for Frasnes, on the Brussels road. The 4th Division, under the orders of General Durutte, was in the lead.

Whilst this move was taking place, the order was received to march towards Quatre Bras; the right [of the army] was closely engaged towards Fleurus. The emperor gave the order to Count d'Erlon to attack the Prussian left and try to seize Bry. The 1st Corps passed close to Villers-Perwin to execute this move. Whilst it was on the march, several messengers arrived in haste from Marshal Ney to stop the corps and have it march back to Quatre Bras. The officers who carried these orders said that Marshal Ney had found superior forces at Quatre Bras and that he was repulsed. This second order put Count d'Erlon in a difficult position, for he received at the same time new calls from the right to march on Bry. Nevertheless, he decided to turn back towards Marshal Ney, but, as he could see, with General Durutte, that the enemy was trying to deploy a column onto the plain that lies between Bry and the wood of Delhutte, which would have cut off the emperor's army from that commanded by Marshal Ney, he decided to leave General Durutte on this plain, leaving under his orders besides his own division, three regiments of cavalry commanded by General Jacquinot.

Before General d'Erlon left, General Durutte asked clearly if he was to march on Bry. General d'Erlon replied that, in view of circumstances, he could not lay down exactly what he should do and that he should rely on his experience and caution. General Durutte sent his cavalry towards the road that went from Sombreffe to Quatre Bras, leaving Wagnée [Wagnelé] and Bry to his right, but bearing towards these two villages; his infantry followed this movement.

General d'Erlon had told him to be cautious because as affairs were going badly at Quatre Bras, General Durutte would do well to observe the Delhutte wood for in the case that Marshal Ney made a retrograde movement, the enemy would be behind him.[7]

The key point from this passage is the caution with which Durutte stresses d'Erlon ordered him to act. Despite all the confusion surrounding d'Erlon's march and counter-march, there was still the time and opportunity for him to strike a telling blow at Ligny, even if it was only delivered by Durutte and Jacquinot. Although they were not on the Prussian rear as directed by Napoleon, they still hovered menacingly on the Prussian flank; the one most closely pressed by Vandamme and the one that had suffered most throughout the day. What was required was a determined and audacious attack against an exhausted and demoralised enemy. Durutte described his contribution:

> Whilst General Jacquinot moved to within artillery range of the road between Sombreffe and Quatre Bras, he encountered a body of enemy with which he exchanged artillery fire for three quarters of an hour. General Durutte advanced his infantry to support him; there was still heavy fighting towards St-Amand.
>
> The enemy troops that exchanged artillery fire with General Jacquinot having withdrawn, General Durutte, receiving no more bad news from the left, decided to march on Bry.
>
> By the movement of our troops, he presumed that we were victorious at Saint-Amand. His skirmishers clashed with Prussian light troops who were still at Wagnelée [Wagnelé]; he took this village as the day ended and being convinced that the enemy were in full retreat, he sent two battalions into Bry who found only a few Prussian stragglers there.
>
> During the night, General Durutte received the order to return to Villars-Perwin on the 17th ...[8]

This action could hardly be described as determined and audacious and it is fair to conclude that Durutte's contribution to the French victory at Ligny was negligible at best. However, Durutte clearly felt he was operating in accordance with his superior commander's intent by not committing his troops more than he did.

Durutte's caution, which may well have been endorsed by d'Erlon, was witnessed with growing frustration by his troops. These were able to see what was going on before them and burned to get into action. Captain Chapuis, who commanded a grenadier company in the 85th Line, which led the 4th Division's column, was a witness to what happened:

> Located at a short distance from the hamlet of Wagnelé, which lies close to the village of Saint-Amand, and awaiting the order that would have us march on Wagnelé, we were all convinced that the 1st Corps had been called on to play a great role in the struggle that was engaged.
>
> ... Our situation behind Wagnelé gave us the absolute assurance that a few minutes would suffice to put the whole of the Prussian right wing between two fires, and there was not one of us, soldier or officer, who could not see that acting with promptitude and vigour, the salvation of the enemy would be gravely compromised.

This order, on which we expected to obtain such admirable results, arrived, but unfortunately, it was not executed because, on one part, General Drouet d'Erlon had left to return to join Marshal Ney at Quatre Bras, under the orders of whom was found the 1st and 2nd Corps, and on the other, General Durutte did not dare to take it upon himself to order such a movement; refusing the responsibility as a divisional commander rather than the commanding general of the 1st Corps. Consequently, he sent an officer to Quatre Bras carrying this order and demanding instructions that others, put in his position, would not have hesitated to carry out.

… This intense struggle [Ligny], that we were able to follow through its various phases by the rising and falling intensity of the firing, electrolysed our soldiers; they impatiently awaited the moment that they would enter the fray, and they expressed their surprise in loud voices that they remained with downed arms when their assistance would render such great services. This order, carried and given in the presence of the whole of the head of the 4th Division, but ignored, was, shortly after, followed by a second so imperative, that General Durutte finally took the resolution to execute it.

Everything was ready for the attack, which we awaited with the highest enthusiasm; but our hopes were to be dashed. [Chapuis goes on to explain the prevarication of Durutte and the excuses he used not to launch his division into the fray] … During this interval, we watched the Prussian corps quietly executing their retreat, of which not a single man would have escaped us. Also, since the two *voltigeur* companies of the 85th, supported by the grenadier company that I commanded, penetrated into the hamlet of Wagnelé at the end of the day, these companies only found there a weak rearguard which made little resistance before retiring.

Master of this position, the 4th Division established itself there.

Whilst this position was being taken, an angrier scene was taking place between our divisional commander, Durutte, and our brigade commander, Brue. The latter, frustrated at the hesitation of his superior, criticised him loudly. He shouted, 'It is intolerable that we witness the retreat of a beaten army and do nothing, when everything indicates that if it was attacked it would be destroyed.'

General Durutte could only offer as an excuse in response to General Brue; 'It is lucky for you that you are not responsible!'

'I wish to God that I was' said this last, 'we would already be fighting!'

This altercation was overheard by the senior officers of the 85th that were at the head of the regiment … It proved, besides, to those who reflected on it, that an enormous fault had been committed in employing certain chiefs for whom, for many years, the words 'glory' and 'la Patrie' no longer had the same significance as to their subordinates.

This suspicion received further confirmation when we learnt the next day, the 17th, that Colonel Gordon, chief-of-staff of the 4th Division, and *chef de bataillon* Gaugler, first ADC to General Durutte, had passed to the enemy the previous morning[9] and this had been hidden from us for the last twenty four hours [He goes on to say that this was interpreted as implicating Durutte himself as he worked so closely with them]. The desertion of two men in positions so close to General Durutte, his hesitation a few hours later to execute orders which previously he would have done quickly, produced such an impression on the 85th Regiment, that it took all the efforts of the officers to restore the soldiers' morale.[10]

Chapuis's view was endorsed by *maréchal de camp* Brue, who later wrote in a letter:

If General Durutte had attacked the Prussian army at the moment when, beaten at Ligny and retiring, this army would have been annihilated; all those who were not killed would have been forced to lay down their arms and would have been captured.[11]

It might be considered doubtful that an infantry division and three regiments of cavalry might have had this much impact on the outcome of the battle of Ligny, particularly as it was made by someone who might be accused of promoting his own contribution to the debate. However, the Prussian right was occupied by Zieten's I Corps, the corps that had already taken quite heavy casualties during the day before, had borne the brunt of fighting during that day and was withdrawing in a state of some disorganisation. Pressed more rigorously by Durutte, there is certainly an argument that this corps may have been so disorganised that it was unable to take any further part in the campaign. The claim that the whole army would have been destroyed is certainly fanciful.

Whilst Durutte dithered, the rest of the 1st Corps retraced its route back to Quatre Bras, arriving tired and frustrated just as darkness fell and the fighting had come to an end.

D'Erlon's Dilemma – Analysis
French writers generally agree that if Ligny had been a decisive victory for Napoleon, Waterloo would not have been fought and the campaign could have been won. The reason they give for why Ligny was not a decisive victory is that d'Erlon's 1st Corps did not make the contribution Napoleon planned, and it is hard to deny that if the 1st Corps had continued its march to the battlefield a major part of the Prussian army could well have been destroyed. Equally, if d'Erlon's 20,000 men had continued their original march and

arrived at Quatre Bras at about 5pm, it is also possible that Wellington could have been overwhelmed. It is therefore unsurprising that the French post-mortem of the events of the day has focussed on this issue. Although we can only speculate on just how decisive d'Erlon's arrival at either battlefield would have been, we can make a considered judgement, based on the considerable evidence that is available, on who was really to blame for this catastrophic failure.

There is no doubt that Napoleon's basic strategic plan was excellent and based on a sound anticipation of the likely reactions of his opponents, the natural aggression and urge to engage of Blücher and a certain caution in Wellington. However, at the end of the 15th, and even well into the morning of the 16th, the situation was not so clear that Napoleon was confident that a major battle was going to be fought against the Prussians. Therefore his plan evolved with the developing situation and it was only at about three o'clock, after his reconnaissance of the Prussian position, that he fully developed the idea of a part of Ney's force falling on the right rear of the Prussians. Napoleon cannot be accused of coming up with the plan too late for its execution.

By 3pm Napoleon expected Ney to have seized Quatre Bras in pursuance of his previous orders, and would have been able to march d'Erlon's corps down the Nivelles to Namur road, which would have brought him onto the Prussian right rear. However, as we have seen, at that time d'Erlon had not yet reached the battlefield of Quatre Bras, let alone been able to take the route Napoleon expected. This was the result of Ney's failure to concentrate his entire force and seize the vital crossroads, but this might not have been significant if d'Erlon had pursued his course from Villers-Perwin; this would have brought him onto the Prussian flank, rather than right rear, but still early enough to strike a telling blow. Even the delay that this unexpected direction of advance had on the launching of Napoleon's final attack need not have prevented a significant contribution if he had not turned back towards Quatre Bras, leaving only a relatively small force with orders to be cautious close to the Ligny battlefield.

If Ney had already concentrated his wing when Napoleon's orders arrived, the 1st Corps would have been close to, or even on the battlefield; he might even have been partially committed. But at least Ney would have been better placed to decide how to proceed. Whilst he may well have decided to ignore the order, he would also have had the ability to adapt the way he was fighting, perhaps by going on to the defensive, and to take the final decision on whether he could afford to send d'Erlon to Napoleon. But at least he would not have been put in such a difficult position at a critical time in his own battle. In a calmer state of mind, he might well have realised the importance of supporting Napoleon whilst he blocked Wellington and could also have conferred with all his key commanders. It is still impossible to conclude that he would have sent d'Erlon, but at least he would have had the opportunity to make a far more rational and considered decision.

In his book *Swords Around a Throne*, the respected American author, John Elting, suggests Ney was badly hungover on the 16th, having stayed the previous night at an inn with a reputation for a good wine cellar, and that this accounts for his lethargic performance. However, this is mere speculation as no eyewitnesses, supporters or detractors, mention it. But as we have already discussed, Ney's personal situation was certainly a difficult one, and there is plenty of evidence that he was distracted. Colonel Crabbé, who had been sent to Ney by Napoleon, wrote:

> He hardly returned my salute, read his orders without saying a word and dismissed me.
>
> He appeared very demoralised, without willpower, almost lacking courage and resolution. I had a disagreeable impression.[12]

Later, Baudus described Ney exclaiming in the heat of battle, 'What! Is there neither a bullet nor a ball for me!'[13]

When Ney heard about the march of d'Erlon's corps towards Ligny, his frustration can be well understood; he was impatiently awaiting its arrival at Quatre Bras to turn the tide of that battle in his favour, his attacks up to that point having been countered by the opportune arrival of a succession of allied reinforcements. However, he should not have been too surprised by Napoleon's actions. After all, just that morning the emperor had twice referred to the option he reserved of drawing on the troops of one wing to strengthen his own, writing in his letter to the marshal, 'You should dispose your troops in the following manner: the first division at two leagues in advance of Quatre Bras, if there is no hindrance; six divisions of infantry about Quatre Bras, and one division at Marbais, *so that I may draw them to me at Sombreffe if I want them*' [my emphasis] and 'I shall draw troops from one wing to strengthen my reserve'.

We can also see that Napoleon, convinced that d'Erlon's manoeuvre would deliver the crushing victory over the Prussians that he desired, sent a number of officers to ensure this march was carried out. Laurent, Forbin-Janson, Baudus, Crabbé and Labédoyère are all mentioned by eyewitnesses or in their own accounts as having done so. Although it is suspected that naming Labédoyère was a mistake on d'Erlon's part, the rest all seem genuine enough. Surely, such a succession of staff officers from the emperor's headquarters should have been enough to convince Ney not to overturn Napoleon's orders, even if they had been delivered in an unconventional way in bypassing the chain-of-command. Although the written orders carried by Forbin-Janson did not reach Ney until the evening, the other messengers would also have been briefed not only to deliver a written order, but also to impress on Ney the importance of d'Erlon's march. We have heard Baudus's brief from

Napoleon and its clarity in impressing on him the secondary importance of a victory over Wellington, and as another example we may refer to General Flahaut's mission in the morning; he wrote:

> But as regards orders for the movement of troops, I was directed to give them to Marshal Ney by word of mouth. I therefore gave him as from the emperor the order to move to Quatre Bras, to hold this important point in strength and (should the enemy allow him to do so) to support with every man at his disposal the emperor's offensive against the Prussian army.[14]

Though his frustration may be understood, we must conclude that Ney totally failed to grasp the critical importance of d'Erlon's march towards Ligny and made a fatal error in demanding its return.

Heymès wrote of Quatre Bras:

> One can see that with 17,000 men, plus Kellerman's brigade of cuirassiers, the marshal had come close to victory and that one can judge what would have been achieved if the 1st Corps had arrived![15]

However, Heymès is missing the point. Napoleon had made it clear that the action at Quatre Bras was of little importance if he succeeded in destroying the Prussian army. Napoleon never planned to fight two major battles on the same day and Wellington's army was in no danger of being destroyed. Two partial victories were no use to him; he needed to concentrate sufficient force against one enemy army in order to destroy it and then turn on the other. This was always his aim and Ney was well aware of it. Ney's mission was not to defeat Wellington's army, but to seize Quatre Bras to facilitate the move of part of his force to ensure the destruction of the Prussians. This in turn would prevent any of Wellington's troops supporting Blücher. Ney was angry and frustrated at losing the services of d'Erlon's troops and it is clear he did not fully grasp the importance of the opportunity that Napoleon had been offered at Ligny. But it is also true to say that both he and Colonel Heymès were guilty of not keeping Napoleon informed of the situation on the left wing, despite Soult writing at 2pm, 'Immediately inform the emperor of your dispositions and what is happening to your front.' There is no evidence that Ney passed any information to Napoleon upon which the emperor could base a considered decision.

Ney was clearly so absorbed in his own battle that he catastrophically failed to understand the strategic importance of d'Erlon intervening at Ligny. His decision to recall his subordinate was rash and made in frustration and anger, not the cool, detached and calculating demeanour of an experienced senior commander.

We must now examine the decision making of Count d'Erlon. If Ney had made a rash and ill-considered decision to recall d'Erlon, this general, a very experienced commander, still had the opportunity to use his own judgement and initiative and decide which course he should follow. By his own account, he claims he was not involved in the decision to turn towards Ligny because this change of direction was made in his absence; he claims he had ridden ahead of his own troops towards Quatre Bras. He was later to claim that the emperor's ADC had no authority to change the march of his corps without his own consent, but even if it was the relatively junior and inexperienced Forbin-Janson who ordered this, d'Erlon's position is not sound.

A commander's personal staff officers (ADCs and *officiers d'ordonnance*) spoke with their superior officer's authority, despite the fact that they were almost inevitably delivering an order to an officer of higher rank and experience than themselves. Napoleon's ADCs certainly had the authority and influence to take the initiative and give orders and had done so throughout the Napoleonic wars. Any senior officer was risking Napoleon's wrath if he ignored or contravened orders given by one of the emperor's personal staff officers. Having said that, Forbin-Janson was an unfortunate choice for such a critical mission and perhaps he should not be blamed for an inability to expand on the message he was carrying.

In his own analysis of the campaign, Ropes feels that d'Erlon made the claim that he was not with his troops when their march was diverted to absolve himself of any responsibility for his corps making this move without the consent or knowledge of his immediate commander (Marshal Ney). However, in his second account, d'Erlon writes,

> There is no doubt that if the emperor had addressed his orders directly to me, as he said in several accounts of this battle, they would have been punctually executed and that this battle (Ligny) would have had the most important results.[16]

This suggests that d'Erlon blames the mix-up on the fact that Napoleon's orders were addressed to Ney and therefore, until Ney had ordered the move, no one should have taken it upon themselves to redirect the march of his corps. He clearly states that if the orders had been addressed to him, he would have carried them out without hesitation. But it seems clear that Napoleon did address his orders directly to d'Erlon and ordered Forbin-Janson to then deliver them to Ney to keep him informed. He had taken this sensible step to inform the marshal of what he was doing, but would certainly not have expected him to countermand his orders.

In the protocol and standard military procedures of the day, the chain of command must always be followed to avoid just this sort of misunderstanding and mix-up. However, there are many occasions when standard operating procedure was ignored and individuals used their initiative. When this turned out for the good, it was conveniently overlooked, but when it had bad results, as in this case, the blame is quickly laid at the door of the officer concerned.

A useful example is the concentration of Perponcher's division at Quatre Bras in direct contravention of Wellington's orders; this disobedience of orders was overlooked by Wellington, normally a stickler for military protocol, because it certainly avoided a crucial strategic mistake that could have had huge consequences. If d'Erlon's corps had continued to Ligny and sealed a crushing victory for Napoleon, having been directed there on the initiative of Forbin-Janson, both these officers would have become national heroes; in the event both have been desecrated.

But ultimately, we must put aside the various means by which the orders were delivered. The fact is that Napoleon's orders made it clear that d'Erlon's corps was to play an absolutely pivotal role in the destruction of the Prussian army, and yet d'Erlon decided to put Ney's orders before those of the emperor. What's more, by the time he received Ney's orders to return, d'Erlon must have realised that if he turned back towards Quatre Bras he would hardly arrive before it got dark and he would be too late to make any contribution at all. By continuing his march towards Ligny, he still had a chance to strike a telling blow. Whatever the circumstances, d'Erlon catastrophically failed to make a rational and fully considered decision that had fatal consequences for the outcome of the campaign.

Even d'Erlon's compromise course of leaving Durutte's division with cavalry support might have been able to make a significant contribution, if ultimately less decisive, if his prevarication had not led him to urge caution on his subordinate.

Durutte's inactivity on the periphery of the battlefield is perhaps understandable given the orders he had received from his senior commander to be cautious. The frustration of his troops, and even his junior commanders, is also understandable, although doubtlessly fuelled in part by their suspicion of his complicity in the desertion of his chief-of-staff. However, what is less explicable is the fact that, whilst hovering on the edge of the battlefield, watching the disordered withdrawal of the Prussians before him, that he did not send an officer to Napoleon, giving details of his strength and location and seeking orders. Some 4,000 relatively fresh infantry, about 1,000 cavalry and two batteries must have been capable of making a significant impression on an exhausted, withdrawing force. Although some Prussian units had maintained their cohesion, some had clearly not; a Prussian unit commander wrote:

> The enemy pursuit broke off, but all order had been lost. Even individual sections could not maintain order in that terrain ... There was no chance to rally the men, because everybody was being carried along in a great stream of humanity ... The retreat went in wild disorder to the village of Tilly ...[17]

Even Hofschröer, a renowned Prussian apologist, wrote, 'The command structure of the Prussian army had now broken down.'[18] Durutte's relatively small force could undoubtedly have struck a telling blow if, even constrained from immediate action by d'Erlon's entreaties to be cautious, he had sought direction from Napoleon; the thrust of whose orders can easily be imagined. Well might French historians speculate on what the whole of d'Erlon's 20,000 men could have achieved.

Ney and d'Erlon must share the blame for the catastrophic failure of the 1st Corps to intervene at either battle. Ney made a rash and illogical decision to recall the corps to Quatre Bras, where its intervention would not have had the strategic advantages Napoleon so desperately sought. D'Erlon made an equally irrational decision to turn away from the battle where the strategic gain would have been incalculable and return towards a battlefield that he could not reach in time to intervene and where tactical defeat was irrelevant if the Prussian army had been destroyed.

Chapter 15

Evening

When the fighting died down the French units found themselves on the line from which they had begun their attack in the morning; from the Laraille farm, along the heights of that name, past the Balcan inn and across the main road down to Grand Pierrepont. Along this line a chain of outposts was established to provide security and the main body fell back around Frasnes. It may be remembered that Colonel Jolyet's 1st Battalion of the 1st *légère* had occupied Grand Pierrepont at the end of the fighting, but he understandably felt somewhat isolated and as he was unsure of where the rest of the regiment was he decided to withdraw under the cover of darkness:

> Then [when it got dark] I started my retreat and I was soon joined by our colonel [Cubiérès] who had been wounded at the beginning of the assault and who, despite this, came to find us. He told me that the rest of the corps was camped behind Frasnes. After having recalled the 2nd Battalion which had remained on the edge of the wood, we re-joined the rest of the corps.[1]

For the soldiers, the priority now was to see to their wounded and get something to eat. Casualty figures are generally consistent in all accounts; the French lost about 4,200 (Gourgaud gives 4,020) and Wellington's army about 500 more. General Foy wrote:

> My division had done well on this day; it had lost more than 800 men killed and wounded seriously enough to end their campaign. The other two divisions had lost 1,100 to 1,200 each. The troops had almost no rations.[2]

Gourgaud gives the casualties of Guiton's cuirassier brigade as 300 out of the 770 (its strength on the day varies slightly between sources). The French archives give the casualties for the 6th Chasseurs for the campaign as 297 men out of 560 at its commencement. As Piré's division was only lightly engaged at Waterloo we can safely say that the majority of these casualties were sustained at Quatre Bras. These are a very high proportion of casualties for cavalry units, which tended to suffer less than their infantry counterparts; they are testament to the determination and high morale of these regiments.

On the allied side it was the British infantry battalions that suffered most; the highest percentage of casualties was suffered by the 42nd who lost 55 per cent of their strength (288 of 526) as the French lancers nearly broke their square; the 92nd lost 48 per cent in their gallant counter-attack through La Bergerie. Given their relatively short involvement in the battle, the 2nd and 3rd Battalions of the 1st Guards also lost very heavily in the Bossu wood (285 and 262 respectively, from 976 and 1,021 according to Siborne). All these units were heavily engaged two days later at Waterloo.

The effect on the survivors of these units can be imagined, but for many, the priority now was food. Unlike the British troops, who were generally well provisioned, the French were given only basic rations which they had to supplement themselves. It will be remembered that Napoleon had specified that each soldier should be issued two days' rations on the 15th, but many had thrown them away to lighten their load, and we have already heard how many provisions had been lost with the 1st Corps baggage. The soldiers had to therefore find what they could to eat.

> The wounded were bandaged and bivouacs established. Unfortunately they had no rations; the soldiers started to spread out across the country-side to maraud ...[3]

As they arrived at Frasnes, the tired and frustrated troops of the 1st Corps passed some of the wounded:

> Occupying our new bivouac, we noticed on the edge of the road a young soldier, or rather part of a man, for the unfortunate had had both legs taken off by a cannon ball! His wounds had not been treated, someone had only tried to stop the bleeding by wrapping the wounds with a shirt. This poor man also had signs of recent wounds to the face and chest. He must have had extraordinary strength to have survived his wounds and the loss of blood that had resulted. Seeing us passing close by, he raised himself on his hands excitedly and shouted in a loud voice, '*Vive l'empereur*! I have lost both my legs, I am finished! Victory is ours! *Vive l'empereur*!' The face, the words of this brave man who, without doubt, died unaware of what happened, have remained engraved in my memory, and, as I write these lines, I still cannot master my emotions at the memory of the sentiments of patriotism so courageously expressed.[4]

The men of this corps were particularly unhappy; they had missed the battle and lost their rations and baggage.

> Night brought an end to the rout of the baggage as it did to the battle; but the damage caused by this panic could not be repaired; everything that had been abandoned or thrown onto the route was pillaged by the drivers who had not fled or had not been as scared as the others; nothing escaped their rapacity; the trunks and *porte manteaux* of the headquarters were all empty, first to last, and the rations spread out on the road or in the fields were lost entirely ...[5]

Their late arrival meant it was a double blow for the exhausted soldiers of these units as their search for food started after that of those who had fought through the day.

Arriving at our destination we took off our packs and stacked our arms; then some bands of men left marauding. I took four men with me and we went off on an adventure, leaving our muskets in the care of our friends. There is an old proverb that says it is very difficult to comb a devil that has no hair; *ma foi*, I think that it was even more difficult to find something to eat, for every house, every barn that we visited had already been visited by others. [Finally they found a ruined barn with a sack of flour inside and returned covered in flour to the amusement of their friends.][6]

Having not fired a shot during the day, the soldiers of the 1st Corps also took over the security outposts:

On the return of my corps to Frasnes, I took responsibility for the advance posts, relieving the 2nd Corps which had suffered much. We learnt during the night that the battle at Ligny had forced the Prussian army to retreat.[7]

The minds of the senior officers also turned to supper:

The marshal invited Prince Jérôme to supper. The table consisted of a plank supported on two empty barrels and lit by candles stuck into the neck of empty bottles. Night had come.[8]

But the marshal's supper was to be interrupted; finally, after the battle and the day had finished, Colonel Forbin-Janson had returned to complete the mission he had so catastrophically failed to complete earlier in the day.

We began our frugal meal when Count Forbin-Janson was brought before Ney carrying the order from the emperor to march on Bry ... M. Forbin-Janson arrived with us when it was dark, since we had started supper by candlelight. It was too late to make the move that was ordered; besides, the 1st Corps had still not reached us ... Thus this order arrived six hours too late and nothing could be done without d'Erlon's participation.[9]

We are not told how he was received and it is quite possible that the storyteller, Prince Jérôme's ADC, was not aware of the full background to the affair.

After his repulse and the continuous reinforcement of Wellington's army through the afternoon and evening, it was now quite possible that Ney was facing 60–70,000 men; it was perfectly feasible that he might face an allied offensive the next morning. He had not received any news about the outcome of the action around Ligny and at this stage could not be absolutely sure that Napoleon would come to his aid. He felt sufficiently concerned to take some precautions in the event of Wellington attacking him at daybreak. At midnight he called for *chef de bataillon* Répécaud of the 2nd Corps engineers, and ordered him:

> To return immediately to Gosselies with several engineer officers and two companies of *sapeurs*, to erect some defences. The marshal anticipated that he might have need of defences to resist, in case of retreat, an enemy of superior strength, not knowing that the Prussians had been forced from their position at Ligny.[10]

However, soon after, Ney had the party recalled. We do not know why the order was rescinded. It is possible that Ney had been informed of the outcome at Ligny, and, realising that the threat was now considerably reduced, he cancelled the order, but most accounts claim Ney did not know about the victory at Ligny until the next morning.

Most of the earlier accounts of the campaign claim that Ney did not send a report on the battle to Imperial Headquarters and concluded that this was due to Ney's frustration at having lost the use of d'Erlon's corps and the consequent loss of the battle. Some, those sympathetic to Napoleon, used the lack of information as an excuse for the emperor's apparent hesitation and waste of time the following morning. However, General Albert Pollio, an Italian who wrote his own history in 1905, includes in his book the following report, written to Soult by Ney, including a facsimile copy of the original:

> Frasnes, 16 June, 10pm.
>
> Marshal, I have attacked the English position at Quatre Bras with the greatest vigour; but an error of Count d'Erlon's deprived me of a fine victory, for at the very moment when the 5th and 9th Divisons of General Reille's corps had overthrown everything in front of them, the 1st Corps marched off to St Amand to support His Majesty's left; but the really fatal thing was that this corps, having then counter-marched to rejoin my wing, gave no useful assistance on either field.
>
> Prince Jérôme's division fought with great valour; His Royal Highness has been slightly wounded.
>
> Actually there have been engaged here only three infantry divisions, a brigade of cuirassiers and General Piré's cavalry. The Count of Valmy delivered a fine charge. All have done their duty except the 1st Corps.
>
> The enemy has lost heavily; we have captured some guns and a colour.
>
> We have lost only about 2,000 killed and 4,000 wounded. I have called for reports from Generals Reille and d'Erlon and will forward them to Your Excellency.
>
> *Maréchal Prince de la Moskowa*, Ney[11]

From the time given, this report was clearly written immediately after the battle had finished and his blistering criticism of d'Erlon's corps and, by inference, d'Erlon himself, probably accurately reflects Ney's frustration and anger. Even nearly a week after the cataclysmic defeat at Waterloo, Ney was still smarting from his defeat, writing to Police Minister Fouché on 26 June:

> On the 16th I received the order to attack the English in their position of Quatre Bras; we marched on the enemy with an enthusiasm that is difficult to describe: nothing could resist our determination. The battle became general and our victory was not in doubt, when at the moment when I was going to advance the 1st Corps, which until then had been left by me in reserve at Frasnes, I learnt that the General had deployed it without warning me, as well as Girard's division of the 2nd Corps, towards St Amand to support the right wing that was committed to action against the Prussians. The blow this struck me was terrible; having only three divisions under my orders, instead of the eight on which I counted, I was obliged to let victory escape and despite all my efforts, despite the devotion of my troops, I was then just able to maintain my position until the end of the day. Towards 9pm the 1st Corps was sent back to me by the Commander-in-Chief, to whom it had been of no utility. Thus 25 to 30,000 men had been effectively paralysed and marched throughout the battle with shouldered arms, from the left to the right, and the right to the left, without firing a shot ...[12]

Ney seems to have had no plan for the following morning and there is no evidence to suggest that he sent out any written orders. The recall of the engineers that had been sent back to Gosselies to prepare defences suggests that he had received at least a rumour of Napoleon's victory at Ligny, although subsequent communications suggest he had not heard officially. He had known for some time that once the emperor had disposed of the Prussians he planned to turn with his reserve to support him against the Anglo-Netherlands army, and so it seems the rumour of a victory was enough for him to await further orders before doing anything. We can safely presume that he briefed each of his senior commanders with the precautions to be taken for the night, but it seems difficult to believe that he made no provisional plans or preparations for the next day. It appears that the left wing settled down for the night just waiting for Napoleon to arrive the next day and launch a new assault on Wellington's now isolated troops. This inactivity, both in thought and action, reinforces the impression of an irresolute and lethargic Marshal Ney, in such contrast to the energy and aggression that had marked so much of his previous service.

Chapter 16

Analysis of the Battle

Tactical Conduct

General Albert Pollio, an Italian historian who wrote an excellent and objective account of the campaign, whilst often critical of Ney's performance, wrote:

> I hasten to add that in my opinion, the battle of Quatre Bras represents for the French one of the best tactical actions that military history relates, as much to the direction as to the execution.
>
> During seven hours of combat, Lord Wellington employed almost double the forces as those of the French and these forces were of excellent quality; and yet after seven hours, things were at the point where they had started.
>
> It is difficult to find in history a tactical direction more skilful, more masterly, more determined, more energetic, than that exercised by Marshal Ney on 16th June 1815.
>
> I firmly believe that no other general in the world could have achieved as much as this giant of battles that was Ney, and with such weak forces! The moral picture of this French general is dazzling!
>
> It is also difficult to imagine a more perfect unity in the action of the three arms, which invigorated this small French force that was immortalised during this day ...
>
> The courage and resistance displayed by the French troops was truly extraordinary.
>
> The performance of the French cavalry was also extraordinary, the cuirassiers as much as Piré's division, but the latter even more so than the former ... I am not aware of a more beautiful employment of cavalry, more tenacious, more intelligent than that of Marshal Ney and General Piré of these squadrons whose effect on this day, literally multiplied their number.[1]

This analysis seems to fly in the face of most assessments of the way the French fought this battle, so perhaps it is worth basing our own analysis on this passage.

Whilst Pollio's suggestion that Ney fought outnumbered for seven hours is misleading, it is certainly useful to examine the balance of forces as the battle progressed. The figures below show how both sides received reinforcements;

Time	French	Anglo-Netherlands
2pm	10,000 infantry, 2,000 cavalry, 42 guns (+Guard Cavalry 2,000, 'not to be used')	8,000 infantry, 0 cavalry and 16 guns
3pm	16,500 infantry, 2,777 cavalry, 50 guns (+Guard Cavalry 2,000)	13,000 infantry, 1,100 cavalry, 28 guns
4pm	16,500 infantry, 2,777 cavalry, 50 guns (+Guard Cavalry 2,000)	17,000 infantry, 2,000 cavalry, 28 guns
5pm	16,500 infantry, 2,777 cavalry, 50 guns (+Guard Cavalry 2,000)	22,500 infantry, 2,000 cavalry, 40 guns
6pm	16,500 infantry, 2,777 cavalry, 50 guns (+Guard Cavalry 2,000) (less casualties)	28,500 infantry, 2,000 cavalry, 68 guns (less casualties)

We can see that although Wellington was always outnumbered in cavalry, and also in guns until late in the afternoon, from 4pm he enjoyed an increasing superiority in infantry, and although it can be argued that some of his original force had become combat non-effective, the French had had to fight without any reinforcements from 3pm. It is somewhat surprising that from 5pm, when Wellington had an appreciable superiority in infantry, he did not become more aggressive in order to open the Namur road and endeavour to support the Prussians by putting the French under more pressure. Ney's aggressive tactics no doubt had something to do with this and kept Wellington on the defensive until shortly before the end of the battle.

Whilst Ney stands accused of not attacking much earlier than he did, when he had an appreciable advantage in numbers, there is no doubt that, during the battle, Wellington received timely reinforcements at the two most critical moments. Without the arrival of Picton and the Brunswickers at about 3.30pm, Ney would undoubtedly have taken Quatre Bras, and two hours later Wellington was again saved by the arrival of Alten. Twice Ney had come within a whisker of winning the battle.

Pollio also praises the combined arms approach used by Ney. Whilst it is fair to say that each of the three arms fought well, and in the case of the cavalry and artillery outstandingly well, it is hard to agree that all three combined to best effect. The aim of combined arms tactics is that each compliments the other, making best use of their strengths whilst compensating for each others' shortcomings, so that their combined effectiveness is greater than the sum of their individual parts. Thus the artillery prepares the attack by concentrating its fire on the point selected for the assault and causing heavy casualties; the cavalry advances to force the enemy infantry into square, in which formation they become more vulnerable to artillery fire and are at the mercy of an infantry assault; the enemy breaks and the cavalry pursue.

Allied accounts all describe the accuracy and overwhelming firepower of the French artillery and it has already been shown that for much of the battle the French had a much higher number of guns available than the allies. It is especially noticeable how effective their guns were in counter-battery fire. The use of the Bossu wood by the allies to hide their troops, the undulating ground and the tall crops, all made engaging infantry targets difficult. The French artillery therefore seemed to concentrate their fire on the most easily identifiable targets, their allied counterparts. Dutch and British accounts describe a number of guns dismounted, limbers and caissons destroyed and high casualties in both gun crew and horses, all of which seems to fly in face of the commonly accepted view that counter-battery fire was not especially effective.

The French artillery also showed an impressive desire to manoeuvre and they were quick to move guns forward as ground was secured by the infantry advance in order to engage the allied line at shorter range. They were helped by the rolling terrain, the low ridges which offered good fire positions and allowed them to shoot over the heads of their infantry. The power of the French artillery contributed to the repulse of Picton's attack and ensured the allied counter-attack at the end of the battle remained slow and cautious. The fact that Quatre Bras was not a typical Wellingtonian position, with most of his force hidden in dead ground behind a ridge, exposed more of his force and allowed the French guns to manoeuvre closer to his main line.

Pollio rightly commends the handling and courage of the French cavalry and particularly Piré's lancers and chasseurs. These showed an aggression and courage which quickly earned the respect and admiration of the allied infantry. Perhaps only at Albuera did the French cavalry so roughly handle British infantry. Piré commanded his division with great daring, exploiting every opportunity to charge and making repeated efforts to break the allied squares, coming close to succeeding on a number of occasions. Several batteries were overrun and battalions ridden down, although French casualties were high. It is true that there were only inferior numbers of allied cavalry to oppose them and these were inevitably overwhelmed, leaving the allied infantry with little dependable cavalry support and giving Piré's troopers freedom to manoeuvre, but this should not detract from an admirable performance.

A study of what detail we know of the fighting also reveals a tactical innovation used by Piré that does not appear to have been seen on a previous battlefield. This was the way in which the chasseurs and lancers were used to complement each other. Although brigaded separately, almost all accounts reveal one regiment of chasseurs appearing to operate with one of lancers. Thus it seems that the chasseurs were used in front, to break the momentum of the opposing charge or disorder an infantry unit, and the lancers followed up to exploit the discomfited unit; a task well suited to lancers who were always most effective when the opposition had lost their close formation, as the Union Brigade were to find out at Waterloo. Tactical innovation will be seen again in the way the French fought during this battle.

Kellerman's cuirassiers made a much briefer, but no less impressive, contribution to the battle than Piré's light cavalry. Leaving them no time to reflect on what they were being asked to do, Kellerman led them in an all-out charge that smashed into the very centre of the allied line. The French cavalry rarely charged at more than a trot, but the circumstances were exceptional; just two regiments, counting less than 800 sabres, launched a virtually unsupported charge against nearly 30,000 men. The charge managed to destroy the 2/69th Regiment and capture one of their colours. Several other British infantry regiments were thrown into disorder, a battery was overrun and the cuirassiers came close to breaking right through the allied line, reaching Quatre Bras itself. Whilst the courage and determination of this fine cavalry must be applauded, and whilst Piré's exhausted troopers charged again in its support, crucially it was not well seconded by the infantry and its final repulse and panicked flight should not overshadow its achievements. Indeed, given the lack of support, Kellerman described its flight in the following words, 'The brigade, having suffered enormous casualties, and seeing itself without support, retired in the disorder inevitable in such circumstances.'[2]

In his own study of cavalry in the Waterloo campaign, General Sir Evelyn Wood VC also lavishly praises the French cavalry for their battlefield performance at Quatre Bras. However, he is less complimentary about their failure to carry out their primary role as light cavalry: reconnaissance.[3] Piré's cavalry were one of Ney's foremost elements on the morning of Quatre Bras and well placed to send out patrols in order to give Ney a full description of the strength and deployment of the small allied force there. Given the relatively narrow frontage that the Prince of Orange was covering and his lack of cavalry, Piré's troops had plenty of time and opportunity to outflank the Netherlands force and gather sufficient information to allow Ney to have made some much better-informed decisions on when and how to act. Indeed, this single, apparently small point, could well have changed the result of the day.

A study of French infantry tactics at Quatre Bras seems to reveal a unique way of operating, which suggests there had been some tactical discussion prior to the battle on how to counter the British tactics that had so often bettered them in Spain. Ney, Reille and Foy (as well as d'Erlon) had all fought the British there and it would be surprising if such a discussion had not taken place. During the Peninsular War, Wellington had developed a tactical system designed to counter the French tactics that had been so successful against the other military powers of Europe: a thick line of skirmishers countered the French skirmish line and prevented the French from knowing the exact deployment of the main British line, which was hidden on the reverse slope of a ridge or some high ground. This would only reveal itself at the last moment, pour in one or more devastating volleys and then charge downhill with bayonets lowered against a surprised and staggered enemy.

As always the French infantry displayed much courage and élan, fighting hard right up to the end of the battle when they were considerably outnumbered. However, whilst the French artillery and cavalry quickly earned the respect of the allied soldiers, the ubiquitous French infantry columns always seem to be described as hovering in the background rather than pressing forward their attack.

The most successful and commented on tactic of the French infantry was the effectiveness of their skirmishers. All allied accounts describe the heavy casualties taken by officers and gun crews; as an example, in the British 44th Regiment, Colonel O'Malley, the commanding officer, was the only unwounded field officer in the battalion, and of twenty-five officers present, only the colonel and six others were untouched: by the end of the battle, four companies were commanded by sergeants. The *tirailleurs* fought in numbers that overwhelmed their allied counterparts, and as they never seemed to be able to achieve this in five years in Spain, it is hard not to conclude that a greater number were deployed as a deliberate effort to achieve this. This then left them free to cause attrition on the main allied line, aiming specifically at officers to weaken the cohesion and resolve of the enemy units. When these felt sufficiently weakened or threatened, they withdrew; the French *tirailleurs* would follow them up, giving them no respite, whilst the following columns would occupy the ground recently surrendered. The columns themselves appear to have done little fighting, but were merely used to occupy ground and reinforce the skirmisher screen as required. But most importantly, the columns were uncommitted and available to counter any sudden appearance of the main British force which had unfailingly caught them out in the Peninsula.

The key problem with these tactics is that a screen of skirmishers, no matter how strong, is never likely to be decisive. At Quatre Bras they were successful against the inexperienced troops of the Netherlands and Brunswick units, but not so against the British. In order to break an enemy's will to resist it either needs to have suffered an unbearable level of casualties due to heavy volley fire, or its cohesion must be shattered by a failure to meet an opponent's mass that threatens to overwhelm it. Skirmisher fire was annoying and might cause significant casualties amongst officers, but this was unlikely to break a unit's cohesion, just as it lacked sufficient mass and momentum to enter or threaten a decisive hand-to-hand fight. Thus this type of advance might push the enemy back, but was unlikely to break him, and, particularly significant for the French on this day, the advance was likely to be a slow one. Ney needed a quick, decisive attack if he was going to seize Quatre Bras before Wellington had concentrated sufficient troops to deny it to him; this secure, but rather laboured approach was unlikely to achieve his aim.

In stark contrast to both the cavalry and artillery, and even their own skirmisher screen, the infantry columns seem to have been handled with caution. Whilst the French skirmishers outperformed their allied counterparts, the battle re-emphasised the superiority of the British infantry over their French equivalents. This was not just a tactical issue, the superiority of the line over the column, but also a moral one. The British had clearly not lost the moral ascendency that they had acquired in the Peninsula, and always seemed to have the confidence that they would win whatever the French threw at them. It may be that there were times when things were not looking good for the British troops, but whenever they were called upon to hold firm or move forward, whatever the odds, they always seemed to answer the call. The French infantry were noted for their élan and enthusiasm, and this is noted by many allied eyewitnesses, and yet when they launched what appeared to be their main attack, virtually the whole of Bachelu's division was thrown back by three British battalions. Without wishing to denigrate the young and relatively inexperienced Dutch and Brunswick battalions, they were overwhelmed by the French, but despite their apparent élan, the French columns appear to have lacked the determination and resilience to really come to grips with the British infantry, and this lost them the battle.

Both allied and French eyewitnesses describe the French infantry using line in both the advance and in defence; this was virtually unheard of in Spain and perhaps reflects another effort to counter British fire superiority by those French commanders who fought them there. Without it being mentioned specifically, this may suggest the French use of *ordre mixte*, a formation favoured by Napoleon which was an attempt to exploit the firepower of the line and the momentum and mass of the column (see Figure 2). An allied account of the battle describes some of Foy's troops advancing 'a battalion in line, supported by two columns', suggesting this was the formation used.

But perhaps the most notable failure of the French infantry was their reluctance to advance in support of the cavalry. Both Piré's and Kellerman's troopers achieved considerable success in disordering a number of battalions and pinning others in square where they would have been vulnerable to an infantry assault. This was a failure of co-ordination. Piré's main charge was an opportunistic one and Kellerman's was hastily launched, but both Ney and the infantry divisional commanders failed to spot the opportunity and launch a determined infantry assault when the allies were most vulnerable. The failure of the infantry to support the attacks of the cavalry undermines Pollio's praise for the combined arms aspects of the battle and is reminiscent of the great cavalry charges that were to come at Waterloo.

Ney's direction of the battle is also interesting. Once again we see his legendary heroism and courage; prepared to expose himself to the hottest fire and always wanting to be in a position that gave him the best view of what was going on, urging his troops forward. But a truly effective commander needs

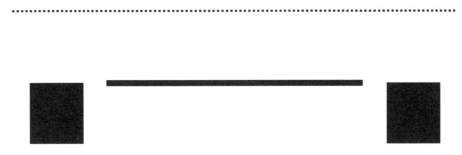

Figure 2. *Ordre Mixte.*

more than courage. At the beginning of the day, Ney's mission was to seize Quatre Bras, concentrate his entire wing around the crossroads and to defeat any allied troops that he encountered. By the afternoon, that mission had evolved; not least because Napoleon presumed that his first mission had been achieved. His new mission was that having seized Quatre Bras he was to send d'Erlon's 1st Corps onto the Prussian right rear at Ligny. It appears that Ney failed to achieve either of his stated missions.

After delivering the emperor's orders to Ney on the morning of the 16th, General Flahaut, the emperor's ADC, remained at the battle for the rest of the day and was thus a witness to proceedings. In his account of the campaign, Thiers writes:

> ... Count Flahaut, who had left Ney during the night after having witnessed the events at Quatre Bras, arrived at General Headquarters at 6am [on the morning of the 17th]. Without wishing to insult Ney, whose heroism touched even those who did not approve of his manner of operations, he did not conceal from the emperor how the dispositions of the marshal had been mediocre at the combat at Quatre Bras; how above all he seemed struck by agitation in his thoughts, adding that he was clearly energetic in his devotion, but that this affected the clarity of his military judgement ...[4]

Although Thiers should not normally be considered as authoritative, this account was specifically endorsed by Flahaut in a letter to Thiers dated London, 27 August 1862. From this passage we must assume that Flahaut was trying to respectfully say that Ney was not thinking or planning clearly and his direction of the battle was poor. Flahaut himself wrote:

> There was no cohesion to the affair. It was like attempting, as the saying goes, to 'take the bull by the horns'. Our forces were thrown into battle piecemeal as they arrived upon the scene, and in spite of the bravery they displayed no result was obtained.[5]

No doubt based on Flahaut's report, Napoleon had the following letter written to Ney the following morning:

> The emperor is disappointed that you did not concentrate your divisions yesterday; they acted individually and so you suffered casualties.
>
> If the corps of Counts d'Erlon and Reille had been together, not an Englishman of the corps that attacked you would have escaped. If the Count d'Erlon had executed the movement on Saint-Amand that the emperor had ordered, the Prussian army would have been totally destroyed and we would have made perhaps 30,000 prisoners.
>
> The corps of Generals Gérard, Vandamme and the Imperial Guard were always concentrated; one exposes oneself to a reverse when detachments are made.[6]

Strategic Issues

Napoleon's main criticism was that Ney had failed to concentrate his entire force and that if he had achieved this, Quatre Bras would have been taken and d'Erlon could have safely been sent to the emperor's support. In his memoirs, Napoleon identifies Ney's fundamental error:

> In other times, this general would have occupied the position before Quatre Bras at 6am, would have defeated and taken the whole Belgian division; and would have turned the Prussian army by sending a detachment by the Namur road which would have fallen upon the rear of the line of battle, or, by moving quickly on the Genappes road, he would have surprised the Brunswick Division and the 5th English Division on the march ... Always the first under fire, Ney forgot the troops who were not under his eye. The bravery which a general-in-chief ought to display is different from that which a divisional general must have, just as that of the latter ought not to be the same as that of a captain of grenadiers.[7]

Here we see Napoleon explaining that Ney had ignored or not grasped the bigger picture; the changing strategic situation and his part in it. In his growing frustration he entirely failed to understand and keep in mind what in modern military parlance is called his superior commander's intent; Napoleon's need to destroy the Prussian army. He thus failed to realise that, once Wellington's force was fixed in place around Quatre Bras, his part in achieving this was the despatch of d'Erlon's corps onto the Prussian rear and that he should have adapted his own operations to this end. We can only speculate on the reasons for this, but eyewitness accounts suggest it was his complete distraction with, and absorption in, what was happening in front of him, that resulted in his rash decision to recall d'Erlon without considering the wider consequences.

Ney was transfixed by the need to seize Quatre Bras, rather than the essential need to send d'Erlon to support Napoleon. Having failed to achieve the former, he should have considered how to achieve the latter, which had become the priority. It is therefore rather surprising how little emphasis was put on the eastern flank by either side and where there was little serious fighting. Yet for Ney, the Namur road was the key route for his despatch of a force to support Napoleon against the Prussians, as laid down in Napoleon's orders of the morning, just as it was the route down which the Prussians were expecting support from Wellington. Ney appears to have allocated fewer than four battalions to secure his eastern flank; far too small a force to clear the allied troops off it and keep it open for his own use. The fighting here was essentially an action between light infantry forces that was unlikely to be decisive for either side. Having failed to secure the route for d'Erlon, the next best thing would have been to send him down the road that he actually took on to the Prussian flank, but from which Ney recalled him.

Ney never appeared to claim any credit for stopping any of Wellington's army reinforcing the Prussians at Ligny; nor does he appear to have been given any credit for it by Napoleon. All he got from the latter, as we shall see later, was criticism. For Ney, an aggressive commander who liked to be in the front line, it seemed like a defeat and many of his officers and men felt the same (although much of the following comment by them was written with the benefit of hindsight). *Chef d'escadron* Lemonnier-Delafosse, Foy's chief-of-staff wrote:

> What precious time lost!
> At Quatre Bras on the 16th June, a battle was necessary, where, the day before, it would only have been an affair of the advance guard. On this day, in the morning, one could still have succeeded although it would have undoubtedly been more difficult: our troops were full of enthusiasm and could not have been stopped; containing their *élan* was an irreparable fault. Besides, the pressing orders of the emperor did not allow the marshal to remain in thought before the enemy; he wanted to make up for lost time and without making a proper reconnaissance of either the position or the strength of the English, he threw himself, head lowered, upon them ... Thus, by an inconceivable feebleness, one had fought to no advantage from 2pm until 9pm.[8]

Even more junior officers who fought there had similar views; Lieutenant Puvis of the 93rd Line penned similar criticism:

> It had seemed to us that with the spirit which animated our army, it would have been possible, without too much resistance to fear, to have seized the enemy position. Why was this not done? ... The old soldiers blamed the hesitation that Marshal Ney displayed before the position of Quatre Bras. Indeed, if he had taken the place the same day we would have gained a march on the enemy.[9]

The view of those supportive of Napoleon, and consequently critical of Ney, is best summed up by Colonel Combes-Brassard, the *sous chef-d'etat* of the 6th Corps, who, writing much later and having no doubt read all the accounts, wrote in his own history of the campaign:

> Marshal Ney was indecisive, irresolute in his attacks during the day of the battle of Ligny. This circumstance is strange in a man whose audacious determination in war was well known. His groping around before an enemy much weaker than himself was inexplicable in a general who was accustomed to saying that the only enemy he feared was the one he could not see.[10]

General Foy, however, seems to give a more balanced, if still rather downbeat, summary of the day:

> It was, at least with us, a poor start to the campaign. I do not know what passed elsewhere. Marshal Ney's attack had been hasty and lacking sense; one does not proceed thus against the English. We were able to colour this affair as we liked, for we had taken two cannon and the enemy had taken none of ours; he had suffered a greater loss than us thanks to the superiority of our artillery; we had maintained, to the end of the day, more ground than we had held before we started our attack. But these arguments are grabbing at straws. We had lost the battle, since we had been stopped from achieving our mission of seizing Quatre Bras.[11]

With the benefit of hindsight, his recall of d'Erlon was Ney's greatest failure on this day and probably cost Napoleon the campaign. However, we have already stated that Ney failed to achieve either of his two missions. This is not strictly true. In Napoleon's orders of the morning of the 16th, Ney's task was merely to advance to the Quatre Bras crossroads and to deploy his troops around it. However, at about the same time as he received these original orders, which did not suggest he would have to fight for the crossroads, he received another order from Napoleon which gave him much clearer direction;

> Concentrate the corps of Counts Reille and d'Erlon and that of Count Valmy, who is just marching to join you. With these forces you must engage and destroy all enemy forces that present themselves. Blücher was at Namur yesterday and it is unlikely that he has sent any troops towards Quatre Bras. Thus you will only have to deal with the forces coming from Brussels.

Whilst this direction is unequivocal, crucially it does not explain *why* the marshal should do this, beyond the original orders stating he should be ready for the emperor to join him and then march on Brussels. The unstated 'why' was that the occupation of Quatre Bras would prevent Wellington's army from marching to Blücher's aid and would allow Ney to send troops to Napoleon's support. In the former point Ney was entirely successful, causing Wellington considerable casualties into the bargain, but he failed in the latter. These were certainly Napoleon's aims, but he did not specify the former, only the latter in more general terms. Napoleon just expected Ney to obey his orders. We must not pretend that if Ney was clear he was to stop Wellington marching to the aid of the Prussians that he would have acted any differently, and as already stated, in this he was successful anyway. Whilst in modern battle procedure a subordinate would expect his mission statement to lay down what he had to achieve and why, we must make our judgement based on the processes and procedures of the day, and there can be little argument that Napoleon's orders were not clear.

Looking at the battle from Wellington's perspective, it was fought solely to give support to the Prussians, and in this he clearly failed. The result of the fighting was a repulse for the French, but for the allies it was a strategic failure. Wellington did not fight at Quatre Bras to deny Napoleon the support of part of Ney's force; that Ney recalled d'Erlon from his march was that marshal's disobedience of orders and his failure to fully understand the emperor's scheme. Most British writers conclude that the battle was a victory for Wellington and make no mention of his failure to support the Prussians, although Chesney at least admits, 'Truly, in holding his own, the great Englishman owed something that day to Fortune.'[12]

Ney's failure to concentrate his whole force, his poor decision-making and Wellington's constant trickle of reinforcements had prevented the French defeating the allied army at Quatre Bras. But Ney's job was to hold back the British and send support to Napoleon at Ligny. He succeeded in the former, but failed in the latter due to his rash and ill-considered decision to recall d'Erlon. But if it was not a French victory, neither was it an allied victory. Whilst Ney had failed to capture Quatre Bras and send a force to support Napoleon, so Wellington had singularly failed to carry out any manoeuvre that supported the Prussians as he intended and Blücher had requested. The French troops had fought well against increasing odds and had scored some notable successes, and the fact that history has marked the battle as a defeat has far more to do with Ney's command than the courage or fighting ability of his soldiers. It seems that real efforts were made by the French chain-of-command to adapt their tactics to counter those used by the British in Spain, and although they achieved some tactical success, significantly, they were unable to challenge the significant psychological advantage that the British continued to hold over them.

Chapter 17

The Morning of the 17th

The 17th dawned with no orders from Napoleon. All the French participants who left accounts are mysteriously silent on what they did first thing in the morning. No doubt for those soldiers who had marched all day on the 14th, marched and skirmished on the 15th, and fought throughout the day of the 16th, the rest would have been very welcome. The 1st Corps were providing the security, and d'Erlon wrote that morning:

> Dated 'in bivouac', before Frasnes, 17 June, morning.
> M. le Maréchal, conforming to the orders of His Majesty, the 1st Corps is holding the first line astride the Brussels road; the 1st Cavalry Division is covering its front and flanks.
>
> I have the honour to inform Your Excellency that the 1st Cavalry Division made a number of successful charges and that it captured a number of wagons and prisoners. [Presumably from the Prussians][1]

Colonel Heymès tells us 'On the morning of the 17th, the marshal had ordered his troops to be under arms early; he was himself at the advance posts first thing.'[2] Surprisingly, there is no other account of the rest of the left wing standing to and preparing to meet an allied counter-offensive. It is possible that Ney believed that Wellington would not dare to attack having learnt of the Prussian defeat, but this would seem to have been a risky assumption and it is not clear that Ney knew of the result of the previous day for certain either. Some in the 1st Corps were more worried about their baggage:

> On the 17th, sent in the morning by my general to look for our baggage, I travelled up and down the road taken by the fugitives without finding what I was looking for and without obtaining any information that would help me; returning once again to the road on which was spread all the broken trunks and rags, open *porte manteaux*, I found mine in the ditch next to the road on the right, but cut open by a knife along its entire length and turned inside out, I had lost all of my possessions, my papers and the little money that I possessed; and to complete my misery, my general and his second ADC had also lost their baggage and everything that we would need to look after ourselves.[3]

French accounts give no mention of any fighting or alarm, so we must turn to those of the allies to confirm that the outposts were active:

... a popping fire of musketry, apparently close at hand, aroused me again to consciousness of my situation ... From whatever the musketry might proceed we could see nothing – not even the flashes ... A smart skirmish was going on amongst the hedges, etc., already mentioned, and this was the firing we had heard all the morning. Our infantry were lying about, cleaning their arms, cooking, or amusing themselves, totally regardless of the skirmish ... After much firing from the edge of the wood, opposite which our riflemen occupied all the hedges, I saw the French chasseurs suddenly make a rush forward in all directions, whilst the fire of our people became thicker and faster than ever. Many of the former scampered across the open fields until they reached the nearest hedges, whilst others ran crouching under cover of those perpendicular to their front, and the whole succeeded in establishing themselves – thus forcing back and gaining ground on our men. The fire then again became sharper than ever – sometimes the French were driven back ...[4]

Although many other allied accounts talk of almost continuous skirmishing between the outposts, it seems that the main forces of both sides were more concerned with resting than fighting. Although Ney had been substantially outnumbered at the end of the battle the previous day, now that d'Erlon had arrived he had concentrated about 35,000 men after the casualties of the previous day are deducted. Girard had died a heroic death leading his division the day before and they had suffered such heavy casualties that they were left at Ligny to recover and did not rejoin their corps until after Waterloo. Durutte's division did not rejoin until late on the 17th. In contrast, Wellington had received further reinforcements during the night and in the morning had between 42 and 47,000 men around Quatre Bras.

Ney understandably feared that Wellington was now considerably stronger than himself and did not dare to provoke the allied commander into attacking him. However, as this must have been a real possibility, it is surprising that the marshal appears not to have taken any defensive measures, such as deploying his force to meet such an attack. We can only speculate that Ney intended to withdraw if Wellington showed any indication of stirring himself. As it was, Wellington too was awaiting definite news of Blücher's situation before committing himself to action; he did not want to find the Prussians had been beaten having already compromised himself. And so the two armies sat tranquilly watching each other, waiting for news of the outcome of Ligny before deciding what to do.

General Flahaut had spent the whole of the 16th with Ney at Quatre Bras and had observed all that had gone on there. He returned to imperial headquarters in the morning and informed the emperor of what he had seen. In particular, he reported that Ney had still not been informed of the result of Ligny and consequently remained unsure of what he should do; until he had been given some orders he was inclined to remain on the defensive. This alarmed Napoleon, who had presumed that Ney had retaken the offensive to fix Wellington in place so that the emperor could march along the Namur road and attack Wellington's flank whilst he was engaged to his front with Ney. Napoleon immediately had Soult write to Ney to make clear the victory that he had won and to press the commander of the left wing to immediately attack the forces in front of him.

Fleurus, 17 June 1815.

M. le Maréchal,

General Flahaut, who has just arrived, has informed us that you are still unsure on the results of yesterday. I thought you had been warned of the victory that the emperor has won. The Prussian army has been routed, General Pajol is in pursuit on the roads to Namur and Liège. We have already taken several thousand prisoners and 30 cannon. Our troops were well led: a charge of six battalions of the Guard, the service squadrons and Delort's cavalry division broke the enemy line, throwing their ranks into disorder and taking the position.

The emperor is going to the mill at Bry where the main road which goes from Namur to Quatre Bras passes. It is thus possible that the English army will act in front of you, if this is the case, the emperor will march directly against it by the main road to Quatre Bras, whilst you attack it from the front with your divisions which, currently, should be concentrated, and this army will be destroyed in an instant. Thus, inform His Majesty of the exact location of your divisions, and all that happens to your front.

The emperor is disappointed that you did not concentrate your divisions yesterday; they acted individually and so you suffered casualties.

If the corps of Counts d'Erlon and Reille had been together, not an Englishman of the corps that attacked you would have escaped. If the Count d'Erlon had executed the movement on Saint-Amand that the emperor had ordered, the Prussian army would have been totally destroyed and we would have made perhaps 30,000 prisoners.

The corps of Generals Gérard, Vandamme and the Imperial Guard were always concentrated; one exposes oneself to a reverse when detachments are made.

The emperor hopes and desires that your seven infantry divisions and the cavalry are well concentrated and formed and that together they do not occupy more than a league of ground, in order to have them well in hand and available to use in case of need.

The intention of His Majesty is that you take position at Quatre Bras, as soon as the order is given; but if this is not possible, send details immediately and the emperor will move there as I have already told you. If, to the contrary, there is only a rear-guard, attack it and take position there.

It is necessary to finish this operation today and to resupply ammunition, rally isolated troops and call in detachments. Give the necessary orders to assure yourself that all the wounded have been tended to and transported to the rear; there are complaints that the ambulances have not done their duty.

The famous partisan Lutzow, who has been captured, said that the Prussian army is lost and that Blücher has exposed the Prussian monarch for the second time.

> *Le Maréchal d'empire, major général, Duc de Dalmatie*[5]

Soult's intimation that he 'thought you had been warned of the victory that the emperor has won' suggests that some effort had already been made to inform Ney of the previous day's result, but it might also have been an attempt by Soult to cover up his own failing. More important is the effect of this reprimand on Ney after his frustrations of the previous day. Although this letter does not have a time attached to it, various French writers have estimated that it was written between seven and eight o'clock, after Flahaut had returned to imperial headquarters. Heymès says that it arrived with Ney 'towards 9am'.[6] Perhaps more drawn to the paragraph on resupplying, rallying and tending to the wounded, inexplicably Ney took absolutely no action to confront Wellington after receiving this order. Whether this was anger and frustration or an unwillingness to goad the army in front of him is unclear, but the majority of his troops appear to have sat in their bivouacs, cleaning their weapons and no doubt trying to procure some breakfast. Lieutenant Henckens and his fellow chasseurs were lucky enough to be issued some rations:

> The night of the 16th to the 17th was very quiet; the morning of the 17th at an early hour there was a distribution of rations for men and horses from which we profited immediately, awaiting new orders.[7]

But Napoleon too is universally accused of wasting the morning. The French emperor had conducted some relentless pursuits in his heyday; perhaps the most famous against the Prussians in 1806 after the victories of Jena and Aüerstadt. Now another was needed; having failed to gain the decisive victory he desperately sought, an aggressive pursuit could have denied the Prussians the opportunity to collect and rally. But Napoleon allowed his tired troops to rest whilst he awaited the news on which direction the Prussians had retreated in and visited the battlefield of the previous day.

For his part, Wellington awoke the next morning concerned that Ney would attack again and was relieved when he was informed that the French showed no inclination to continue the fight. He needed to know what had happened at Ligny before he could decide on what his next action should be. It was not until seven-thirty that he was informed of Blücher's defeat and, although he knew this meant he must retreat, French inactivity convinced him there was time for his troops to have breakfast, and he set the time for the first units to fall back as ten o'clock. This might have been considered rather risky, but there is no doubt that he felt confident that with the force he now had he could comfortably resist any French attack.

It was only at midday that Napoleon turned his mind back to Ney and Wellington. He had Soult write:

> In front of Ligny, 17 June, midday.
>
> *Monsieur le Maréchal*, the emperor is going to take position in front of Marbais with an infantry corps and the Imperial Guard. His Majesty directs me to inform you that his intention is that you are to attack the enemy at Quatre Bras, chase them from their position, and that the corps which is at Marbais will second your operations. His Majesty will move to Marbais, and awaits your reports with impatience.
>
> *Le Maréchal d'empire, major général, Duc de Dalmatie*[8]

Whilst his plan to fall on Wellington's flank was sound and in line with his original intent, it was carried out five hours too late. For this only Napoleon can take the blame.

Once Grouchy's pursuit of the Prussians had been sent off, Napoleon put himself at the head of the 6th Corps, Imperial Guard and Milhaud's cuirassiers, and marched towards Quatre Bras. He stopped at Marbais, surprised that he could not hear any firing to indicate Ney had started his attack. He sent the 7th Hussars forward to meet up with Ney's troops and ironically the hussars exchanged shots with Ney's outposts, who had mistaken them for the enemy. An English woman who had been with the allied army had been captured and was brought before Napoleon; she revealed that only a rear-guard composed of cavalry and artillery still occupied Quatre Bras. Angry, Napoleon galloped forward to join the left wing. Gourgaud takes up the story:

> The emperor was greatly astonished to find that Marshal Ney's corps was still bivouacking before Frasnes. Irritated at this delay, he instantly ordered the troops to march forward and join him. He had to wait upwards of an hour for them.[9]

Lieutenant Philippe-Gustave Le Doulcet de Pontécoulant of the Guard Horse Artillery was a part of the force that Napoleon led towards Quatre Bras and took a leading role in the subsequent pursuit of Wellington's army to Waterloo. He wrote:

> Marshal Ney had been warned of these movements by the *major général* who had at the same time reiterated the order to advance against the enemy who was at Quatre Bras with vigour, and announced to him the

co-operation of Count Lobau who was at Marbais in order to support him.

Despite these formal and repeated instructions no activity was apparent towards Quatre Bras; all appeared calm and in perfect tranquillity. Napoleon, astonished to see his intentions so badly seconded, then set off in the lead with all the troops that he had immediately to hand.[10]

It will be remembered that General d'Erlon's 1st Corps was the foremost of Ney's troops and he later wrote:

He [Napoleon] then came with the rest of his army, to rejoin Marshal Ney at Quatre Bras, which had already been evacuated by the English. The emperor found me before this position and said to me with great sorrow, these words which have been forever engraved in my memory, 'France is lost; go my dear general, put yourself at the head of this cavalry and press the English rear-guard hard.[11]

In his account of the campaign, Gourgaud states that Napoleon criticised d'Erlon for his failures of the day before, but perhaps it is unsurprising that d'Erlon does not mention this. However, both Foy and Desalles appear to have been witness to this criticism. The latter wrote:

He [Napoleon] expressed his discontent to Count d'Erlon, who explained that he found himself in an embarrassing position, since he was under the orders of Marshal Ney. His Majesty did not reply and gave me his orders: 'Get the horse artillery moving forward and pursue the enemy without respite.'[12]

A little later Napoleon was joined by Ney and the emperor demanded an explanation as to why his orders had not been obeyed; Ney tried to excuse himself by saying he believed he had the whole of the allied army in front of him. But Heymès, in his attempts to defend Ney, claims, 'It is not true that the emperor showed his discontent to Marshal Ney; it is also not true that the troops were still in their bivouacs when he appeared for they were under arms at daybreak.'[13]

Dismissing his lieutenant, Napoleon put himself at the very head of his troops and set off after Wellington. The pursuit of the allies was led by cavalry and horse artillery; Captain Duthilt reported that the 2nd Division of the 1st Corps left, '. . . at 2 o'clock in the afternoon'.[14] The 2nd Corps was left to bring up the rear; General Foy wrote in a letter home, 'The army set off . . . in the afternoon. Why so late? I do not know'.[15] and Colonel Jolyet of the 1st *légère* merely records, 'On the 17th June, we remained in our camp until towards 4pm.'[16]

In the morning General Durutte and his division had been ordered to rejoin the rest of their corps at Quatre Bras, but were then ordered to stop;

presumably to let the 6th Corps and Imperial Guard pass. Captain Chapuis, already frustrated by the failure of Durutte to intervene at Ligny, had even more to complain about:

> Held up in our march by the rain, the mud and the numerous columns that were all advancing towards the same point as us, we arrived so late in the position allocated to us that it was impossible for the soldiers to get any shelter from the poor weather.[17]

The whole of the French army was now in motion following up Wellington's troops. The stage was set for the cataclysmic battle that was to be fought the next day at Waterloo.

Analysis – the 17th

It is hard to censure Ney for not having attacked Wellington before he knew the outcome of Ligny. Whilst he had sufficient forces to impose on his opponent for a time, given that he was outnumbered and may even have been facing virtually the whole of Wellington's army, such an attack, without the promise of a sizeable force coming to support him from Ligny, could have been suicidal. What's more, Napoleon's first order of the day merely directed him to, 'take position at Quatre Bras, as soon as the order is given; but if this is not possible, send details immediately and the emperor will move there as I have already told you.' In these circumstances, Ney probably felt justified in not attacking Wellington; although he does not appear to have made this clear in any communications with Napoleon, leaving the latter unclear on the situation he was facing. However, as we have seen, the order went on to say, 'If, to the contrary, there is only a rear-guard, attack it and take position there.'

It is perfectly reasonable to expect Ney to have taken a close interest in what the allies were doing to his front. The news of the Prussian defeat certainly made an attack by the Anglo-Netherlands army highly unlikely, but equally it made a retreat extremely likely. He should therefore have been looking for signs of this retreat so that he could both warn Napoleon and identify the time to launch an attack that would fix part of the force in place, well set up to be destroyed by the emperor's flanking move. Ney appears to have been struck by a wave of complete apathy; he took no interest in what Wellington was up to at all, made no efforts to comply with Napoleon's orders and had not even bothered to get his formations ready to move. This was unforgiveable and it is no surprise that the emperor was angry and chose to lead the pursuit himself.

But Napoleon was not free from blame for the wasting of time this morning either. He was slow to find out where the Prussians had gone and slow to despatch an effective pursuit. Although his troops had marched and fought for three days, he of all people understood that a commander must not spare his men when the opportunity for a decisive pursuit offered itself. He was also slow to turn on Wellington, giving him the opportunity to slip away from a moribund Ney. Although Ney was complicit in the failings of the day, it was Napoleon's lack of energy and decisiveness that were the key to French failure on the 17th; not Ney's inactivity.

Through the 14th, 15th and even the 16th, Napoleon had maintained the initiative and forced the two allied commanders to dance to his tune. He had outmanoeuvred and outfought them, and although he had not achieved the results he had hoped by first light on the 17th, it is wrong to lay the blame solely at his door; he had still not lost the opportunity to win the campaign. Blücher's army had taken a beating, although it had not been destroyed as Napoleon had wanted, but a swift pursuit should have kept it out of the game whilst he turned with his fresh troops (the 6th Corps and majority of the Imperial Guard) against Wellington with the rest of Ney's wing.

At first light on the 17th, the campaign was still Napoleon's to win, but by lunchtime the Prussians had escaped a punishing pursuit, which would allow them the time to rally and reorganise, and Wellington had started his retreat towards the position at Waterloo without mishap. In a few short hours, and without any fighting, the pendulum had swung decisively in favour of the allies; forty-eight hours later, the French army had been destroyed and Napoleon's hopes lay in ruins.

Chapter 18

Summary and Conclusions

How easy it is to be an armchair general, especially when we have all the benefit of hindsight: a full understanding of what was going on 'on the other side of the hill' and with a comparatively comprehensive record of the communications that went on between the various commanders of both sides. But what we don't have is a full understanding of what it was like to actually be there, knowing what the commanders actually knew and affected by the various pressures and stresses that war inevitably brings to decision-making, and not exposed to what Clausewitz described as the inevitable 'friction' of war.[1]

How much of what went wrong in these few days was the friction of war, and how much was incompetence? All sides and all commanders made mistakes. For the allies, Wellington's tardy concentration and failure to support the Prussians, and the Prussian decision to fight at Ligny even though the IV Corps would not be available and Wellington's support was uncertain, both came close to losing them the campaign. But for the French, the list is longer and cumulatively proved to be fatal, even before Waterloo. We now need to look at why things went wrong for the French left wing after what was an encouraging opening.

Napoleon has inevitably generated a clear divergence of opinion in history and most historians write him up as either a genius or a megalomaniac. The same is true when assessing his performance during 1815; he was either personally faultless and let down by his subordinates, or all the responsibility for the failure lies squarely at his own door. The truth behind this campaign is complicated by the sheer volume of debate it has generated, not only amongst historians, but, given Napoleon's criticism of his subordinates, their own attempts to justify either their own behaviour and decisions, or that of their relatives who, particularly in the case of Marshal Ney, were not able to defend themselves. Although most of the key actors wrote of their own contribution, each of them inevitably weighted their accounts to support their own arguments, positions and hypotheses; 'spin' is not a modern phenomenon!

Perhaps one of the most frustrating aspects of trying to penetrate the many uncertainties that surround this campaign has been the number of significant orders and letters that were sent without the time they were prepared being written on them. On campaign it should have been standard operating procedure to put this small piece of information on orders so that the receiving commander might appreciate how long ago it was written. ADCs and other messengers often got lost or had long distances to travel, so it was not unusual for an order to have been overtaken by events by the time it arrived. A number of key orders sent by Napoleon, Soult and Ney were not timed and this has led the supporters and detractors of all the main actors of this drama to liberally add or subtract considerable lengths of time in using them to support their own arguments or undermine the arguments of others. Napoleon's many comments on time underline its importance in analysing the performance of commanders on campaign and many of his early victories were won by the hard marching of his troops, rather than with the points of their bayonets.

And yet, in Napoleon's view, this campaign was characterised by the excessive caution and lethargy of many of his subordinates, and there is no doubt that he saw these as underpinning the campaign's failure. Napoleon's concentration of the army and strike into the Kingdom of the Netherlands caught the allies off guard, but even on the 15th his army failed to reach all the objectives he had set for it. The time that various orders were sent or received thus becomes of vital interest; the difference of an hour or two is more than enough to mean the difference between success and failure.

One of the prerequisites for offensive operations is the need for a sense of urgency. In order to outmanoeuvre the enemy the commander must seize and maintain the initiative, forcing the enemy to react to his manoeuvres instead of being given the time or opportunity to initiate his own. This requires not only superior strategic thinking, but the energy in a commander that can instil that same sense of urgency in all his subordinates who then pass it on down the chain of command. Keeping one step ahead of your enemy is the sure way of ensuring it is you who sets the agenda. Whilst Blücher may well have wanted to fight an early battle against Napoleon, the latter, whilst wanting the same, by his own manoeuvres was able to force this before the Prussian army was concentrated (despite the problems he faced in achieving the same), whilst Wellington, due to his concerns for his right flank towards Mons, was strategically outmanoeuvred by Napoleon and it was only thanks to the insubordination of some of his more junior commanders, the fighting spirit of his troops and the failure of Ney to concentrate his own troops that he was able to hold on at Quatre Bras.

So why were so many of Napoleon's senior commanders, experienced in war and well-practised in its execution, apparently so lethargic during this campaign when clear thinking, energy, audacity and a sense of urgency were most needed? Napoleon had no doubt, writing through Gourgaud on St Helena:

> In these actions, the French soldiers fought with as much courage and confidence in victory as they ever displayed in their most celebrated battles; but several of their generals, and even Marshal Ney himself, were

no longer the same men. They had lost that energy and that spirit of brilliant enterprise, which once distinguished them, and which had so materially contributed to the achievement of great triumphs. They had become timid and circumspect in all their operations; their personal bravery alone remained. The question with them now was, who should least compromise himself?[2]

Napoleon returns to this theme many times in his writings on the campaign and in this passage goes on to list the many times when precious time was lost to show how this was the case. One is reminded of Napoleon's statement that the reason he beat the Austrians is because they did not know the value of five minutes. However, it is in his last sentence that he probably best identifies the reason for their lack of energy. It appears that few of his generals really believed that they could win; many had been reluctant to serve again and were fearful of the consequences of failure. Ney is the best illustration of this and we have already explored his state of mind during this fateful campaign. It seems that the majority of the emperor's most senior generals had one eye on their future should Napoleon be defeated, and rather than fully commit themselves they almost sought expressions of their reluctance, justifying their actions through a desire to protect *la patrie* rather than serve Napoleon. Colonel Gordon, who deserted to the allies, wrote at the time, 'Most of the general officers are undecided and love neither the king nor Bonaparte.'[3]

What is also clear is that Napoleon singled out Marshal Ney for particular criticism. We must now decide if this criticism was fair. The failings and issues of controversy have already been discussed at the end of the relevant chapters and do not need to be repeated. Marshal Ney had enjoyed a most illustrious and successful career that had earned him a reputation as an energetic, brave and charismatic commander that would have ordinarily well suited him for the command of the left wing during this campaign. That he underperformed is beyond question and the fundamental reason has already been discussed; he was distracted by the implications of changing his allegiance, doubtful of a successful outcome of the campaign and mindful of the possible consequences. Consequently, his leadership and decision-making can best be described as desperate rather than cool and calculated.

Let us summarise the results of our analysis on the issues on which Ney has faced the most censure.

- Criticism that he did not seize Quatre Bras on the evening of the 15th is unfounded. Whilst with the benefit of hindsight it can be seen that it would ultimately have been advantageous, at the time Napoleon did not categorically order him to do this and appeared content that it had not been achieved.
- The uncertainty surrounding the meeting between Napoleon and Ney during the night of the 15th/16th is unfortunate. Napoleon

specifically criticised Ney for not seizing the crossroads first thing in the morning of the 16th, but Ney's actions that morning are sufficient to convince this author that he had no definitive orders to do so until he received Napoleon's letter at about 10.30am.

Deciding on a fair and objective judgement on Ney's failure to seize Quatre Bras relies almost entirely on whether or not Napoleon and Ney met at midnight on the night of the 15th/16th. And yet, whilst not wishing to revisit the evidence, it is impossible to reach an absolutely indisputable conclusion. To most historians it seems inexplicable that if they did meet, they did not discuss the strategic importance of Quatre Bras and the need for it to be occupied as soon as possible. Supporters of Napoleon will always contend that if Ney had seized Quatre Bras and been able to then fall on the Prussian rear at Ligny, Waterloo would not have been fought and Napoleon would have won the campaign. His detractors will always maintain that Ney's failures were due to Napoleon's lack of clear, timely direction. Thus the sense of uncertainty that surrounds this vital aspect of the campaign will surely remain.

- On the morning of the 16th, Ney can be criticised for not closing up his command in anticipation of what those orders would be. He did not need to be ordered to do this (although he was). This loss of time was to have significant implications for how the rest of the day unfolded.

By leaving the divisions of Jérôme and Foy at Gosselies instead of bringing them up to Frasnes early in the morning, by leaving that of Durutte at Jumet, and the other three of d'Erlon's divisions still further in the rear until after the last regiments of 2nd Corps had left Gosselies, Ney ensured that a prompt and bloodless occupation of Quatre Bras was almost impossible. If he had concentrated his whole force as he had been ordered, the Prince of Orange would not have been able to contest Quatre Bras and would have been forced to retire from the crossroads before reinforcements could arrive. Ney would then have been well placed to send a corps to support Napoleon as he was subsequently ordered. Exactly how far he was responsible for the gap between his two corps we cannot be absolutely sure, but we can certainly say that a diligent and experienced officer in Ney's place would have known to a half hour just how long after the arrival of the last division of the 2nd Corps the van of the 1st Corps might be expected. Ropes, whom we should remember is a truly objective observer, wrote, 'The whole management of Marshal Ney on this day shows distrust of the emperor's judgement, unwillingness to take the most obvious steps, finally, disobedience of orders.'[4]

- In the circumstances, the battle of Quatre Bras was not the disaster for the French that many historians, and even French participants, have painted it. The French fought valiantly and achieved some notable successes, and ultimately, although outnumbered and failing to seize the crossroads, succeeded in denying the Prussians any support from Wellington's army.

By denying the opportunity for Wellington to support the Prussians Ney made a vital contribution to Napoleon's victory at Ligny. He achieved this without the help of d'Erlon's corps. Napoleon's criticism of Ney at Quatre Bras was exclusively based on his failure to have concentrated the whole of the left wing prior to the battle. Criticism by subsequent writers, based on a mis-interpretation of Napoleon's words and with the benefit of hindsight, are undeserved:

> Marshal Ney was indecisive, irresolute in his attacks ... This was strange in a man whose audacious determination in war was well known. His groping around before an enemy weaker than himself was inexplicable in a general who was accustomed to saying that the only enemy he feared was one he could not see.[5]

- Marshal Ney's most fateful decision was his rash and frustrated recall of d'Erlon's march towards Ligny.

Ultimately, and with all the benefit of hindsight, it seems that the failure of d'Erlon's 1st Corps to intervene at Ligny was probably the pivotal moment of the campaign. We can discount the impact he would have had at Quatre Bras, whether he had marched straight there or had returned there in sufficient time to fight, as there was never any expectation of destroying Wellington's army, with or without his intervention. Napoleon needed to destroy one of the two allied armies and it was the Prussians that had given him the opportunity. That d'Erlon was marching on to the Prussian flank, rather than their rear, would probably not have reduced the impact of his arrival, as it was here that the Prussian retreat was most chaotic. The 1st Corps's intervention would have made the subsequent unmolested retreat to Wavre impossible for the Prussians.

But it is not true to say that with only a partial victory over the Prussians at Ligny that Napoleon had lost the opportunity to win the campaign. A more effective pursuit of the Prussians, that denied them the ability to intervene at Waterloo, might well have given Napoleon the opportunity to have turned that battle into a victory. If Wellington had chosen not to fight at Waterloo because of the lack of Prussian support, then we can only speculate on what might subsequently have happened.

The mistakes and failures we have identified of all the commanders prior to d'Erlon's recall could be considered the inevitable friction of war, were repairable and were mirrored by problems experienced by the two allies. But the timely appearance of the 1st Corps at Ligny would almost certainly have had a significant impact on the campaign, which could well have resulted in a decisive French victory.

So why did Ney recall d'Erlon? Through his frustration and anger, Ney failed to grasp his superior commander's intent: he was entirely focussed on seizing Quatre Bras rather than helping Napoleon to destroy the Prussians. Throughout the campaign Ney inevitably displayed his legendary courage, but courage, though indispensible, is no substitute for cool judgement and presence of mind. He once again repeatedly lost sight of the bigger picture and seemed unable to prioritise anything above the immediate tactical fight that was right before his eyes. His behaviour was almost frenetic at times and he was prone to desperate exhortations at both Quatre Bras and Waterloo. This was hardly the behaviour of a calm and composed battlefield commander who could take timely and calculated decisions based on a broad understanding of the situation across the entire battlefield. Although his state of mind can only be guessed at, his behaviour during the campaign clearly demonstrates that he was unable to meet the demands of the moment and was probably distracted by the possible consequences of his actions.

Ney's late entry into the campaign resulted in a lack of knowledge of his men; a lack of bonding and understanding which would have created an efficient working relationship (the moral strength of which must not be underestimated). This, and the lack of an established headquarters staff are powerful mitigating circumstances, but in themselves do not relieve him of culpability.

Napoleon's criticism of Ney in his writings on St Helena polarised opinion in all the authors that wrote a history of the campaign; between those that were sympathetic to the emperor and wished to endorse his accounts, and those whose long antagonism towards him inevitably led them to lay all blame for failure at his own door. Almost inevitably in such cases, the truth lies somewhere in between, and with such contrary arguments and the passage of time, we will never know the exact truth. Certainly, Ney started with a tremendous disadvantage; coming late into the campaign he did not know his commanders or his troops, and his lack of a properly constituted staff and headquarters goes a long way towards explaining some of the failures of the left wing during these early days. We must also not underestimate his state of mind; some of his actions and decisions were so out of character that it seems there can be little argument that this was the cause of at least some of them. With these things in mind, perhaps we should forgive Ney his failure to concentrate all his forces prior to the battle of Quatre Bras, as even having failed to do this it was a very close-fought battle and succeeded in preventing Wellington from supporting the Prussians at Ligny; a singular achievement for which he has appeared to receive absolutely no credit. His key failing was, as we have already seen, his rash and unthinking recall of d'Erlon, an act which probably changed history, and for this I cannot find any truly miti-gating circumstances.

Napoleon

All historians and critics agree that Napoleon's strategic concept for the cam-paign saw him back at his best. However, he is certainly not free of any blame for some of the failures of the early days of the campaign, although as with Ney, he is certainly not as guilty as his detractors have branded him. Much of this has been addressed in the analysis sections and will not be repeated here, but there are two issues which do require a little scrutiny.

The first is that in his orders to Ney, Napoleon failed to make his direction and intent absolutely clear and generally arrived too late to give the marshal a fair opportunity to carry them out. In 1820, Colonel Janin, who worked in the headquarters of Lobau's 6th Corps, wrote a short pamphlet to challenge some of the assertions made in Gourgaud's (i.e. Napoleon's) account of the cam-paign. In it he concludes that, 'Marshal Ney did not receive orders that were precise enough nor instructions that were detailed enough, on the operations that he was to have carried out.'[6]

A rereading of Napoleon's orders to Ney on the 16th undermines Janin's argument. The orders reflect the growing clarity of the situation facing Napoleon and the actions he wants Ney to carry out in order to support the destruction of the Prussian army. To grasp the full context of Napoleon's orders it is necessary to read them in full, but for brevity's sake let us look at extracts from the relevant orders that Napoleon sent, or had sent, to Ney on the 16th.

Napoleon's letter to Ney. Arrives about 10.30am.

I wish to write to you in detail because it is of the highest importance.

... You should dispose your troops in the following manner: the first division at two leagues in advance of Quatre Bras, if there is no hin-drance; six divisions of infantry about Quatre Bras, and one division at Marbais, so that I may draw them to me at Sombreffe if I want them.

... I desire your dispositions may be made so that your eight divisions can march on Brussels as soon as it is ordered ...

At this point Napoleon does not believe Ney will have to fight for posses-sion of Quatre Bras and therefore supposes that he will just have to move forward to occupy it. He was then to deploy his troops as directed, including some specifically so that Napoleon could call on them to help him against the Prussians if required. Some sense of urgency is specified as Napoleon orders he should be ready to move from Quatre Bras, 'as soon as it is ordered.'

Soult's letter to Ney. Arrives about 11am.

Soult reiterates the direction given in Napoleon's letter.

Soult's order to Ney. Arrives about 11.30am.

Concentrate the corps of Counts Reille and d'Erlon and that of Count Valmy, who is just marching to join you. With these forces you must engage and destroy all enemy forces that present themselves.

Although there is no mention of the turning movement there is clearly an imperative to take decisive action.

Soult's order timed at 2pm. Arrives about 3.30pm.

His Majesty's intent is that you should attack all that is in front of you, and then, after having vigorously pushed it back, you should advance towards us to assist in enveloping the force I have just mentioned.

Only now is Napoleon clear that virtually the whole Prussian army is before him and that he has an opportunity to outflank and destroy it. This is the first order that categorically directs Ney to fall on the Prussian rear; it is clear and unequivocal. At this point at Quatre Bras, the arrival of British reinforcements has just saved Wellington from unmistakeable defeat. Although Ney does not know exactly where d'Erlon is, he is uncommitted and therefore available to conduct this movement. Ney merely awaits the arrival of the 1st Corps and does not seem to consider any further options for its use or the obedience of this order.

Soult's order timed at 3.15pm. Arrives about 5pm.

His Majesty has directed me to tell you that you must manoeuvre onto the field in such a manner as to envelop the enemy's right and to fall with full force on his rear. The enemy army will be lost if you act vigorously. The fate of France is in your hands. Therefore, do not hesitate an instant to move as the Emperor has ordered, and head toward the heights of Bry and Saint-Amand to co-operate in a victory that may be decisive. The enemy has been caught *en flagrant délit* while trying to unite with the English.

The importance and imperative of this order is unmistakeable. Unfortunately, the time of arrival of this order is crucial in assessing Ney's response. The evidence suggests that by the time he reads it, Ney has already recalled d'Erlon. But even given the imperative of the order – 'The enemy army will be lost if you act vigorously. The fate of France is in your hands . . . do not hesitate a moment . . .' – Ney chooses not to rescind his order and, still focussed on the battle before him, launches Kellerman in his gallant, but suicidal charge.

Baudus's brief from Napoleon. Baudus arrives with Ney about 7.15pm.

I have sent Count d'Erlon the order to move with his entire corps onto the rear of the Prussian army's right; you go and take a duplicate of this order to Marshal Ney which has to be communicated to him. You are to tell him that, whatever the situation he is facing, it is absolutely necessary that this direction is executed; that I attach no great importance to what happens on his flank today; that the key is what happens where I am, because I need to finish off the Prussian army. As for him, he should, if he cannot do better, be content with containing the English army.

Only now does Napoleon make clear to Ney the secondary importance of his battle at Quatre Bras. Unfortunately, given d'Erlon's march and counter-march, it is too late for Ney to act. If Ney had fully understood that Napoleon's aim was to destroy the Prussian army, and had carried out the 3.15pm order, this explanation would not have been necessary.

Having successfully concentrated his army and crossed the border into the Kingdom of the Netherlands, we know that Napoleon's next immediate aim was to destroy one of the allied armies. Although he expected Blücher to confront him first, he could not know for sure that this would be the case. Therefore from hour to hour he had to await events and give orders based on the information he received and his own best guess, using his intuition as much as absolute facts on which to base them. It is this moment to moment decision-making, based on incomplete information, that the armchair general cannot fully comprehend nor experience. Should a decision be made now and orders sent immediately, or should you await one more piece of intelligence and risk losing the initiative? Thus, in offensive operations, timely decision-making is vital and it is inevitable that some orders will require almost instant compliance; that some orders appeared to be very short notice was inevitable. It is necessary to judge each order on the basis of what was known at that moment in time and without the benefit of hindsight, before we can truly say how apposite they were; this is virtually impossible for someone who was not there.

As for the precision and detail of Napoleon's and Soult's orders, judgement inevitably becomes very much more subjective. We have already discussed that it was not the convention of the time to explain why each action had to be carried out. There was a danger orders would become very long and take too much time to write and copy; brevity was a virtue. It was most important for an order to be obeyed without the temptation to question what was behind it. Some years before, Marshal Berthier, then the chief-of-staff, said to Ney, that Napoleon 'in his general projects requires neither advice nor plans of campaign; no one else knows his designs, and it is our duty to obey.'[7]

Within the uncertainties of the timing of the sending and arrival of orders already discussed, if Ney and his subordinates had had their formations in hand and executed their orders as soon as they were received, however uncertain the reasons for them, most of the key failures would not have occurred. Read without context or without an understanding of the bigger picture, Napoleon's scheme of manoeuvre on the day of Quatre Bras can seem somewhat unclear, but an understanding of the situation faced by Napoleon and the fact that any situation is constantly changing, explains the logic of them. Ultimately, as emperor and commander-in-chief, Napoleon just expected his orders to be obeyed; by definition orders should be carried out immediately, without question, and with energy and determination. If Ney had done this, things would have been very different.

If Marshal Ney's big mistake was the recall of d'Erlon, then Napoleon's was surely his failure to relentlessly pursue the Prussians overnight on the 16/17 June. Whilst this does not directly relate to our study of Quatre Bras and the operations of the left wing during these early days of the campaign, the fallout of this failure surely was. We have already discussed the need for a pursuit to be immediate and merciless. Napoleon's apologists give two reasons for his failure to pursue the Prussians: the need to rest his troops after three days of relentless activity and the need to be sure of what line of retreat the Prussians had taken.

There is no doubt that those of Napoleon's men that had marched to Ligny, and then fought there, were exhausted and needed rest. But Lobau's 6th Corps had not been engaged, much of the cavalry reserve, the troops best suited to an immediate pursuit, had been only lightly engaged, and the imperial guard had only been committed at the very end of the battle; all of these were available for immediate tasking. Only relatively late in the morning did Napoleon order most of these troops to Marbais to be prepared to march on to Wellington's flank by the Namur to Nivelles road, and only sometime about one o'clock did he join them having finally set off Grouchy's pursuit of the Prussians.

Although we have established that Ney did send a report on the battle he had fought at Quatre Bras on the evening of the 16th,[8] it gave no information on what Wellington had done at the end of the battle (stayed in position or withdrawn). Early the following morning, perhaps around three o'clock, Ney should have confirmed that Wellington's forces were still before him and immediately informed the emperor, who had always envisaged marching against Wellington having defeated the Prussians and had warned Ney of this in his orders of the morning of the 16th.[9] Thus Ney failed to inform Napoleon that an opportunity still presented itself; Wellington had still not gathered his entire army and was still in position before him.

Without this information it was only sometime between seven and eight in the morning that Soult had written to Ney:

> It is thus possible that the English army will act in front of you, if this is the case, the emperor will march directly against it by the main road to Quatre Bras, whilst you attack it from the front with your divisions which, currently, should be concentrated, and this army will be destroyed in an instant ...
>
> The intention of His Majesty is that you take position at Quatre Bras, as soon as the order is given; but if this is not possible, send details

immediately   ·d the emperor will move there as I have already told you.
I·   .ary, there is only a rear-guard, attack it and take position

Having only heard of the Prussian defeat at about eight o'clock, Wellington chose to start his retreat at ten. If Napoleon, warned by Ney that part of the Anglo-Netherlands army was still before him, had chosen to march immediately and co-ordinated his attack with Ney, then Wellington would have been in serious trouble. But Ney's failure to inform Napoleon, a recurring theme, and Napoleon's preoccupation with the Prussians, had denied the emperor the opportunity. The late hour that Napoleon reached Quatre Bras and Ney's failure to carry out his orders to attack the rear-guard had let the opportunity to destroy a large proportion of Wellington's army slip through his fingers.

Napoleon's strategic design for this campaign was worthy of his greatest days and he knew it. Confident in its success, it is unsurprising that in the idleness of his exile he cast around for scapegoats in light of its failure. Ney and Grouchy were the obvious candidates and with the amount of criticism he heaped upon them it was inevitable that others would leap to their defence and equally unsurprising that they turned this criticism back onto Napoleon. Despite his writings, it is impossible to truly understand his thoughts or penetrate the reasons for the decisions he took. His detractors have been quick to accuse him of prevarication and indecision on the mornings of both 16 and 17 June. The uncertainties of an ever-developing situation and the natural inclination to wait for just one more piece of critical information before making a decision seem to be the reasons for this. However, there is little doubt that in his heyday he would not have hesitated; in 1815 Napoleon undoubtedly lacked the *coup d'oeil*, energy and decisiveness that had marked him at his brilliant best. The final verdict, however, is an individual one that must fall to those who have studied this fascinating piece of history. But whatever that verdict, there is no doubt that Napoleon's stinging criticism of his subordinates was unworthy of one of history's greatest captains.

Orders of Battle

Although most orders of battle available agree on the composition of each army, virtually none of them agree on unit strengths. I have taken the French strengths from Mark Adkin's excellent book *The Waterloo Companion*, and the allied strengths from Siborne's meticulously researched *History of the Waterloo Campaign*.

THE FRENCH LEFT WING
Commander
Marshal Ney, *Duc d'Elchingen* and *Prince de la Moskowa*

CAVALRY OF THE GUARD
Light Cavalry Division (Lieutenant General Count de Lefebvre-Desnouëttes)
  Chevaux-Légers Lanciers (The Red Lancers) (880)
  Guard *Chasseurs à Cheval* (1,197)
  2 Horse Artillery Batteries (12 guns)

II CORPS
(Lieutenant General Count Reille)
5th Division (Lieutenant General Baron Bachelu)
1st Brigade (*Maréchal de Camp* Baron Husson)
  2nd *Légère* (4 bns, 2,294)
  61st Line (2 bns, 830)
2nd Brigade (*Maréchal de Camp* Baron Campi)
  72nd Line (2 bns, 970)
  108th Line (3 bns, 1,072)

6th Division (Lieutenant General Prince Jérôme Bonaparte)
1st Brigade (*Maréchal de Camp* Baron Bauduin)
  1st *Légère* (3 bns, 1,852)
  3rd Line (2 bns, 1,114)
2nd Brigade (*Maréchal de Camp* Baron Soye)
  1st Line (3 bns, 1,766)
  2nd Line (3 bns, 1,765)

9th Division (Lieutenant General Count Foy)
1st Brigade (*Maréchal de Camp* Baron Gauthier)
  92nd Line (2 bns, 1,018)
  93rd Line (3 bns, 1,461)

2nd Brigade (*Maréchal de Camp* Baron Jamin)
  100th Line (3 bns, 1,093)
  4th *Légère* (3 bns, 1,604)

2nd Cavalry Division (Lieutenant General Baron Piré)
1st Brigade (*Maréchal de Camp* Baron Hubert)
  1st *Chasseurs à Cheval* (4 sqns, 485)
  6th *Chasseurs à Cheval* (4 sqns, 560)
2nd Brigade (*Maréchal de Camp* Baron Wathier)
  5th *Lanciers* (3 sqns, 412)
  6th *Lanciers* (4 sqns, 405)

II Corps Artillery (Corps Pelletier) 4 Foot Btys and 1 Horse Bty

From the **11th Cavalry Division** (Lieutenant General Baron l'Héritier) of
the **III CAVALRY CORPS** (Lieutenant General Kellerman, Count Valmy)
2nd Brigade (*Maréchal de Camp* Guiton)
  8th Cuirassiers (3 sqns, 452)
  11th Cuirassiers (2 sqns, 325)
  1 Horse Bty

I CORPS
(Lieutenant General Drouet d'Erlon)
1st Division (*Maréchal de Camp* Baron Quiot du Passage)
1st Brigade (Colonel Charlet)
  54th Line (2 bns, 962)
  55th Line (2 bns, 1,149)
2nd Brigade (*Maréchal de Camp* Bourgeois)
  28th Line (2 bns, 898)
  105th Line (4 bns)

2nd Division (Lieutenant General Baron Donzelot)
1st Brigade (*Maréchal de Camp* Schmitz)
  13th *Légère* (3 bns, 1,875)
  17th Line (2 bns, 1,002)
2nd Brigade (*Maréchal de Camp* Baron Aulard)
  19th Line (2 bns, 1,032)
  51st Line (2 bns, 1,168)

3rd Division (Lieutenant General Baron Marcognet)
1st Brigade (*Maréchal de Camp* Nogues)
  21st Line (2 bns, 1,137)
  46th Line (2 bns, 888)
2nd Brigade (*Maréchal de Camp* Grenier)
  25th Line (2 bns, 974)
  45th Line (2 bns, 1,003)

4th Division (Lieutenant General Count Durutte)
1st Brigade (*Maréchal de Camp* Pégot)
  8th Line (2 bns, 983)
  29th Line (2 bns, 1,146)
2nd Brigade (*Maréchal de Camp* Brue)
  85th Line (2 bns, 631)
  95th Line (2 bns, 1,100)

1st Cavalry Division (Lieutenant General Baron Jacquinot)
1st Brigade (*Maréchal de Camp* Baron Bruno)
  7th Hussars (3 sqns, 804)
  3rd *Chasseurs à Cheval* (3 sqns, 365)
2nd Brigade (*Maréchal de Camp* Gobrecht)
  3rd *Lanciers* (3 sqns, 406)
  4th *Lanciers* (2 sqns, 296)

I Corps Artillery (Colonel Desalle) 5 Foot Btys and 1 Horse Bty

THE ALLIED ARMY
(in order of arrival)
Commander-in-Chief
The Duke of Wellington

1st Corps Commander
William, Prince of Orange
2nd Netherlands Division (Lieutenant General Baron
  Perponcher-Sedlnitzky)
1st Brigade (Major General van Bijlandt)
  27th Dutch Jägers (809)
  7th Belgian Line (701)
  5th Dutch Militia (482)
  7th Dutch Militia (675)
  8th Dutch Militia (566)
2nd Brigade (Major General H.S.H Prince Bernard of Saxe-Weimar)
  2nd Nassau-Usingen Regiment (3 bns, 2,709)
  28th Orange-Nassau Regiment (2 bns, 1 coy Jäger, 1,591)

Divisional Artillery 2 Foot Btys (Bijlveld, Stevenaar)

Netherlands Light Cavalry (Major General van Merlen)
Part of the Netherlands Cavalry Division
5th Belgian Light Dragoons (3 sqns, 441)
6th Netherlands Hussars (4 sqns, 641)
Section of guns from Petter's horse bty

5th British Infantry Division (Lieutenant General Sir Thomas Picton)
8th British Brigade (Major General Sir James Kempt)
  1/28th (North Gloucestershire) (557)
  1/32nd (Cornwall) (662)
  1/79th (Cameron Highlanders) (703)
  1/95th Rifles (6 coys, 549)
9th British Brigade (Major General Sir Denis Pack)
  3/1st (Royal Scots) (604)
  1/42nd (Highland) (526)
  2/44th (East Essex) (455)
  92nd (Highland) (588)
4th Hanoverian Brigade (Colonel Best)
  Verden Landwehr (621)
  Lüneberg Landwehr (624)
  Münden Landwehr (660)
  Osterode Landwehr (660)

Divisional Artillery 2 Foot Btys (Rogers, Braun)

Brunswick Corps (H.S.H The Duke of Brunswick)
[This corps did not all arrive together; see narrative.]
Avantgarde Bn (635)
Lieb Infantry Bn (565)
  Light Infantry Regiment (3 bns, 2,000)
  Line Infantry Regiment (3 bns, 1,753)
  Uhlans (1 sqn, 232)
  2nd Brunswick Hussars (4 sqns, 690)

Corps Artillery 1 Foot Bty (Moll), 1 Horse Bty (Heinemann)

3rd British Division (Lieutenant General Count Alten)
[The 2nd Kings German Legion Brigade did not arrive in time to take part in the battle.]
5th British Brigade (Major General Sir Colin Halkett)
  2/30th (Cambridgeshire) (615)
  1/33rd (Yorkshire (West Riding)) (561)
  2/69th (South Lincolnshire) (516)
  2/73rd (Highland) (562)
1st Hanoverian Brigade (Major General Count Kielmannsegge)
  Duke of York's Field Battalion (Osnabruck) (607)
  Grubenhagen Field Battalion (621)
  Bremen Field Battalion (512)
  Verden Field Battalion (533)
  Lüneberg Field Battalion (595)
  2 coys Field Jäger (321)

Divisional Artillery 2 Foot Btys (Lloyd, Cleeves)

1st British Infantry (Guards) Division (Major General Cooke)
1st British Brigade (Major General Maitland)
   2/1st Foot Guards (976)
   3/1st Foot Guards (1,021)
   2nd British Brigade (Major General Sir John Byng)
   2/Coldstream Guards (1,003)
   2/3rd Guards (1,061)

Divisional Artillery 1 Horse Bty KGL (Kuhlman), 1 Foot Bty (Sandham)

A Quick Visit to the Battlefield

I have visited the Quatre Bras battlefield a number of times; the earliest visit was a formal battlefield tour and the latest was after I had completed the narrative of this book. This most recent visit was a revelation. After the study and research in preparation for writing, and then the writing itself, I was able to return to the battlefield with a real feel for what happened there, and this thorough understanding of the detail and the flow of the fighting finally brought the battlefield to life. Suddenly, the lie of the land, the undulations, the dead ground, the ridgelines – all helped to explain how things unfolded and convinced me, if I needed convincing, that a tour of a field of battle after a thorough study of the fighting is absolutely vital to truly understand it. For those with the passion to pursue this understanding, the opportunity to stand on the actual ground and to be able to visualise the enthusiastic advance; the reluctant retreat; the inevitable chaos and confusion; the splendour and courage; the fear and despair; and the death and destruction, offers a feeling that your research has given you something that is rare in military history. It is perhaps the nearest we can come to 'closure' in our study of a battle, given that we could not actually be there to witness it.

Like many battlefields, Quatre Bras has been scarred by modern development; the Bossu wood has been cut down, the Quatre Bras farmhouse has been condemned and is awaiting demolition (and may well have been demolished by the time this book is published), the Charleroi to Brussels road is very busy and access to many areas is restricted. Nonetheless, Quatre Bras is still a good battlefield to visit.

The Bossu wood was part of an award to the Duke of Wellington from a grateful King of the Netherlands after the battle of Waterloo. It is slightly ironic that the Duke, who is quoted as saying 'they have destroyed my battlefield' when he saw the Lion Mound at Waterloo, was responsible for having the Bossu wood cut down and the timber sold soon after he became its owner! The absence of such a key feature is a sad loss when trying to envisage the progress of the battle.

The Gémioncourt farm still stands proud and strong in the very centre of the battlefield and it is a shame that it is privately owned and access is denied. The line of the Gémioncourt stream and the Étang Materne still exist, as does La Bergerie.

There are monuments to the British army and the Netherlands cavalry to the west of the crossroads on the Nivelles road and a very impressive memorial to the Duke of Brunswick on the main Charleroi to Brussels road, close to where he fell. Unfortunately, there are no memorials to the French army.

Most interesting of all, however, is the lie of the ground; one can see the limitations of what Wellington could observe from Quatre Bras and the French guns could engage from the heights above Lairalle, the dominance of the ridges of Gémioncourt and the Bati-Saint-Bernard. One can see how both sides used dead ground to shelter their troops from fire and how the French cavalry were able to launch their charges almost without warning. It is obvious why a strong farm like Grand Pierrepont was actually of little tactical value, and why, once the French artillery had been brought forward, it had such an influence on the battle.

Lying little more than a ten-minute drive south of Waterloo, a visit to Quatre Bras can be tacked onto a visit to its 'big brother'. Pen and Sword have published a comprehensive battlefield tour guide by Peter Hofschröer that covers the battlefields of both Quatre Bras and Ligny, as well as the other minor actions and movements that led to Waterloo. I highly recommend a visit.

Notes

Introduction

1. Napoleon, *Napoleon's Memoirs*, edited by Somerset de Chair (London: Soho Books, 1986), pp. 544–5.
2. Ropes, *The Campaign of Waterloo, A Military History* (New York: Charles Scribner's Sons, 1892), p. 352.

Chapter 1

1. Gourgaud, *The Campaign of 1815; or a Narrative of the Military operations which took place in France and Belgium during the Hundred Days* (London: James Ridgeway, 1818), pp. 43–4.
2. Clausewitz, translation in *On Waterloo, Clausewitz, Wellington and the Campaign of 1815*, Christopher Bassford, Daniel Moran and Gregory W. Pedlow (USA: Clausewitz.com, 2010), pp. 69–70.
3. Jomini, *The Campaign of Waterloo 1815; A Political and Military History* (Reprinted, by Leonaur, 2010), p. 79.
4. Houssaye, *1815 Waterloo*, translated from the 31st Edition (London: Adam and Charles Black, 1900), p. 59.
5. Chevalier, *Lieutenant Chevalier, Souvenirs des guerres napoléoniennes* (Paris: Hachette, 1970), p. 313.
6. Combe, *Mémoires du Colonel Combe sur les campagnes de Russie 1812, de Saxe 1813, de France 1814 et 1815* (Paris: Plon, 1896), p. 295.
7. Nöel, *Souvenirs Militaires d'un Officier du Premier Empire*, reprinted by A la Librairie des Deux Empires, Paris, 1999, p. 182.
8. Chapuis, *Notice sur le 85e de ligne pendant la champagne de 1815* (Annonay, Ranchon, 1863), p. 25.
9. Fantin des Odoards, *Journal du Général Fantin des Odoards, Etapes d'un officier de la Grande Armée 1800–1830* (Paris: Plon, 1895), p. 427.
10. Girod de l'Ain, *Vie Militaire du Général Foy* (Paris: Plon, 1900), pp. 269–70.
11. Lemonnier-Delafosse, *Souvenirs militaries du Capitaine Jean-Baptiste Lemonnier-Delafosse*, reprint presented by Christophe Bourachot (Saint-Amand-Montrond: Le Livre Chez Vous, 2002), p. 201.
12. Anon, *Rectification de quelques faits relatives à la champagne de 1815, par un officier general ayant combattu à Waterloo*, in *Souvenirs et correspondence sur la bataille de Waterloo*, p. 93.
13. De Brack, Letter published in *Carnet de la Sabretache*, reproduced in *Waterloo, Récits de Combatants* (Paris: Librairie Historique F. Teissèdre, 1999), p. 93.
14. Lemonnier-Delafosse, op. cit., p. 201.
15. Mauduit, *Histoire des derniers jours de la Grande Armée*, Volume 2 (Paris: Dion-Lambert, 1854), p. 191.
16. Ibid, pp. 200–1.
17. Colonel Gordon, COS to Gen Durutte, 4th Division, I Corps, having deserted on 16 June, in a letter dated 20 June. Mauduit, op. cit., pp. 183–84.

18. Martin, *Souvenirs d'un ex-officier, 1812–1815* (Paris & Geneva: J. Cherbuliez, 1867), p. 273.
19. Houssaye, op. cit., p. 48.

Chapter 2

1. Margerit, *Waterloo, l'Europe contre la France* (Éditions Gallimard, 1964), p. 169.
2. Heymès, *Relation de la campagne de 1815, dite Waterloo, pour server a l'histoire du maréchal Ney* (Paris: Gautier-Laguionie, 1829), pp. 5–6.
3. Lecestre, *Lettres inédits de Napoleon 1er*, Vol. I (Paris: 1897), p. 424.
4. Napoleon, op. cit., p. 527.
5. Chandler, *The Campaigns of Napoleon* (London: Weidenfeld, 1993), p. 1022.
6. Lerreguy de Civrieux, *Souvenirs d'un cadet (1812–1823)* (Paris: Hachette, 1912), p. 151.
7. Crabbé, *Jean-Louis de Crabbé, Colonel d'Empire* (Nantes: 'Editions du Canonnier, 2006), p. 276.
8. Petiet, *Mémoires du general Auguste Petiet, hussar de l'Empire* (Paris: Éditions S.P.M, 1996), p. 434.
9. Thiers, *Waterloo* (Paris: Plon, 1892), pp. 30–31.
10. Guyot, *Général Comte Guyot, Carnets de campagnes (1792–1815)* (Paris: Teissèdre, 1999), p. 290.
11. Crabbé, op. cit., pp. 275–76.

Chapter 3

1. Gerbet, *Souvenirs d'un officier sur la campagne de Belgique en 1815* (Arbois: Javel, 1867) p. 6.
2. Grouchy, *Mémoires du Maréchal de Grouchy*, Vol. 4 (Paris: Dentu, 1874), p. 440.
3. *Correspondance de Napoléon 1er*, publié par ordre de l'Empereur Napoléon III, Vol. 28, p. 325.
4. Houssaye, op. cit., p. 61.
5. Martin, op. cit., p. 274.
6. Gerbet, op. cit., p. 8.
7. Duthilt, *Mémoires du Capitaine Duthilt* (Lille: J. Tallandier, 1909), pp. 297–8.

Chapter 4

1. Gerbet, op. cit., p. 6.
2. Ibid, p. 8.
3. Correspodance de Napoleon, op. cit., p. 324.
4. Bro, *Mémoires du Général Bro (1796–1844)* (Paris: Plon, 1914), pp. 146–47.
5. Canler, *Mémoires de Canler, ancient chef du service de sureté* (Paris, Mercure de France, 1968), pp. 23–4.
6. I cannot find this wood on any contemporary maps.
7. Lemonnier-Delafosse, op. cit., p. 204.
8. *Documents inedits sur la campagne de 1815, publiés par le Duc d'Elchingen* (Paris: 1840), p. 54.
9. This town is named Jamignon, Jamignou or Jamioulx on different contemporary maps.
10. Ibid, pp. 22–23.
11. Martin, op. cit., p. 274.
12. Duthilt, op. cit., p. 298.
13. Martin, op. cit., pp. 274–5.
14. *Documents inédits*, op. cit., p. 24.
15. Lemonnier-Delafosse, op. cit., p. 204.
16. Gerbet, op. cit., p. 5.
17. Biot, *Souvenirs Anecdotiques et Militaires du Colonel Biot* (Paris: Henri Vivien, 1901), p. 234.
18. Ibid, p. 235.
19. Gerbet, op. cit., p. 5.

20. Gourgaud, *Bataille de Waterloo, Relation d'un Officier Général Francais*, printed in *Nouvelle Revue Rétrospective*, Vol. 4 (Paris: 1896), p. 362.
21. Petiet, op. cit., footnote to p. 430.
22. Rumigny, *Souvenirs du Général Comte de Rumigny 1789–1860* (Paris: Émile-Paul Frères, 1921), p. 94.

Chapter 5
 1. Gourgaud in *Nouvelle Review Rétrospective*, op. cit., pp. 362–3.
 2. Correspondance, op. cit., p. 25.
 3. Gerbet, op. cit., pp. 8–9.
 4. Rumigny, op. cit., p. 95.
 5. Hemyès, op. cit., p. 6.
 6. Napoleon, op. cit., p. 505.
 7. Puvis, extract from his *Souvenirs du chef de bataillon Théobald Puvis, du 93ème de ligne (1813–1815)*, reproduced in *Journal de route d'un garde d'honneur (1813–1814)* (Paris: Demi-Solde, 2007) p. 80–1.
 8. Heymès, op. cit., pp. 7–8.
 9. Given in Arcq, *Les Quatre-Bras 16 Juin 1815* (Fontaine-l'Évêque: Historic'One Éditions, 2012) p. 28.
10. Documents inédits, op. cit., p. 25.
11. Martin, op. cit., p. 276.
12. *Correspondance de Napoleon*, op. cit., p. 331.
13. Also known as Jumignon and shown as this on the map.
14. Gourgaud, *The Campaign of 1815*, op. cit., pp. 51–2.
15. Heymès, op. cit., pp. 7–9.
16. Charras, *Histoire de la Campagne de 1815, Waterloo*, Vol. 1 (Brussels: Meline, Cans et Compagnie, 1858), p. 100.
17. Grouchy, Memoirs, op. cit., Vol III, p. 466.
18. Chesney, *Waterloo Lectures*, Fourth Edition (London: Greenhill, 1997), p. 82.
19. Archives de Vincennes, Armée du Terre, Carton C15 de 20 à 33 Armée du Nord.
20. Given in Ropes, op. cit., pp. 57–8.
21. Napoleon, op. cit., p. 507.

Chapter 6
 1. Pontécoulant, op. cit., p. 144.
 2. Duthilt, op. cit., p. 298.
 3. Canler, op. cit., pp. 24–5.
 4. Hemyès, op. cit., p. 11.
 5. *Documents Inédits sur la campagne de 1815* (Paris: 1840), p. 57.
 6. Hemyès, op. cit., p. 10.
 7. *Documents inédits*, op. cit., p. 26.
 8. Ibid, p. 11.
 9. De Bas and T'Serclaes, *La Campagne de 1815 aux Pays Bas, d'après les rapports officials Néerlandais*, Vol. 1, pp. 460–1.
10. Flahault, *The First Napoleon, some unpublished documents from the Bowood papers* (London: Constable, 1925), p. 116.
11. *Correspondance*, op. cit., p. 334.
12. *Documents Inédits*, op. cit., p. 57.
13. Ibid, p. 27.
14. Ibid, p. 38.
15. Heymès, op. cit., p. 12.

16. *Documents inédits*, op. cit., pp. 37–8.
17. Girod de l'Ain, op. cit., p. 269.
18. Puvis, op. cit., p. 80.
19. Trefcon, *Carnet de champagne du colonel Trefcon, 1793–1815* (Paris: Edmond Dubois, 1914), pp. 157–58.
20. *Documents inédits*, op. cit., p. 31.
21. Letter from d'Erlon to Ney's son, dated 9 February 1829, reproduced in *Documents Inédits*, op. cit., p. 64.

Chapter 7
1. Müffling, *The Memoirs of Baron Von Müffling, a Prussian Officer in the Napoleonic Wars* (Reprinted by Greenhill Books, London, 1997), pp. 230–1.
2. General Sir Evelyn Wood, *Cavalry in the Waterloo Campaign* (Reprinted by Worley Publications, Felling, 1998), p. 68.
3. *The Recollections of Sergeant Morris*, edited by John Selby, The Windrush Press, 1967, p. 68.
4. Ibid, p. 69.
5. *Documents Inédits*, op. cit., pp. 57–9.
6. Several authorities have these two brigades interchanged, but the balance of evidence supports what I have represented here.
7. A handwritten note from Napoleon dated 'One hour after midday', the original copy was authenticated by Baron Gourgaud, one of Napoleon's ADCs. The note is reproduced in Chandler; *Waterloo, The Hundred Days* (Oxford: Osprey Publishing, 1980), pp. 88–9.
8. Henckens, *Memoires se rapportant a son service militaires au 6e regt de chasseurs a cheval francais de 1803 a 1816* (La Haye: Martinus Nijhoff, 1910), p. 237.
9. Quoted in Houssaye, op. cit., p. 110.
10. Girod de l'Ain, op. cit., pp. 270–2.
11. Quoted in Hofschröer, *1815, The German Victory, Wellington, his German Allies and the Battles of Ligny and Quatre Bras* (London: Greenhill, 1998), p. 237. In this book, Hofschröer examines the various accounts of what help Wellington promised Blücher in some detail.

Chapter 8
1. *Documents Inédits*, op. cit., pp. 57–9.
2. Girod de l'Ain, op. cit., p. 270.
3. Trefcon, op. cit., pp. 158–9.

Chapter 9
1. *The Conversations of the First Duke of Wellington with George William Chad*, edited by the 7th Duke of Wellington (Cambridge: The Saint Nicholas Press, 1956), p. 7.
2. Puvis, op. cit., p. 81.
3. Henckens, op. cit., pp. 238–9.
4. From Dellevoet, *The Dutch-Belgian Cavalry at Waterloo, A Military History* (The Hague: privately published by the author, 2008), p. 113.
5. *Dictionnaire des Braves de Napoléon*, Vol. I, under the direction of Colonel Molières and de Pleineville (Paris: Le Livre Chez Vous, 2004), p. 177.
6. In Henckens, op. cit., p. 241, he goes on, 'As for the encounter between the Netherlands hussars and dragoons and Piré's chasseurs and lancers, one has very often been involved in bloody combats between former comrades who had served together in France. [After the war …] I was, on one of the first days after my arrival, stopped by an officer who had a scar on his face, and he alleged that it was me that had administered the blow; although I made the observation to him that I did not pay attention to those with whom I exchanged blows in

a combat, he maintained his story and invited me the same day to dine with the officers where all their feats of arms, and ours, were recalled.'

7. Quoted in Arcq, *op. cit.*, p. 64.
8. Lord Fitzroy Somerset's account in Dellevoet, *The Dutch-Belgian Cavalry at Waterloo, A Military History* (The Hague: privately published by the author, 2008), p. 114.

Chapter 11
1. *Documents inédits*, op. cit., p. 40.
2. Maxwell, *The Life of Wellington*, Vol. II (London: Sampson, Low Marston and Company, 1900), pp. 20–1.
3. Mauduit, op. cit., footnote to pp. 148–50. Mauduit was a sergeant in the prestigious 1st regiment of Foot Grenadiers of the Old Guard during this campaign. Although he was not present at Quatre Bras, he was later commissioned and became the editor of *La Sentinelle de l'armée* and as such he communicated with a wide range of participants in the battle; basing his own account of the campaign on the correspondence in the same way that Siborne did from the British side.
4. Trefcon, op. cit., pp. 158–9.
5. Private Vallence, quoted in Robinson, *The Battle of Quatre Bras 1815* (Stroud: The History Press, 2009), p. 245.
6. Girod de l'Ain, op. cit., pp. 270–2.
7. *Documents Inédits*, op. cit., pp. 57–9.
8. Mauduit, op. cit., footnote to p. 150.
9. Private Vallence quoted in Robinson, op. cit., p. 246.
10. Lemonnier-Delafosse, op. cit., p. 206.
11. Bourdon de Vatry, quoted in Brett-James, *Waterloo Raconté par les Combattants* (La Palatine, 1969), pp. 34–5.
12. Wood, op. cit., p. 82.
13. Henckens, op. cit., pp. 241–2.
14. Jolyet, given in *Souvenirs et Correspondance sur la Bataille de Waterloo* (Paris: Editions Historiques Teissedre, 2000), pp. 75–6.

Chapter 12
1. *The Waterloo Letters*, edited by H.T. Siborne, reprinted by Arms and Armour Press, London, 1983, Letter 138, p. 326.
2. *Documents inédits*, op. cit., p. 42.
3. Houssaye, op. cit., p. 119.
4. Kellerman's account of Waterloo, reproduced in *Souvenirs Napoleonien No. 438*, p. 26–7.
5. Ibid, pp. 26–7.
6. Houssaye, op. cit., p. 120.
7. Wheatley, *The Wheatley Diary*, edited by Hibbert (Gloucestershire: The Windrush Press, 1967), p. 77.
8. Kellerman, op. cit., pp. 26–7.
9. Hope-Pattison, *Personal Recollections of the Waterloo Campaign*, Edited and Reprinted by Bob Elmer (Glasgow: Blackie and Co., 1997), p. 7.
10. Private Hemingway quoted in Robinson, op. cit., p. 330.
11. Morris, *The Recollections of Sergeant Morris*, edited by John Selby (Moreton-in-Marsh: Longmans, 1967), p. 68.
12. Kellerman, op. cit., pp. 26–7.
13. Report of Colonel Van Zuylen van Nyevelt, COS of the 2nd Netherlands Division, given in *Waterloo – Récits de Comabattants* (Paris: Teissedre, 1999), p. 74.
14. Kellerman, op. cit., pp. 26–7.

15. Report from Kellerman, addressed to Ney, dated 'close to Frasnes, 16 June, 10pm'. Given in Pontécoulant, *Napoléon à Waterloo 1815* (Paris: la Librairie des Deux Empires, 2004), pp. 379–80.
16. Henckens, op. cit., p. 242.
17. Heymès, op. cit., p. 13.
18. Berton, *Précis Historique, Militaire et Critique des Batailles de Fleurus et de Waterloo, dans la Campagne de Flandres, en Juin 1815* (Reprinted by LACF Editions, 2009), p. 31.
19. Duthilt; op. cit., pp. 299–300.
20. Girod de l'Ain, op. cit., p. 272.
21. Levavasseur, *Souvenirs Militaires d'Octave Levavasseur, officier d'artillerie aide de camp du maréchal Ney (1802–1815)* (Paris: Plon, 1914), p. 290.
22. Gourgaud, *Campaign of 1815*, op. cit.
23. Berton, op. cit., p. 31.
24. Girod de l'Ain, op. cit., p. 272.

Chapter 13
1. Myddleton, quoted in Robinson, op. cit., p. 322.
2. Letter 108, from Captain H.W. Powell in *The Waterloo Letters*, edited by Siborne (Reprinted by Arms and Armour Press, Lodon, 1983), p. 251.
3. Lemonnier-Delafosse, op. cit., p. 207.
4. Jolyet, in *Souvenirs et Correspondance*, op. cit., pp. 75–6.
5. Girod de l'Ain, op. cit., pp. 270–2.
6. Trefcon, op. cit., pp. 158–89.
7. Captain H.W. Powell in *The Waterloo Letters*, op. cit., pp. 251–2.
8. Jolyet, in *Souvenirs et Correspondance*, op. cit., p. 76.

Chapter 14
1. Heymès, op. cit., p. 14.
2. *Documents inédits*, op. cit., pp. 64–5.
3. Deselles in *Souvenirs et Correspondance*, op. cit., pp. 50–1.
4. Crabbé, op. cit., p. 277.
5. Baudus in *Waterloo Recontée par les combattants*, op. cit., p. 120.
6. Ibid, pp. 120–22.
7. Durutte, extract from *La Sentinelle de l'Armée*, 8 March 1838, in *Documents Inédits*, op. cit., pp. 71–2.
8. Ibid, pp. 72–3.
9. Charras, *Histoire de la Campagne de 1815, Waterloo* (Brussels: Meline, Cans et Compagnie, 1858), tells us that Gordon and Gaugler only deserted as they approached the Ligny battlefield, and not on the morning of the 16th as Chapuis claims.
10. Chapuis, op. cit., pp. 26–30, wrote his own account to challenge that of Durutte.
11. Brue, in a letter dated Toulose, 3 November 1837, published in Chapuis, op. cit. p. 52.
12. Crabbé, op. cit., p. 277.
13. Houssaye, op. cit., End Note 58, p. 366.
14. Flahaut, op. cit., p. 116.
15. Heymès, op. cit., p. 14.
16. D'Erlon, *Le Maréchal Drouet, comte d'Erlon. Vie militaire écrit par lui-même et dédiée à ses amis.* (Paris: Gustarve Barba, 1844).
17. Carl Friccius, 3rd Westphalian Landwehr, quoted in Hofschröer, op. cit., pp. 323–4.
18. Hofschröer, op. cit., p. 324.

Chapter 15

 1. Jolyet, *Souvenirs et Correspondance*, op. cit, p. 76.
 2. Girod de l'Ain, op. cit., p. 272.
 3. Bourdon de Vatry, in Brett-James, op. cit., p. 35.
 4. Canler, op. cit., pp. 24–5.
 5. Duthilt, op. cit., p. 300.
 6. Canler, op. cit., p. 25.
 7. D'Erlon, *Le Maréchal* Drouet, *Comte d'Erlon Vie militaire ecrit par lui-même*.
 8. Bourdon de Vatry, in Brett-James, op. cit., p. 35.
 9. Ibid.
10. Répécaud, *Napoléon à Ligny et le Maréchal Ney à Quatre Bras. Notice historique et critique, par le colonel du genie Répécaud* (Arras: Mme Veuve Degeorge, 1849), p. 42.
11. Pollio, *Waterloo (1815)* (Paris: Charles-Lavauzelle, undated), pp. 247–8.
12. Given in Berton, op. cit., p. 32.

Chapter 16

 1. Pollio, op. cit., pp. 254–5.
 2. Report of Count Valmy to Marshal Ney, dated 'close to Frasnes', 10pm, 16 June 1815. Published in Pontécoulant, op. cit., pp. 379–80.
 3. Wood, op. cit.
 4. Thiers, op. cit., pp. 167–8.
 5. Flahaut, op. cit., p. 116.
 6. Soult's letter to Ney, dated Fleurus, 17 June 1815. This document is actually misdated the 15th. *Documents Inédits*, op. cit., p. 45–6.
 7. Napoleon, op. cit., p. 544.
 8. Lemonnier-Delafosse, op. cit., pp. 205–8.
 9. Puvis, op. cit., pp. 81–2.
10. Combes-Brassard, in *Souvenirs et Correspondance*, op. cit., p. 13.
11. Girod de l'Ain, op. cit., pp. 273–4.
12. Chesney, *Waterloo Lectures*, Fourth Edition (London: Greenhill, 1997), p. 129.

Chapter 17

 1. Pontecoulant, op. cit., p. 384.
 2. Heymès, op. cit., p. 17.
 3. Duthilt, op. cit., pp. 299–300.
 4. Mercer, *Journal of the Waterloo Campaign* (Edinburgh and London: William Blackwood), p. 140–2.
 5. *Documents inédits*, op. cit., p. 45.
 6. Heymès, op. cit., p. 17.
 7. Henckens, op. cit., p. 243.
 8. *Documents Inédits*, op. cit., p. 44.
 9. Gourgaud, *Campaign of 1815*, op. cit., pp. 80–1.
10. Pontécoulant, op. cit., p. 155.
11. D'Erlon, *Le Maréchal Drouet, Comte d'Erlon Vie militaire écrit par luimême*, op. cit.
12. Deselles, Souvenirs et Correspondance, op. cit., p. 51.
13. Heymès, op. cit., p. 17.
14. Duthilt, op. cit., p. 300.
15. Girod de l'Ain, op. cit., p. 275.
16. Jolyet, op. cit., p. 76.
17. Chapuis, op. cit., p. 44.

Chapter 18

1. In his classic study of war, Clausewitz describes 'friction' as those many things that could disrupt even the most carefully made plans of the commander without him being able to influence them. This may be an act of god such as the weather, an unpreventable accident or any number of other unforeseen incidents that could affect every level from an individual to a corps or even the army.
2. Gourgaud, *Campaign of 1815*, op. cit., p. 70.
3. Colonel Gordon, COS to Gen Durutte, 4th Division, I Corps, having deserted on 16 June, in a letter dated 20 June. Given in Mauduit, op. cit., p. 185.
4. Ropes, op. cit., p. 187.
5. Coombe-Brassard, op. cit., p. 13.
6. Gourgaud, *Campaign of 1815*, op. cit., p. 47.
7. Petre, Napoleon's Conquest of Prussia – 1806 (London: The Bodley Head, 1907), p. 30.
8. *Ante* p. 169.
9. *Ante* p. 80.
10. *Documents Inédits*, op. cit., p. 27.

Select Bibliography

The French Army
Bowden, *Armies at Waterloo* (Arlington: Empire Press, 1982).
Couderc de Saint-Chamant, *Napoléon ses dernières armées* (Paris: Flammarion, undated).
Haythornthwaite, *The Waterloo Armies* (Barnsley: Pen and Sword, 2007).
Lachouque, *The Anatomy of Glory* (London: Lund Humpries, 1962).

Campaign Analyses
Chesney, *Waterloo Lectures*, Fourth Edition (London: Greenhill, 1997).
Clausewitz, translation in, *On Waterloo, Clausewitz, Wellington and the Campaign of 1815*, Christopher Bassford, Daniel Moran and Gregory W. Pedlow (USA: Clausewitz.com, 2010).
Jomini, reprint, *The Campaign of Waterloo 1815, A Political and Military History* (Leonaur, 2010).
Ropes, *The Campaign of Waterloo, A Military History* (New York: Charles Scribner's Sons, 1892).

Campaign/Battle Studies
Arcq, *Les Quatre-Bras 16 Juin 1815* (Fontaine-l'Évêque: Historic'One Éditions, 2012).
Becke, *Napoleon and Waterloo* (repr London: Greenhill, 1995).
Chandler, The Campaigns of Napoleon (London: Weidenfeld, 1993).
Charras, *Histoire de la Campagne de 1815, Waterloo* (Brussels: Meline, Cans et Compagnie, 1858).
Cotton, *A Voice from Waterloo*, Revised edition by S. Monick (The Naval and Military Press, 2001).
De Bas and T'Serclaes, *La Campagne de 1815 aux Pays Bas, d'après les rapports officials Néerlandais*, Vol. 1 (Brussels: Albert Dewit, 1908).
Dellevoet, *The Dutch-Belgian Cavalry at Waterloo, A Military History* (The Hague: privately published by the author, 2008).
Hofschröer, *1815, The German Victory, Wellington, his German Allies and the battles of Ligny and Quatre Bras* (London: Greenhill, 1998).
Houssaye, *1815 Waterloo* (London: Adam & Charles Black, 1900).
Lachouque, *Waterloo*, English Edition (London: Arms and Armour Press, 1975).
Logie, the English version, *Waterloo, The 1815 Campaign* (Spellmount, 2006).
Margerit, *Waterloo, l'Europe contre la France* (Éditions Gallimard, 1964).
Muilwijk, *Quatre Bras, Perponcher's Gamble* (Bleiswijk: Sovereign House Books, 2013).
Pollio, *Waterloo (1815)* (Paris: Charles-Lavauzelle, undated).
Robinson, *The Battle of Quatre Bras 1815* (Stroud: The History Press, 2009).
Shaw-Kennedy, *Notes on the Battle of Waterloo* (London: John Murray, 1865).
Siborne, *Histroy of the Waterloo Campaign*, reprinted by Greenhill Books, 1995.
Thiers, *Waterloo* (Paris: Plon, 1892).
Tondeur, Courcelle and Meganck, *Charleroi, la Journée du 15 Juin 1815*, No. 12 of the *Carnets de la Campagne* Series (Brussels: Tondeur Editions, 2011).
Uffindell, *The Eagle's Last Triumph* (London: Greenhill, 2006).
Vaulabelle, *1815, Ligny-Waterloo* (Paris: Garnier Frères, undated).

French Primary Sources

Anon, *Rectification de quelques faits relatives à la champagne de 1815, par un officier general ayant combattu à Waterloo*, in *Souvenirs et correspondence sur la bataille de Waterloo*.

Baudus, *Études sur Napoleon* (Paris: Debécourt, 1841).

Berton, *Précis Historique, Militaire et Critique des Batailles de Fleurus et de Waterloo, dans la Campagne de Flandres, en Juin 1815* (Reprinted by LACF Editions, 2009).

Biot, *Souvenirs Anecdotiques et Militaires du Colonel Biot* (Paris: Henri Vivien, 1901).

Bourdon de Vatry, quoted in *Mémoires et correspondence du roi Jérôme et la reine Catherine* (Paris: E. Dentu, 1861–1866).

Bro, *Mémoires du Général Bro (1796–1844)* (Paris: Plon, 1914).

Canler, *Mémoires de Canler, ancient chef du service de sureté* (Paris, Mercure de France, 1968).

Chapuis, *Notice sur le 85e de ligne pendant la champagne de 1815* (Annonay, Ranchon, 1863).

Chavalier, *Lieutenant Chevalier, Souvenirs des guerres napoléoniennes* (Paris: Hachette, 1970).

Combe, *Mémoires du Colonel Combe sur les campagnes de Russie 1812, de Saxe 1813, de France 1814 et 1815* (Paris: Plon, 1896).

Combes-Brassard, *Notice sur la bataille de Mont Saint-Jean*, published in *Souvenirs et correspondence sur la bataille de Waterloo* (Paris: Teissèdre, 2000).

Correspondance de Napoléon 1er, publié par ordre de l'Empereur Napoléon III.

Crabbé, *Jean-Louis de Crabbé, Colonel d'Empire* (Nantes: 'Editions du Canonnier, 2006).

Drouet, *Le Maréchal Drouet, comte d'Erlon. Vie militaire écrit par lui-même et dédiée à ses amis*. (Paris: Gustarve Barba, 1844).

Duthilt, *Mémoires du Capitaine Duthilt* (Lille: J. Tallandier, 1909).

Fantin des Odoards, *Journal du Général Fantin des Odoards, Etapes d'un officier de la Grande Armée 1800–1830* (Paris: Plon, 1895).

Flahault, *The First Napoleon, some unpublished documents from the Bowood papers* (London: Constable, 1925).

Fleury de Chaboulon, *Mémoires* (Paris: Edouard Rouveyre, 1901).

Gerbet, *Souvenirs d'un officier sur la campagne de Belgique en 1815* (Arbois: Javel, 1867).

Girod de l'Ain, *Vie Militaire du Général Foy* (Paris: Plon, 1900).

Gourgaud, *The Campaign of 1815* (London: James Ridgeway, 1818).

Gourgaud, *Bataille de Waterloo, Relation d'un Officier Général Francais*, printed in *Nouvelle Revue Rétrospective*, Vol. 4 (Paris: 1896).

Janin, *Campagne de Waterloo: Remarques Critiques et Historiques sur l'Ouvrage du Général Gourgaud* (Paris: Chaumerot Jeune Libraire, 1820).

Grouchy, *Mémoires du Maréchal de Grouchy* (Paris: Dentu, 1874) Vols 3 and 4.

Guyot, *Général Comte Guyot, Carnets de campagnes (1792–1815)* (Paris: Teissèdre, 1999).

Henckens, *Memoires se rapportant a son service miltaires au 6e regt de chasseurs a cheval francais de 1803 a 1816* (La Haye: Martinus Nijhoff, 1910).

Heymès, *Relation de la campagne de 1815, dite Waterloo, pour server a l'histoire du maréchal Ney* (Paris: Gautier-Laguionie, 1829).

Janin, *Campagne de Waterloo ou Remarques Critiques et Historiques sur l'ouvrage du Général Gourgaud* (Paris: Chaument jeune, 1820).

Jérôme, *Mémoires et correspondence du roi Jérôme et la reine Catherine* (Paris: E. Dentu, 1861–1866).

Jolyet, *Souvenirs et correspondence sur la bataille de Waterloo*.

Kellerman's account of Waterloo, reproduced in *Souvenirs Napoleonien No. 438*.

Ney, Joseph Napoléon, *Documents inédits sur la Campagne de 1815, publiés par le Duc d'Elchingen* (Paris: Anselin and Laguione, 1840).

Lemonnier-Delafosse, *Souvenirs militaries du Capitaine Jean-Baptiste Lemonnier-Delafosse*, reprint presented by Christophe Bourachot (Saint-Amand-Montrond: Le Livre Chez Vous, 2002).

Lerreguy de Civrieux, *Souvenirs d'un cadet (1812–1823)* (Paris: Hachette, 1912).

Levavasseur, *Souvenirs Militaires d'Octave Levavasseur, officier d'artillerie aide de camp du maréchal Ney (1802–1815)* (Paris: Plon, 1914).

Martin, *Souvenirs d'un ex-officier, 1812–1815* (Paris & Geneva: J. Cherbuliez, 1867).

Mauduit, *Histoire des derniers jours de la Grande Armée* (Paris: Dion-Lambert, 1854).

Napoleon, *Napoleon's Memoirs*, edited by Somerset de Chair (London: Soho Books, 1986).

Napoleon, *Correspondance de Napoléon 1er*, Vols 27 & 31 (Paris: Plon, 1858–1870).

Nöel, *Souvenirs Militaires d'un Officier du Premier Empire*, reprinted by A la Librairie des Deux Empires, Paris, 1999.

Petiet, *Mémoires du general Auguste Petiet, hussar de l'Empire* (Paris: Éditions S.P.M, 1996).

Pontécoulant, *Napoléon à Waterloo 1815* (Paris: la Librairie des Deux Empires, 2004).

Puvis, extract from his *Souvenirs du chef de bataillon Théobald Puvis, du 93ème de ligne (1813–1815)*, reproduced in *Journal de route d'un garde d'honneur (1813–1814)* (Paris: Demi-Solde, 2007).

Reille's account in *Documents Inédits sur la campagne de 1815* (Paris: 1840).

Répécaud, *Napoléon à Ligny et le Maréchal Ney à Quatre Bras. Notice historique et critique, par le colonel du genie Répécaud* (Arras: Mme Veuve Degeorge, 1849).

Rumigny, *Souvenirs du Général Comte de Rumigny 1789–1860* (Paris: Émile-Paul Frères, 1921).

Témoin Oculaire [an 'eyewitness'; attributed to René Bourgeois, a Chiurgien-Major in the cuirassiers], *Relation fidèle et détaillée de la dernier champagne de Buonaparte, terminée par la Bataille de Mont-Saint-Jean, dite de Waterloo ou de la bataille de la Belle Alliance, par un Témoin Oculaire* (Brussels: Chez P.J. de Mat, 1816), Fifth Edition.

Trefcon, *Carnet de champagne du colonel Trefcon, 1793–1815* (Paris: Edmond Dubois, 1914).

Allied Primary Sources

Kincaid, *Adventures in the Rifle Brigade and Random Shots from a Rifleman* (London: Maclaren and Company, undated).

Hope-Pattison, *Personal Recollections of the Waterloo Campaign*, Edited and Reprinted by Bob Elmer (Glasgow: Blackie and Co., 1997).

Morris, *The Recollections of Sergeant Morris*, edited by John Selby (Moreton-in-Marsh: Longmans, 1967).

Mercer, *Journal of the Waterloo Campaign* (Edinburgh and London: William Blackwood).

Müffling, *The Memoirs of Baron Von Müffling, a Prussian Officer in the Napoleonic Wars* (Reprinted by Greenhill Books, London, 1997).

Siborne, *The Waterloo Letters* (repr. London: Arms and Armour Press, 1983).

Collections

Souvenirs et Correspondance sur la Bataille de Waterloo (Paris: Editions Historiques Teissedre, 2000).

Waterloo, Récits de Combattants (Paris: Teissedre, 1999).

Other Books of Particular Note

Clausewitz, *On War*, Everyman's Library Edition (London: Everyman's Library, 1993).

Hofschröer, *Waterloo 1815, Quatre Bras and Ligny* (Barnsley: Pen and Sword, 2005). A useful guide to visiting these two battlefields.

Meulenaere, *Bibliographie Analytique des Témoignages Oculaires Imprimés de la Campagne de Waterloo* (Paris: Teissedre, 2004).

Adkin, *The Waterloo Companion* (London: Aurum Press, 2001).

Index